A LIE WILL SUFFICE

A DiGiovanni Family History

J A Y   W I L K I N S O N

Fulton Books
Meadville, PA

Published by Fulton Books 2022

Library of Congress Registration Number: TXu 2-279-684

ISBN 978-1-63985-662-6 (paperback)
ISBN 978-1-63985-664-0 (hardcover)
ISBN 978-1-63985-663-3 (digital)

Printed in the United States of America

"Truthfulness should be ordinarily preferred,
without abandoning deception altogether."

—Francesco Guicciardini

For my mother

CONTENTS

ILLUSTRATIONS

PROLOGUE

Picchi didi a verita quanna a farfantaria cia basta.
(Why tell the truth when a lie will suffice).[1]

"My people lied to me my whole life." My mother was near tears, seated at the end of the old sofa in my living room. She was old herself by this time, still grieving over the recent death of my father, her husband of fifty-four years. "Why did they have to lie to me so much?"

"What lies are you talking about?" I asked her with fear and concern. Fear, because throughout our long life together as mother and eldest son, I had never before seen fear in Mom's face or heard it in her voice.

"Never mind," she said, composing herself quickly and reverting to the silence that so often had smothered any urge to voice introspection or secrets that might bubble briefly to her surface. She was Sicilian, after all, reared in the ways of deception and *omerta*, the code of silence that governed communication with strangers, authority figures, even family. Was I all three to Mom?

She had trudged to the sofa in silence after knocking on my back door and handing me a crisp manila folder. It contained a few photocopies from public library microfilm of newspaper articles from the 1920s. Four words in the third paragraph of a front-page lead story seared through my dimming eyesight: "[A]ssassination of... **Dominick DiGiovanni**."[2] DiGiovanni. It was her mother's maiden name, a hallowed name in the history of my family; a famous name, as things turned out, in the small Western Sicily town from which they came.

11

"Why all the secrets?" Mom muttered from her spot at the end of the sofa. "Why all the lies?"

By the early twenty-first century, the grandchildren and great-grandchildren of Gaetano and Angela DiGiovanni had become settled, secure, prosperous, even prominent. Among them were a retired lieutenant colonel of the United States Air Force; a top chef at a venerable French-Creole restaurant in the Vieux Carre of New Orleans; one of Louisiana's first licensed nurse practitioners, retired from the prestigious Tulane University Medical School and Hospital; a United States magistrate judge; the deputy assistant secretary of the Louisiana Department of Family Services; the chief of staff of the United States Sentencing Commission; holders of advanced degrees, including a PhD, several MBAs, JDs and CPAs; successful and respected businessmen and professionals; loving mothers and fathers; pillars of every American community in which they lived. All this had sprung from what had been a dream of Western Sicilian peasants more than a century earlier.

When I was a kid, I thought I was Italian. Whenever the subject of ethnicity came up—in social studies class in a discussion of the old-fashioned theory of America as the melting pot, before "diversity is our strength" became a popular slogan, on St. Patrick's Day or Columbus Day—when asked by teachers or classmates what I was, I told them I was Italian.

Apart from my parents, the most influential people in my life as a child were my mother's parents, Natale and Antonia "Lena" or "Nia" Guinta, and Nia's loud and rollicking family, the DiGiovannis. Every Sunday afternoon, every holiday, every special day of any importance—birthdays, anniversaries, First Communion celebrations—even random summer days of no importance, when school was not in session and Mom simply needed a break provided by willing babysitters, were spent at the welcoming Uptown New Orleans home of the Guintas, where my great-grandmother, Angela Bucaro DiGiovanni, also lived. A Sicilian dialect of Italian was spoken there. Nia presided over a kitchen that was always filled with treats and games for her grandchildren. Homemade discs of ricotta cheese, hand-crafted from goat's milk by "Old Grandma" DiGiovanni herself, fermenting in shallow dishes, were placed in the refrigerator next to frosty bottles of Delaware Punch, Natale's favorite soft drink. Natale himself, "Pa-Paw," held sway over the side yard, where he grew fruits and vegetables, including snap beans climbing the fence on leafy vines, a Sicilian squash called cucuzza snaking across the tin roof of his wood-frame garage, bloodred tomatoes on grass green stalks propped up to the hot New Orleans sun by thin stakes of hand-cut wood he had sharpened to a point with a short whittling knife and driven into the ground, figs, Japanese plums and little sprigs of fresh mint. Natale also dictated the evening program selection on the black and white television set, where endless episodes of *Gunsmoke*, *Rawhide*, and *Bonanza* or the other American westerns he preferred for entertainment blared incessantly.

Every Sunday saw huge piles of pasta and tureens of tomato sauce consumed there by an army of relatives, all—except those like my father, who had married into the family—with the Sicilian genes of the DiGiovanni or Guinta *cosca* (a combination of families). The feasts featured mounds of meatballs and Italian sausages, eggplant in all manner of preparation, *panneed* veal and chicken, stuffed slabs of beef pockets called daube, cheeses, black olives, lettuce and tomato salads dripping in Sicilian olive oil poured from a gallon can, all fol-lowed by homemade *biscotti regina* (sesame seed "queen cookies"), almond cakes or creamy, crunchy cannoli, covered in powdered sugar. I sipped my first taste of red wine there, from a small shot glass held to my lips by my beloved Nia.

We all attended the Italian weddings of Mom's dozens of cous-ins and the wakes and funerals of her aged ancestors. The wakes and weddings alike were loud, raucous affairs. Platoons of olive-skinned, dark-haired children like myself and my Guinta cousins were allowed to run and play with a minimum of adult supervision and view the bodies of the dearly departed displayed in open caskets or the bare legs of the young brides as they removed lacy garters from their thighs and tossed them into the wedding party crowds.

"So what are you, with that name, Wilkinson?" some teacher or classmate would ask me at the Catholic grammar schools I attended

13

as a child whenever the subject of ethnicity came up. "Italian," I would say to their disbelief and astonishment. "Sicilian, really."

It was inevitable that I would choose to write about my Sicilians. It became a necessity, almost a command or obsession on the day Mom presented me with her thin file of 1920s newspaper articles. I had recently completed a book about my father, a sad and gentle ode of love and respect driven by my grief over Dad's dying and death. "Someday you're gonna write a book about my family," Mom said, "and it won't be so pretty."

I set about the task in the usual way, searching out the old family photos and documents, the birth, baptismal, and death certificates; the passports and alien registration cards; the property transfers; cemetery burial deeds; obituaries and succession records. I uncovered more newspaper articles from the 1920s and '30s, using the few that Mom had given me as a starting point. The newspaper stories led me to the old court records and arrest registers, which were easy enough for a person of my background and position to obtain and understand. The documentary evidence was thin but helpful. More problematic, however, were the oral histories, the interviews—only a couple of which, with Nia and her sister, Aunt Lou, had been tape-recorded, the informal conversations, the stories passed from mouth to mouth over the years. The oral lore was problematic because it was often filled with sarcasm, omission, coded language, selective and subjective recollection, obscure Italian phraseology, rehearsal, woodshedding, subtle deception, and outright misrepresentation. "Why all the secrets?" Mom had asked that day from her spot at the end of my sofa. "Why all the lies?"

For me, the answer to Mom's questions had to be found in the history books, the academic, sociological, and journalistic studies of the culture, environment, and thought processes of the people who came to Louisiana from late-nineteenth- and early-twentieth-century Western Sicily. The conclusions of the experts were similar.

As a general matter, according to the experts, Italians of all origin, from the north, south, and the Mediterranean islands, have been "accused of not having a sufficient respect for the truth.... And yet they know the truth when they see it. They are no fools (*fessi*)....

But collectively they seem sometimes to forget truth's unique importance. They often ignore it, embellish it, embroider around it, deny
it, as the case may be. They lie to please, to round off a picture, to
provoke an emotion, to prove a point.... [T]hey must keep secrets."[3]
According to Francesco Guicciardini, the early-sixteenth-century
Florentine patrician, politician, and philosopher, the formula for
Southern Italian success was that "truthfulness should be ordinarily
preferred, without abandoning deception altogether.... [I]n the
ordinary circumstances of life, use truthfulness in such a way as to
gain the reputation of a guileless man. In a few important cases, use
deceit. Deceit is the more fruitful and successful the more you enjoy
the reputation of an honest and truthful man; you are more easily
believed."[4] For a significant segment of Western Sicilians of the late
nineteenth and early twentieth centuries, "truth is a peculiarly precious and dangerous commodity.... [Its telling must be tempered by
being] prodigiously good at keeping their mouths shut [and by the
ability to] communicate in codes, hints, fragments of phrases, stony
stares, significant silences.... [Thus, interpreting what these Sicilians
said and did] is now seen to be about making out a pattern among
the truths and the tactical lies, and finding other evidence to corrob-
orate that pattern."[5]

For more specific answers and filling in the blanks about the
DiGiovannis and Natale Guinta particularly, in an attempt to rec-
oncile the inconsistencies, nonsense, and out-and-out contradic-
tions that the family history sometimes produced, I fell back on the
fact-finding and research methods I had learned as a lawyer, judge,
newspaper reporter, and journalism student. I relied on the history
and sociology books to understand the character of my Sicilians, some
of whom I had known only as a child or not at all, and of the settings
in which they were born, lived, and died. I visited the places in New
Orleans where they had lived, worked, and were buried. I studied
pictures, photographs, postcards, travel guides, Atlas maps, Google
Earth, and films of Sicily. I absorbed the verbal descriptions of relatives who had visited or lived on the island, all while I planned my
own trip to Sicily for my sixty-seventh birthday. In most instances,
I was left to employ inference, surmise, and the reaching of conclu-

sions based on my own limited powers of analysis, reasoning, and educated speculation. In law, we call this the "*ratio decidendi*,...the ground(s) of the decision, the point(s)...which determine the judgment(s)."[6] I remembered and applied some of the same instructions I have given as a judge addressing juries, just before they are sent off for secluded deliberation and decision at the conclusion of trial:

> You must consider only the evidence.... There are two types of evidence.... One is direct evidence—such as testimony of an eyewitness. The other is indirect or circumstantial evidence— proof of circumstances that tend to prove or disprove the existence or nonexistence of certain other facts. The law makes no distinction between direct and circumstantial evidence,...and you must consider both.... This does not mean, however, that you must accept all of the evidence as true or accurate. You are the sole judges of the credibility or "believability" of each witness and the weight to be given to his or her testimony. In weighing the testimony of a witness, you should consider his relationship to a party; his interest, if any, in the outcome...; his manner of testifying; his opportunity to observe or acquire knowledge concerning the facts about which he testified; his candor, fairness and intelligence; and the extent to which he has been supported or contradicted by other credible evidence. You may, in short, accept or reject the testimony of any witness in whole or in part.... You cannot be governed by sympathy or prejudice or any motive whatsoever, except a fair and impartial consideration of the evidence, and you must not allow any sympathy that you may have for any party to influence you in any degree whatsoever. You are expected to use your good sense. Give the evidence...a reasonable and

fair interpretation in the light of your own knowledge of the natural tendencies of human beings....
[Y]ou may draw such reasonable inferences...
as you feel are justified in the light of common
experience. You may make deductions and reach
conclusions that reason and common sense lead
you to make.... [D]ecide...for yourself.... [D]o
not hesitate to re-examine your own opinion and
change your mind if you become convinced that
you are wrong. However, do not give up your honest beliefs solely because...others think differently.
Remember,...you are judges—judges of the facts.
Your only interest is to seek the truth....[7]

In short, "[w]hat follows here is...a mixture of knowledge and
supposition."[8] The writer, historian and intellectual, Luigi Barzini, is
one of the legion of geniuses Italy has produced over the centuries.
In *The Italians*, his masterpiece of insight and understanding, Barzini
explains his feelings on writing about his own country and countrymen, all in a way that also describes what it has been for me to write
about the DiGiovannis and Natale Guinta. As Barzini said,

I have felt at times like the man who does
that most exacting of all things, the "Portrait of
the Artist's Mother." The Mother, in this case, is
notoriously distinguished. Her past is glorious,
her achievements are dazzling, her traditions
noble,...and her charm irresistible. I have known
her and admired her for a long time. I love her
dearly. As I grew older, however...I became dis-
enchanted with some of her habits, shocked by
some of her secret vices, repelled by her corruption,...and hurt when I discovered that she was
not, after all, the shining paragon I believed her
to be when I was young. Still, I could have no
other mother. I could not stop loving her. When

17

I was writing this book, I did not want to hurt her feelings, I did not want to be unnecessarily cruel, I did not want to forget her good points; but, at the same time, I tried hard not to flatter her, not to be seduced by her magical charms or misled by my own sentiments. I was determined to do the most honest job of portraiture I possibly could.[9]

Here is my portrait.

CHAPTER 1

WESTERN SICILY 1893

Gaetano DiGiovanni sat atop his stout little horse in the middle of the familiar nowhere he knew so well as the Sicilian countryside, outside the town of Ciminna. He was barely twenty-five, an age of certain manhood for Sicilian males of that time and place. Gaetano was covered in dust, which clung to his clothes and the thin layer of oily sweat that coated his skin. He was tall and thick when compared to his *paisani* (countrymen)—five feet six inches tall and 160 pounds—though he always seemed taller and huskier in person. A full head of jet-black hair protruded from beneath his floppy fedora. His face was hard and weathered but handsome, naturally dark, and made darker still by his daily exposure to the Mediterranean sun. His right cheek already bore the jagged two-inch scar that would mark him for life. The scar was the product of a youthful mishap when he took his father's shotgun, the deadly *lupara*, fired it without holding it tightly, and the hammer caught his mouth. On this night, that same kind of short-barreled *lupara*, which rural Sicilian men of that time preferred both for hunting and as a weapon of protection, hung across his back from a leather strap draped across his left shoulder. He smelled of goat cheese and olive oil, the basic components of his most recent meal. His clothing was rough and rustic, befitting his standing and occupation. His appearance belied the sharpness of his intelligence, shrewdness of his judgment, and audacity of his ambition, three characteristics for which he was becoming increasingly recognized in the small village that was his home base, San Cipirello in the Palermo Province of Western Sicily. Gaetano recognized the importance of the decision he had made and the action he would take to effectuate that decision on this night.

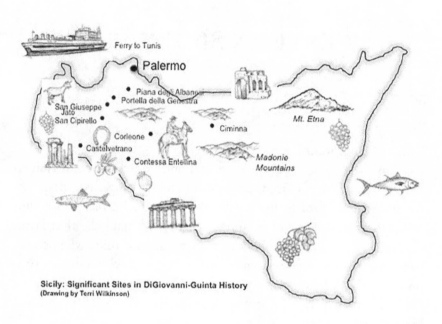

Sicily: Significant Sites in DiGiovanni-Guinta History
(Drawing by Terri Wilkinson)

He was born in San Cipirello on June 14, 1868, eight years after eight hundred armed guerillas of Garibaldi's red shirts stormed ashore at Marsala near Palermo from the Italian mainland. Garibaldi's guerillas routed the loyalists of the Sicilian Bourbon princes, replacing the golden lily on the white field flag of the old Sicilian aristocracy with the tricolor red, white, and green banner of Italian national unification under King Victor Emmanuel. San Cipirello was a humble village, recently created by disaster. Located about thirty-two kilometers southwest of Palermo, the town had been established in 1838 when a tragic landslide destroyed part of nearby San Giuseppe Jato, causing some of its residents to move slightly south. In 1864, the town became a self-governing community, deriving its name from an important local landowner, Sancio Pirrello. Located in the shadow of the ruins of both a Saracen castle and a Greek temple of the Goddess Aphrodite, San Cipirello became a place where corn, grapes, olives, and melons were grown. Goat cheese production was common in most households.[10]

Gaetano's father was Domenico DiGiovanni, whose namesake was a barber and famous satirical poet of the Medici Era. The oldest known Domenico DiGiovanni (1404–49) was "*Il Burchiello* (the barge)" of Florence. He was called *Burchiello* because the sign that hung over his barbershop included a painted picture of a flat-bottomed boat. His barbershop became a gathering spot for Florence's leading artists and poets. In Florentine politics, Domenico supported the Albizzi family against the Medici, which sometimes got him into trouble. His most noteworthy sonnets included *La Poesia Contende col Rasojo* (Poetry Argues with the Razor) and *O Humil Popul* (Oh Humble People), which criticized the powerful and influential Cosimo de Medici and characterized him as a hawk posing as a dove. When Cosimo de Medici took official power in 1434, *Burchiello* was forced into exile. Eventually, he relocated to Rome, where he died in poverty.[11]

The nineteenth-century Domenico DiGiovanni who was Gaetano's father had not achieved the notoriety of the fifteenth-century poet, except perhaps in marriage. According to family oral lore, Domenico was one of the hundreds of prisoners of the mid-nineteenth-century Bourbon establishment in Sicily freed by Garibaldi's invading forces. Domenico's most memorable characteristic was his height. He was a tall man by Sicilian standards, so tall that when he rode a donkey, his feet dragged the ground. With the same shrewdness of judgment and bold action that Gaetano was contemplating on that starry night in 1893, Domenico about three decades earlier had recognized and embraced that oldest of Sicilian realities: "Often, the only way for an ambitious man to succeed is to marry one of the daughters of the men at the top."[12] Thus, Domenico abandoned the desolate and impoverished circumstances of his birthplace in Santa Margherita[13] and traveled to nearby San Cipirello, where he married Giuseppina Randazzo,[14] daughter of one of the region's "*uomini rispettati*"—that is, "men who can keep a secret, do favors, accept favors, but also have power and authority of their own.... [M]en who exact respect from others and should not be harmed."[15]

Domenico had been responsible for acquiring for his descendants an originally derogatory sobriquet, which his son, Gaetano, would later make synonymous with dauntlessness and respect. "You see, but the DiGiovannis were called Baioccos," Nia said mysteriously, without prompting and unresponsively to the question just asked, during her taped interview more than a century later. "That was their nickname," Nia said, hesitatingly, thoughtfully. "But,... well, let's don't start.... Joe [her son, my Uncle Joe Guinta] wanted...." She hesitated again. "The Mafia was somewhere around, you know."[16] In direct contradiction of herself seven years earlier, Nia had told me quite clearly and pointedly, expressing her disapproval of my involvement as a law clerk to the federal judge presiding over the high profile "BRILAB" trial of the reputed local Mafia don and others, "There's no such thing as the Mafia."

It was Paolo "Paul" DiGiovanni, Mom's first cousin, Uncle Vito's son, Gaetano's grandson, who explained the genesis of the alias "Baiocco" to me years later. Paolo was born in San Cipirello, grew up there, and returned for extended visits with his parents and on his own, years after his family immigrated to New Orleans to make its permanent home in 1953. Paul explained that in Western Sicily in the late nineteenth century, traveling the mountainous and poor roads from Palermo or between villages in the countryside was treacherous business because of the conditions and the bandits. Along those roads, the peasants constructed small chapels, dedicated to the local saints, like San Domenico, San Rosalia, San Vituum, and of course, San Giuseppe (St. Joseph). These chapels were places where travelers could stop for rest and pray for their safety during the journey. Each chapel was equipped with small baskets or alms boxes, where the prayerful travelers could leave small offerings of low denomination coins. Sometimes a dishonest traveler or one of the marauding bandits would liberate the small donations from the isolated little chapels and convert them to his own use. Domenico DiGiovanni apparently was one of these petty thieves. Predominant among the small coins in the alms boxes Domenico would sometimes purloin was the baiocco, the equivalent of today's penny, sometimes called the pope's coin. An individual baiocco was of so little value that it once had been the subject of a stinging insult that caused a dispute between the artist and sculptor Michelangelo and Pope Julius II. Michelangelo had been commissioned to sculpt several statues for display in the Vatican, so he entered a contract and received delivery of thirty-four pieces of marble of various sizes. "Michelangelo wanted the pope to pay him something on account, so that he could in turn pay the carters and the quarrymen, but the papal cash flow suddenly dried up. Michelangelo was greatly perturbed. To make matters worse, Michelangelo heard a rumor from the papal court that Julius had been overheard saying…he 'wasn't going to pay a baiocco for either the large stones or the small ones.' In those days, a baiocco was a very small coin; [and] the word still survives in the popular [Italian] dialect."[17]

In later days, use of the baiocco by the men of the DiGiovanni clan became so prodigious, and their means of acquiring their stash of the small coins such common knowledge, that family members came to be called "Baiocco" as frequently as they were called DiGiovanni. At about that same time, it was the "[l]egendary and still revered…Don Vito Cascio Ferro, perhaps the greatest head the Mafia ever had, who reigned from the end of the [nineteenth] Century till the late [nineteen] twenties…, [who] organized all crimes, from the largest deals down to the chicken thefts and the purloining of brass coins from the alms boxes in the churches. All criminals were more or less indexed in his memory…; they were all licensed by him, could do nothing without the *societa*'s consent, and incidentally without giving the Mafia the customary cut…. [It was] Don Vito [who] brought the organization to its highest perfection without undue recourse to violence."[18]

Perhaps that had been Domenico's route to the bold and beneficial marriage he was subsequently able to make. No thief of pope's coins, no matter how small, from the alms boxes of the Sicilian countryside could hope to survive in such a trade without a local Mafia chief's blessing and protection. Both could be purchased with a tangible showing of respect by paying a healthy percentage of the take to the don himself. It was Paolo DiGiovanni who confirmed for me in our baiocco conversation that back in those days, one of the leading men of respect in San Cipirello was a Randazzo. Perhaps Gaetano's grandfather on his mother' side was a predecessor or other relative of Don Vincenzo Randazzo, who is identified in the available reference materials as Mafia chief of coastal Cinisi and who died in 1941;[19] or of Calogero and Santo Randazzo, identified in the state archives at Palermo as the 1920s Mafia-affiliated *gabelloti* of *Feudi Montaperto*, a large estate in the San Giuseppe Jato area; or of Filippo Randazzo, identified as one of the Mafia group in San Cipirello in 1926.[20] It was men like the Randazzos who "found it convenient at times to recruit men among the bandits themselves, usually the older bandits who tired of life in the woods, wanted stability and longed for the respectability of family life. They were the only men around who did not fear taking risks."[21]

But what kinds of risks, and what kind of mafia? "The word Mafia notoriously means two things, one, which should be spelled with a lowercase 'm,' being the mother of the second, the capital letter Mafia.... [The uppercase Mafia] is the world-famous illegal organization.... [The lowercase mafia is] a state of mind, a philosophy of life, a conception of life, a moral code, a particular susceptibility, prevailing among all Sicilians."[22] This philosophy required that Sicilians "help each other, stand by their friends and family, fight common enemies, and divulge no secrets—*omerta*. Sicilians were also to stay clear of officials and the law and to protect their honor by means of violence. A man who practiced this philosophy was called *mafioso, uomo di rispetto* [man of respect]."[23]

Substantial evidence—while not rising to the level of beyond a reasonable doubt but certainly reaching a preponderance of, and approaching clear and convincing evidence—supports the conclusion that Gaetano, Domenico, and perhaps others of *my* DiGiovannis were Mafia with a capital M. While the oral and circumstantial evidence is substantial, my years of research reviewing reams of paper

and digital materials have located only one instance of documentation identifying *my* DiGiovannis in a simple list of names of individuals affiliated with the Mafia in the towns of San Giuseppe Jato
and nearby San Cipirello.[24] It can be said without question, however,
that both Domenico and Gaetano, as landless but enterprising and
ambitious Western Sicilian men of the late nineteenth century, were
lower case "m" *mafiosi* in all respects.

According to Nia in her taped interviews, the DiGiovannis
of 1890s San Cipirello were "horse people." Her younger sister,
Aunt Lou, had agreed in shouted merriment during her interview:
"Yay, cowboy."[25] Apparently, horses were important enough to the
DiGiovannis that, when the last of the family immigrated to America
from Sicily for good in the 1950s, an ancient horseshoe from the
family home in San Cipirello was carefully packed and brought with
them. It hung for years, preserved in a cherry wood box frame on the
wall of my judicial chambers until my retirement. What did this all
mean?

"John," Nia had said to her interviewer and grandson, my
cousin John Guinta, with seeming but circumspect sincerity. "The
DiGiovannis were always cattle r..." Nia hesitated after pronouncing
the "r" as if she had caught herself on the precipice of letting slip
some truth she did not wish to reveal. The cogs and axles of her aged
but still sharp mind whirred and ground as she carefully chose her
next words: "cattle ranchers."[26]

Ranchers? When I first played Nia's taped interview twenty
years later for Paolo DiGiovanni, native-born Sicilian, and other relatives, one cousin howled in denial and outrage when Nia called the
DiGiovannis "cattle ranchers."

"That's not right," the cousin said. "Goats. No cows. They had
goats. Fix that. You gotta fix that," as if I could change something
that Nia said.

Paolo merely clucked a sly laugh. I laughed too, remembering
my own angry and disappointed reaction the first time I realized that
my sainted Nia had lied to me directly to my face. Ranchers? How
could the DiGiovannis of late-nineteenth-century Sicily have been
ranchers when they lacked the principal asset necessary to all cattle

ranchers—a ranch; that is, ownership of land sufficient in acreage to call a ranch? Why would they have left Sicily if they had really been landowners of sufficient size to call their land a ranch—or even *gabelloti* (wardens or middlemen who leased large tracts of land owned by others, usually absentee nobility, for short-fixed terms and wrung as much as they could out of it while they had it)?

More likely, the "r" word following "cattle" that Nia had successfully stifled during her taped interview was "rustlers," not ranchers. As early as 1864, Nicolo Turrisi Colonna, Baron of Buonvicino, had written about a "sect of thieves" whose members were "transporting stolen cattle through the countryside to city butchers. Some of the sect members specialized in rustling cattle, others in transporting the animals…, still others in illegal butchery."[27] Cattle rustling became an important means of scratching out a living for lower socioeconomic rural Sicilians who did not own land. At that time, the new Italian national state was too weak or disinterested to protect the interests of the big feudal landowners of Sicily. "Even the police became corrupted…. [T]hey would often broker or impose deals between the victims and perpetrators of theft. For example, rather than send stolen cattle along the chain of intermediaries to the butchers, rustlers could simply ask the captain of the local police to mediate. He would arrange for the stolen animals to be handed back to the original owner in return for money passed on to the rustlers. Naturally, the captain would get a percentage of the deal."[28] "[T]he sect emerged in the Palermo hinterland when the toughest and smartest bandits,…*gabelloti*, smugglers, livestock rustlers, estate wardens, farmers, and lawyers came together…"[29] It was Don Vito Cascio Ferro himself, who "had begun his career in 1892…in Bisaquino not far from Corleone [and within a 45-kilometer radius of both San Cipirello and Ciminna]…and made his fortune smuggling cattle with a small fleet of boats."[30] Cattle rustling remained a mainstay of the Western Sicilian economy, dominated by the vast estates of large feudal landowners, well into the twentieth century.[31]

It was into this environment, this mindset, this restrictive, oppressive, often-violent anthropological condition, this odd philosophy of *cavalleria rusticana* (rustic chivalry), that Gaetano DiGiovanni had been born, reared, and grown to manhood. In Gaetano's Western Sicily of the late nineteenth century, the nobility, the church, and the influential few who benefitted from a generally weak and corrupt government were the formal—if not actual—social powers. Those who held places in those three spheres were a distinct minority. Sicily's 1,200 barons, princes, dukes, and counts and the scions of a few old moneyed business dynasties, founded by past conquerors and occupiers of the island, like the Florios and Whitakers of Palermo, virtually monopolized ownership of its land, natural resources and large business enterprises through great estates. A small percentage of the remainder of the population, through church-based education or highly politicized entry into the University of Palermo, attained "professional" status. They became officials or functionaries of the formal institutions: bishops, monsignors, policemen, teachers, military men, or operatives of the church- or state-bolstered banking, shipping, mining, and railroad interests. The vast majority of the population were *contadini* (peasants) who lived outside and subject to the influence of these three spheres. They faced one of two destinies: either a life of desperate poverty eking out a meager existence as day laborers or subsistence farmers under the brutal thumbs of the overseers of the great estates, the *gabelloti*; or rejection of consignment to this fate and clawing their way upward by whatever means necessary, including self-reliance on their personal powers of intelligence, cunning, toughness and—sometimes—what we would describe today as lawlessness. Gaetano DiGiovanni was among this latter caste.

All this had culminated in that cloudless night in 1893. Gaetano DiGiovanni, also known as Tano Baiocco, cattleman without ranch, frequent user of fistfuls of brass baioccos, grandson of *uomo di rispetto* Don Randazzo, possessor of boldness, judgment, ambition, and intelligence uncommon among the landless men of his small Sicilian village, sat securely in the saddle of his stout little horse somewhere in the Madonie mountain range of Palermo Province, near the town of Ciminna. He gazed clear-eyed at the Sicilian sky, moonless but bright with stars, the source, no doubt, of an overpowering prescience that descended upon him. Gaetano saw his future.

CHAPTER 2

CIMINNA

That same night, Angela Bucaro stared at the same sky from her perch near an open window of her family's home in Ciminna, an ancient and baroque Western Sicily village. She had been born in Ciminna on August 7, 1878, less than two years after the kidnaping of English sulfur company manager John Forester Rose outside the nearby mining town of Lercara Friddi, only twenty kilometers south of her birthplace. Rose had been ransomed and released but only after his reluctant-to-pay family received his severed ears in the mail.[32] Ciminna was a small village, located atop a peak of the Madonie mountain range about forty-two kilometers southeast of Palermo within Palermo Province itself and about sixty kilometers east/southeast of the DiGiovanni home in San Cipirello. Ciminna was centuries old even then, established originally as a hamlet for the Arabs who conquered Sicily in the ninth century. Those Arab origins perhaps accounted for the darkness of the hair, skin, and eyes of its inhabitants, including the Bucaros. Architectural remains from the eras of Punic, Roman, and Norman domination can still be found in its environs. Ciminna became a duchy under the feudal domination of Ventimiglia in the sixteenth century and later the permanent residence of the Griffeo princes of Partanna. It overlooks a fertile valley that has historically produced olives, grapes, almonds, and broad beans. Its inhabitants are sometimes referred to as "*Vituzzi*," a reference to their religious devotion to St. Vito, the town's patron Sicilian saint[33] and the inspiration later for the name of one of Angela's sons. Ciminna is perhaps known best today as the backdrop of director Luchino Visconti's film *Il Gattopardo* (*The Leopard*), the story of a nineteenth-century Sicilian prince coping with the Garibaldi-led revolution, starring Burt Lancaster and Claudia Cardinale.

Angela Bucaro, this girl of Ciminna, was impish in stature, four feet ten inches tall, weighing less than ninety pounds. It was her diminutive size, common to the Bucaros, that prompted her loved ones, then and later, to refer to her as Angelina. Her features were Moorish and dark. Her flowing hair, coal black and long, framed her coffee-colored eyes and hawklike nose. Angelina's beauty was purely Mediterranean. She was doll-like and exotic, but it was the piercing intelligence of her eyes and the unusual broadness of her shoulders for a girl whose build was otherwise so slight, emoting fearlessness and independence bordering on haughtiness, that first attracted the attention of Gaetano DiGiovanni, then struck him like the mythical thunderbolt and moved him inexorably to the position on horseback he then occupied in the Madonie slopes near Ciminna.

On that night, Angelina was fourteen and a half years old, the ripe age of impending marriage for Sicilian girls of her time, place, and standing. Quietly and under her breath, she cursed that fact. She had been promised in marriage by her father to a sturdy and respectable man of the town. Was he a young policeman, a future police captain, or lawyer striving earnestly under her father's thumb? A *gabellato* with whom her father sometimes dealt in his official capacity? A merchant? A bishop's nephew? She did not know. It made no difference. Whatever he was, Angelina knew with certainty the only two things about her betrothed that mattered to her: she did not love him, and because he was her father's choice, she must rebel.

It was not that she did not love and respect her father. Giacomo Bucaro, who had married the stout but spritely Antonia Petrano, was a man of importance in Ciminna. In fact, the entire Bucaro family included people of means and standing. "My mother was a Bucaro. She was high class," Nia had said proudly in her taped interviews.[34] "[M]y mother's father was *la policia*,…a lawyer, not a detective, like an assistant superintendent, a cop…. You might say chief of police.

He was something big." Aunt Lou agreed, "My Grandpa [Bucaro], him. He was a head of the,…he was a government agent, him. He was a big shot, him." Nia added, "[M]y Uncle Frank [Giacomo's son, Francesco Bucaro]…was the head of the *Federia*,…the railroad, you might say the president of some railroad…. [M]y mother's family, they were mostly priests and nuns. Yeah, they were very religious. [Uncle Frank was] the one who was gonna be a priest, [but] he ran away with the bishop's niece…. Yeah, he eloped with the bishop's niece. Her name [was]…Gioranina. I don't know her last name. She was class. She was…a school teacher…. The bishop sent him [Uncle Frank] on an errand. He was gonna say his first Mass, my dear uncle. And then he eloped with the damn bishop's [niece]."[35]

Unlike much of the rest of the population of Ciminna, the Bucaros had means sufficient to take into their home an extra child, an abandoned infant. Angelina "had the adopted brother too," Nia said. "You see, in Italy, when they didn't want a baby, they had a convent, and on that convent…porch, they had a basket of vine, and you could bring that baby there, and it wasn't deserted…. [A]fter that baby stayed [in the convent for a while], it belonged to the government, and my grandmother [Antonia Petrano Bucaro] had nothing but miscarriages. She just had my mother and my Uncle Frank, so they adopted that baby…. His name was Boncorrea…John Boncorrea. His name was Giacomo after my grandfather [re]named him, but his last name was Boncorrea, [which means] good heart…. Yeah, when they put that baby in the basket, they put the baby's name in there, but [the Bucaros] gave him Grandpa's…first name, and let him keep his last name."[36]

Ciminna Police Chief Giacomo Bucaro was the patriarch of this distinguished family. Of course, he was no fool. His eyes were wide open to the realities of his circumstance and his community. As a religious but realistic and doting father, he knew exactly what he had in his beautiful Angelina, his beloved only daughter. As a superintendent of local policemen, it was his job to sense what was going on, even in a culture where informing was virtually unheard of, to track the identities, even to develop a certain professional relationship with all men of the village and the surrounding countryside who might occasionally stray from strict adherence to the law. Certainly, a local police officer's job in Western Sicily in the late nineteenth century had its odd and ironic features. Regardless whether the central government of the new unified Italy was in the hands of the Conservative Right of Prime Minister Giovanni Lanza or the Liberal Left of Interior Minister Giovanni Nicotera, Rome directed that Sicilian crime must be addressed in the same way: "[T]owns were encircled at night and suspects deported en masse.... The police colluded with some criminals against others."[37] Giacomo Bucaro maintained his position in the Sicilian way, by accommodating whatever wind blew from Rome at any given time, while keeping his own counsel. After all, what did Rome know of Sicily? As a Sicilian himself, Giacomo knew that "[o]ften the policeman preferred to help the dishonest countryman with whom he had to live the rest of his life, rather than the guileless foreign[er],...[including those northerners from Rome. He knew that] [i]f most Italians manage at times to weave skillfully in and out of written laws, most Sicilians appear to avoid them all completely. They are the supreme masters of this skill, recognized by all Italians as the unbeatable champions.... [He knew that among the] principles...shared by all Sicilians [including himself], they must...always beware of official authorities and law;... [that often] [t]he police [must confess] themselves impotent..."[38]

Giacomo Bucaro must have known the reputation of the "Baioccos." But was he truly appalled when he first heard the local gossip that his daughter had somehow stricken—and become smitten herself with—the young DiGiovanni known as Tano Baiocco? Could Giacomo have had mixed feelings? On one hand, the young DiGiovanni was said to be a youth of extraordinary courage and conscientiousness. Giacomo's people told him that Tano Baiocco had begun to acquire something of a reputation as a young man of uncommon reason, a calm mediator of small-time local disputes; a go-between for the powerless and a trusted intermediary for his maternal Grandfather Randazzo; an earner in the cattle trade; a man who—because he was thought to be fully capable of violent self-protection of himself and his people—seldom actually had to employ it. While the proof of these characteristics had not yet been firmly established by the passing of time and the accumulation of repeated accomplishments that can only be counted in older age, Gaetano DiGiovanni seemed to have potential. Though uneducated, rough in appearance, and seemingly lacking in tangible resources, young Tano seemed by all reports to possess all the qualities of Sicilian manliness that might someday lead to something. What did it matter, the nickname Baiocco and its origins? What did it matter that Tano Baiocco was said to tend toward a lack of strict obedience to civil authority of the type represented by Giacomo himself? Was this not quintessentially Sicilian? Had Giacomo not detected a similar strain, at least the potential for such actions that in fact would play out in New Orleans early in the next century, among his own namesakes? On the other hand, Angelina was his only daughter. She must do better than a dusty country cowboy, regardless of his ambition, intelligence, and potential; regardless of his rumored connections; regardless of Giacomo's own sometimes cooperation with just such people, all out of the necessity of realism.

Giacomo resolved this internal paternal conflict by deciding to show disapproval and rage when he confronted Angelina with the intelligence he had gathered. His studied rage became reality when she denied it, especially when she did so in a furiously sincere way that convinced Giacomo that she was lying. He flatly forbade any liaison with young Gaetano DiGiovanni. Nia indicated as much in her taped interviews:

"[T]hey [the Bucaros] objected to the marriage, you know, a DiGiovanni wasn't going to marry a cop's daughter."

"Her father thought she made a mistake?" Nia was asked by her interviewer.

"Of course, she made a mistake," Nia answered immediately and forcefully,[39] giving the impression that the Bucaros considered young DiGiovanni "*viddanu*, a term [then in common use] with strong pejorative connotations: *viddanu* (from *villano*, villein, villain), a man from the countryside and lacking any civility."[40]

"She could have had boys," Nia said. "Who the hell was [Gaetano DiGiovanni], you know?... They [the Bucaros] were all professional people, like lawyers and...railroad [managers]...[and]

police. [Grandpa Bucaro] was something big, and the DiGiovannis couldn't stand cops. We don't like the fuzz... The Mafia was somewhere around, you know... The Bucaros, they were, you know, they objected... That's why they didn't like the DiGiovannis. That's why they didn't want my mama to marry him. They said my daddy [di]dn't have the quality... They thought they might have the horse people comin'."[41]

The vehemence of her father's disapproval, the silent reproach in her mother's eyes, and her burning memory of the sight of Gaetano DiGiovanni on horseback, so tall, so dashing, so bold and mysterious, now so forbidden, merely cemented Angelina's resolve. She must rebel against her father's choice, against his disapproval of the notion that she might marry a DiGiovanni. She must rebel, not from lack of love for her father or her family but because of a characteristic set deeply in her cultural and genetic makeup. "'Sicilian man...eternally has rebellion and the unbounded passion of his own ego in his bloodstream—the *mafioso* in a nutshell.'"[42] Could Angelina be anything less than a Sicilian man, just because of her gender?

CHAPTER 3

MADONIE MOUNTAINS 1893

"My Mama said that Paw Paw kidnapped her out of her room," Nia said in her taped interview. Aunt Lou agreed. "They kidnapped her... when she was fourteen and a half." Upon momentary reflection, Nia disagreed. "Well, you know, that's a lie. She met that man halfway... Now, you know, she went down that damn line herself."[43]

Based on these few snippets, I imagine that the courtship of Gaetano DiGiovanni and Angelina Bucaro must have been swift and enigmatic but ultimately decisive. Perhaps Gaetano was on horseback one day, roaming the mountainous countryside outside of Ciminna, in search of stray cattle or path-side chapel baskets half filled with baioccos or on some errand for his Grandfather Randazzo. Perhaps Angelina was wandering those same mountain paths on that same day, leading a pack of village children or a flock of goats, with only two or three older women of the town as chaperones, strolling down from a peak of the Madonie mountain range, where Ciminna sat at the top. Gaetano would have spied her first, perhaps from some distance, her dark beauty and girlish chattering to the goats or little children cutting through the thin mountain air and into Gaetano's senses. *Que bella*, what beauty, beguiling him, a physical beauty he had never before seen: Moorish, exotic, tiny, yet broad-shouldered, like the porcelain dolls he had seen in the windows of Palermo curio shops, so small and delicate that he could imagine cradling her entirely in the palm of one of his rough cowboy's hands, like a velvet purse filled with baioccos. He must get a closer look. Gaetano would have spurred his stout horse, gently but with command, down the mountain slope, around a dusty boulder, just off to the side of the narrow path where the chirping beauty and her following pack would have to pass. He concealed himself behind the boulder. Angelina would have come directly toward his hiding place, into his view, skipping lightly and confidently over the rocks, with the sure-footedness of a mountain goat.

Suddenly, there she was before him. It was then that Gaetano was struck by the proverbial thunderbolt. His mouth opened slightly at the force of the electric shock, which lifted him up high in his horse's saddle. He no longer attempted to conceal himself or his naked feelings. It was then that Angelina first saw him and faltered in her tracks. This was a sort of man she had previously only imagined: tall, dashing, unusually magnetic in his dust-covered roughness, his fedora broad and floppy, a shotgun slung across his left shoulder, so different from the prim village policemen and lawyers she had seen with her father. Angelina stared at Gaetano. Curiosity and fascination bolted from the dark pools of her eyes.

"Angelina!" One of the chaperones would have shrieked at the girl from behind, appalled that a virtuous girl from an upstanding family might come so close to and look so directly at a young man who was not her brother or uncle. Abruptly, Angelina turned and ran, through the bleating of her confused flock or the marveling children, through the invective of the chaperones hurling curses toward Gaetano until she reached a hiding place behind a large rock. Her heart pounded. Her breath raced. She peeked from behind the rock, hoping for another glance of this mysterious cowboy, a sight as exotic to her as she had been to him. But he had disappeared into the Sicilian landscape.

Gaetano needed to see no more. He had pulled the reins of his stout little mount and strategically retreated to a familiar place nearby, the shade of a mountain path chapel, dedicated to the glory of San Francesco di Paolo. He inhaled a heavy breath of the thin mountain air and shook his head from left to right, clearing it of the effects of the thunderbolt. There was no doubt or question in his mind. He must have this girl as his wife. He was twenty-five, well past the age at which he felt he should have married. Long ago, he had foreseen his future as a man of standing, well-dressed in suit, white shirt and tie, a cowboy no longer, but patriarch of a large brood whose security and success he would obtain through the power of his own shrewdness, will, and perseverance, but none of the young women of San Cipirello had met his high standards. Immediately, he set about the task of learning Angelina's identity. He chuckled upon learning that she was a Bucaro, daughter of the Ciminna police superintendent. Gaetano had already dealt satisfactorily in various transactions with several of Giacomo Bucaro's subordinates. Despite the surface cordiality of these dealings, Gaetano knew that marriage to a police chief's daughter was an entirely different matter: personal, familial, not business. He realized that it would be useless to pursue her in the traditional way, to ask her father for the privilege of courting her, under the supervision of her mother and aunts, all of which he knew would be angrily refused. All the better, he thought to himself. Better for a man of action like himself to bypass the slow and deliberate usual route, especially since there was another well-worn way.

For centuries in Sicily, it had been part of the "primitive justice" of the society, "conceived as something innate in man" that "outraged virgins [should be] married off to their seducers,…"[44] Gaetano would steal her away, take her from her home and into his own, in a sudden and forceful fashion that would compel all concerned to assume that Angelina had been "spoiled" for any other possible suitor. With the prescience that Gaetano alone recognized as his special gift, though the two had not yet exchanged a single word, he knew that this girl would be his willing accomplice.

Gaetano spent the following days camped out in the passes of the Madonie mountain range encircling Ciminna, in constant surveillance of the mountaintop town and its surrounding slopes. He ate very little, sustained by the nearness of his petite prize. His active mind spun with schemes, but he settled on the simplest plan of all. Each early afternoon, he spurred his horse to the spot where he had first seen her, but she did not appear there again. He galloped into the town itself, surreptitiously searching her out among the dense layout of the ancient stone buildings in its sloping labyrinth of narrow streets near her home. Finally, one bright afternoon, he spotted her again, walking alone, bearing a wheel of cheese on her head, delivering it from her mother's kitchen to her grandmother's home nearby. Boldly, in the plain view of passersby and a few of the neighborhood women who habitually sat outside their houses at that time of day, Gaetano dismounted and stepped abruptly into her path, no more than a meter from her face. Angelina halted, dead in her tracks, causing the cheese to bobble slightly until she balanced it in her tiny left hand, this time Gaetano delivering the thunderbolt, rather than receiving it.

"Tonight, my beauty," he said to her quickly and quietly. "Unlock the door to your house, just before dawn. Be waiting for me."

She stared directly into his eyes, showing astonishment, but without fear, indicating neither assent nor resistance. Gaetano pulled briefly at the brim of his fedora, nodded slightly, and disappeared into a nearby street. The whole encounter lasted only seconds. With lightning speed, he jumped into the saddle and galloped his horse swiftly away into the mountains.

The stunned Angelina was frozen in place on the narrow Ciminna street. The cheese now balanced uncertainly on her head. It was true that during these past days, she had daydreamed of little else than the rugged cowboy she had bewitched on the mountain path. Their infatuation had been mutual. She had chattered girlishly and improvidently about the meeting with some of her cousins, too near to the neighborhood women sitting in their doorways in the afternoon. The chaperones had started the gossip among the women, and she worried now that her foolish chirping had increased it, leading to the unpleasant scene with her father. It would now intensify. No matter. Angelina felt a compulsion, fueled by adolescent urges of rebellion and romance. She wanted him. She must comply with his whispered command.

That night, Angelina went to her room at the usual hour and feigned sleep excitedly until shortly before midnight. She rose from her bed and crept quietly through the house, assuring herself that the others were asleep. She tiptoed back into her room, dressed in practical outdoor clothing, and then slowly unlocked the front door that opened directly to the nearby street. She sat on a wide chair in the front room and tried to stay awake. She failed and drifted into the deep sleep of the young and innocent, slumping lightly into the cushion of the chair where she had been sitting.

With the same studied deliberateness that he employed in all his affairs, Gaetano rode into Ciminna from his mountain perch, concealed only by the darkness of the night. For this operation, he had borrowed a mule and a small wagon from a friendly carter, leaving his stout little horse as collateral. As he neared the narrow street where the Bucaro house was located, he slowed the mule to a walk and dismounted. Quietly, he led the obedient mule by the reins of the wagon to a spot near the Bucaro house and quickly eyed the front door. Had she unlocked it? After tying the mule lightly to a nearby hitching post, he strode to the entrance of the Bucaro house. He jiggled the latch. The door was not locked. Quietly, he turned the latch and tiptoed into the room. Gaetano saw Angelina asleep in the chair. Angelina, still dozing, felt his strength as he lifted her in his arms. She thought dreamily that it must be her father, lifting her from the chair to carry her to bed. When she awoke, still in his arms but now through the door and into the street, she saw that it was Gaetano. Their eyes met. She nodded. Gently, Gaetano lifted her up into the back of the wagon and laid her on a thick quilt he had carefully placed there for her comfort. Then he leaped in place at the front of the wagon, grasping the leather reins in his strong hands. He urged the mule forward, rushing now through the Ciminna streets, into its surrounding mountain paths, downward, westward, into the Sicilian countryside, the wagon and its occupants racing away before any alarm might be sounded.

They trotted all night and into the next day, cantering intermittently, occasionally dismounting and walking in silence for short periods, before bundling into the wagon again and continuing their journey. They rode and rode, down and away from the Ciminna mountaintop and the Madonie range. They passed the ruins of the

Norman castle at Villafrati and the Greek temple at Cefala Diana, past the outskirts of Marineo and into the rolling plain of Central Palermo Province with its lemon groves, olive orchards, and vast fields of golden wheat, past the roadside shrines of the Blessed Virgin and the various martyred saints, into the Portella della Ginestra, the main pass through the mountains that enveloped the towns of Piana degli Albanesi, San Giuseppe Jato, and San Cipirello. Finally, they reached the safety of the DiGiovanni home. It was dark again, but Angelina, exhausted and covered in dust, had lost track of the precise day and time. They went inside.

Gaetano walked her to a rough wooden table where a clay bowl filled with fresh water and a small white square of clean linen could be used to wash. He fetched a loaf of good bread, a wedge of goat's cheese, and a shallow plate of olive oil and laid it out in front of her to eat. It was the last meal he would ever prepare for her throughout the more than half a century of their marriage.

Gaetano seated himself at a chair nearby and watched her eat. She was so calm, so satisfied, seemingly comfortable in her quiet certitude. After sleep, he would scare up a friendly local priest and persuade him with the commanding reason for which he was well known and a purse full of baioccos to perform the marriage cere-mony. For now, however, he merely gazed in silence at the extraor-dinary sight of his doll-like prize, seated comfortably in his home as she finished her meal.

Angelina gazed back. "What now?" she asked herself, silently, without words or gestures, but clearly and fearlessly, her question apparent in the fiery glow of her intelligent eyes. "What now?"

Gaetano rose from his chair and approached her. He smiled a broad grin, illuminated by the light of his audacity and ambition. He bent forward and kissed her squarely on the thin lips of her long mouth as she remained seated in the chair, her first kiss, which she did not resist, the first of many. Gaetano was swept up in his premo-nition. *Now it can begin*, he thought.

CHAPTER 4

CASTELVETRANO, TRAPANI PROVINCE

Today, Natale Giunta of Castelvetrano is a celebrity chef, the Emeril Lagasse of Western Sicily. Of course, the concept of the "celebrity chef" originated centuries ago in Italy, specifically in the time of the decline of the Roman Republic, shortly before the birth of Christ. Before that time, "[c]elebrity chefs had long been regarded [in Rome] as a particularly pernicious symptom of decadence. [In the last century of the Republic, however, elaborate cookery] 'began to be highly prized, and what had been a mere function instead came to be regarded as high art, [with famous chefs and their exotic recipes and ingredients becoming] an all-consuming craze.'"[45] The early twenty-first-century Natale Giunta, the celebrity chef of Castelvetrano, is a modern-day version of this vestige of Ancient Rome. He is the chef/owner of two acclaimed upscale restaurants of Sicily, one in Castelvetrano and one in Palermo. He hosted the television program "Showcooking with Chef Natale Giunta" and is the author of popular cookbooks. He has been the star attraction at the festive opening of a new multi-plex movie theater in Palermo, fundraisers for the Sicilian National Symphony Orchestra and various charitable endeavors. Chef Natale's infectious smile and laughing visage can be viewed by millions of computer users worldwide via YouTube or "Facebook Fans of Natale Giunta" as he joyously prepares one of his fabulous specialties, like

Aragosta e Caviale di Piselli (lobster and caviar with peas) or *Zuppetta di Fave e Finocchietto Selvatico* (broad beans and wild fennel soup).[46]

One of Chef Natale's late-nineteenth-century ancestors in Castelvetrano was my grandfather, originally Natale Giunta of Castelvetrano, later Natale Guinta of New Orleans, where he married my grandmother Nia (Lena, Antonia), the middle child of Gaetano and Angelina DiGiovanni. In contrast to Chef Natale, about whom almost anything can be known today through the power of the internet and the relentless marketing and publicity so necessary to his status as a celebrity restauranteur, almost nothing is known about my Grandfather Natale's youth in Castelvetrano or his earliest days in America.

"My daddy never talked about his past," Mom told me many times. "It was like he put it all behind him once he left Sicily. Fact is, he didn't say much about his present either. He was a man of few words." Even Nia (Lena), his wife of thirty-four years, knew virtually nothing about Natale when she married him in 1931, except that he was the choice of her father, the redoubtable Gaetano DiGiovanni. It appears from Nia's recorded recollections that what she learned about her husband's premarriage life during the thirty-four years that followed their civil wedding before a judge of the Municipal Court of the City of New Orleans was nothing more than basic information. Like some of the rest of her taped interviews, the accuracy of what Nia remembered or was told about Natale's past may be subject to question.

We know from his official Italian birth certificate that Natale Guinta was born Natale Giunta on October 1, 1888, in Castelvetrano, a small town in Trapani Province, about eighty-nine kilometers southwest of Palermo near the Sicilian coast. His father was Giuseppe Giunta, and his mother was Anna Sanstefano Giunta, both of Castelvetrano.[47] His immediate family included two brothers, Pasquale and Giuseppe, and three sisters, Catarina, who subsequently married a Napolitano; Antonia, who subsequently married a Mangiricino; and Margherita, who subsequently married a Victorino.[48]

The remains of an ancient necropolis discovered in modern Castelvetrano's main piazza indicate that Natale's birthplace was inhabited as early as the seventh century BC. During the Roman

occupation of Sicily, it served as "a camp for the lodgings of veteran soldiers in charge of the stores, which were kept in great cisterns" called "*castrum veteranorum*," the apparent origin of the town's name. "In 1299 it was made a fief of the Tagliavias, who promoted the development of the town," [and] "[i]n 1653 the fief passed by succession to the Pignatelli Aragona family."[49] On July 5, 1950, Castelvetrano was the site of the assassination of the internationally notorious but spectacularly photogenic bandit gang leader, murderer, and Sicilian separatist, Salvatore Giuliano, the subject of Mario Puzo's best-selling novel, *The Sicilian*. Castelvetrano has been famous for centuries, continuing through today, for its olives and fine olive oil, a frequently enjoyed bottle of which sits continuously on a shelf of my kitchen pantry.

Whatever might be said about my Natale's early character, appearance, or personality as a youth of Castelvetrano or his reason for leaving Sicily to come to America is mostly conjecture based upon what we know of his later life. As a young man, he must have cut an imposing figure. His physical strength and capabilities were substantial, and his appearance was powerful. He was five feet four inches tall, and his build was bearish, muscular, barrel-chested, broad-shouldered, thick through the torso, hips, and limbs, a throwback to the twelfth-century Norman conquerors of Sicily. His eyes were gray blue, and his hair was reddish brown in color, odd hues when compared to the dark features of most of his countrymen. His hair was thin and wispy, even when he was young, foretelling the almost absolute baldness of his perfectly round head that would distinguish him in later life.

Unlike today's Chef Natale, there was nothing about my grandfather's personality that reflected the joyousness, piety, or cheer of his first name—the Italian word for Christmas. His bearing was unsmiling, taciturn, even menacing to those who were not his family members. Even as a youth in Castelvetrano, he must have been a man of few words. The words that he did speak were spare and blunt, incisive and directly to the point, wholly lacking in the extraneous charm, politeness and flattery that peppers the speech of so many Italians. The fuse that ran to his considerable temper was short. He brooked no teasing, no careless joking about his appearance, personality, or stony silences.

At an early age, Natale was taken with fishing and hunting, avocations that would stay with him for the rest of his life, not because of any particular sentimentality about the natural world or any need to provide food for himself or his family but because he was good at it. He was a natural predator, content to be alone in the countryside or at the seashore, roaming freely, comfortable in his own thoughts and deeds, unfettered by anyone outside of himself, even those who might love him. He became an expert in the handling and use of hunting weaponry, especially the shotgun, sportsman's knife and small sidearms, and an excellent marksman. His misanthropy was sometimes mistaken for a serious bent of introspection. Natale was wholly sufficient unto himself, finding no need to depend upon or entrust himself to anyone else until much later in life when he became a husband and father. He was no academic or intellectual, but he could read and write. He possessed a wholly practical intelligence and shrewdness that was thoroughly grounded in realism. Today we would call his hardheaded perspicacity "street smarts." The nineteenth-century Natale Giunta of Castelvetrano—just like his later self, Natale Guinta of New Orleans—was not to be trifled with in any way. He could not accept foolishness of any kind, either in himself or in others.

Odd, perhaps, that this kind of character should spring from what his widow later described as an almost privileged upbringing, at least by the nineteenth-century standards of rural Western Sicily.

According to Nia, Natale was the only one of his siblings who ever left Sicily. Although some of the children of Natale's siblings did ultimately emigrate to America, his siblings themselves stayed in Castelvetrano because "they had no need," Nia said. "They were, you know,...they were landowners... [T]hey had olive groves. In fact, Taormina used to get all their olives, all their olive oil from Castelvetrano, from my father-in-law, Pa-Paw's daddy..."[50] Nia said that in later days, after she and Natale were married, the Giuntas back in Castelvetrano were so well off, relatively speaking, that "money Pa-Paw and I used to send [them] for food and things, for Mother's Day,...they didn't need it, and she [her mother-in-law, Anna Sanstefano Giunta] put it away in the *banca*, you see. She says, 'if something happens to me, then you'll all inherit'... But, they [the Giuntas] didn't have no need to come to America... Natale's [siblings] never did come to the United States."[51]

"[O]n Natale's...side, his family,...what did they do over in Sicily?" her interviewer, my cousin John Guinta, asked Nia.

"They lived on a farm," Nia said. "Well, they were landowners... [T]hey farmed olives, you know, wheat especially, grapes, making wine and olive oil and everything you can imagine a farm is... They were self-employed people. They didn't have to work 9 to 5. They had their own land...not really a farmer, landowners."[52]

Landowners? In nineteenth-century Sicily? The Giuntas, landowners, at a time when only the nobility owned the vast majority of acreage sufficient in size to grow large and varied crops of wheat, grapes, and olives, enough olives in fact to supply all of Taormina's olive oil needs? Perhaps the Giuntas of Castelvetrano owned some land. We know, in fact, from legal documents in the family records that Natale executed a power of attorney in 1954 in favor of a Sicilian lawyer, Rizzo Baldasare, so that his own inherited interest in the Giunta property in Sicily could be donated to his siblings. But it was not a tract of land as rich and vast in size as Nia described. More likely, Giuseppe Giunta, Natale's father, and his sons, were *gabelloti*.

In nineteenth-century Sicily, "the big landowners...typically spent their time in Palermo and leased out their estates...to middlemen or *gabelloti*...[who] had to wring money out of the peasants... The average *gabelloto* was a ruthless, self-made man; this was a job you could not do without making enemies."[53] These *gabelloti* were "strong men or 'violent peasant entrepreneurs' who were willing to use violence and take people under their protection to compensate for the weakness of the state... The central government was too weak... to protect landowners and guarantee that they received regular rent payments from their tenants. So, landowners hired these strong men...to protect them and guarantee the payment of rents. Indeed, many landowners went off to live in the cities, leaving the *gabelloti* virtually in charge of their estates. As long as the rents flowed in, all was well."[54] "*Gabelloti* were such pivotal figures in Sicily's violent economy that it was often assumed that being a *mafiosi* and being a *gabelloti* were the same thing. It is more accurate to say that joining the Mafia enabled a *gabelloto* to do his job better."[55] However, they "were certainly not simply bandits and criminals. They had a more sophisticated role in protecting the interests of landowners..."[56]

Why would the eldest son of a prominent *gabelloto* or the son of an owner of land, a son who stood to inherit either position or property, whose siblings saw no need to emigrate to America to earn a living since their living was being well-made in Castelvetrano, choose to leave? And when did Natale leave? For years, with no success, I spent day after day in two libraries scanning the indices and pages of the multiple volumes of Glazier and Filbey's *Italians to America: Lists of Passengers Arriving at U.S. Ports* in search of Natale's name. The encyclopedic collection of the identities of Italian immigrants contains several Giuntas and Guintas, even a couple of Pasquales and Giuseppes, the name of his father that Natale would sometimes use himself later in life, but none from Castelvetrano who might have been about the correct age Natale would have been when he arrived in America. One year, on a trip to Ellis Island, my sister Judy found the name Natale Guinta inscribed in a brass plaque, along with the names of many others. The plaque contained no date of arrival, no place of departure, no age or village of origin. "Just the name of my grandfather," Judy said. "Nothing else." Someday, I will have to go to Ellis Island myself and trudge through its voluminous records in search of something certain.

On the other hand, maybe such a search would be futile. In 1940, on the verge of American involvement in World War II, like all other US noncitizens born in one of the belligerent nations of the Axis Powers, Natale was required by Act of Congress to register with the United States Department of Justice.[57] Like almost every other document and bit of oral lore describing the family history, certain oddities in Natale's Alien Registration Form cast doubt on its complete veracity even though Natale signed it as a notarized affidavit, swearing that all statements contained in it "are true and complete to the best of my knowledge and belief."[58] The form lists his name as Natali Giunta, not Natale Guinta. It correctly lists his home address as 1169 Tchoupitoulas Street in New Orleans, his birthplace as Castelvetrano, his occupation as a bartender, and that he had a wife and two children. However, the form falsely represents his birth date as October 1, 1892, not 1888. The form states that he arrived in New York on October 17, 1919, aboard the SS *Locan* or *Logan* as one of its crewmembers and that he "entered the United States under the name of Antonino Calia."[59]

The form also reports that Natale served in the Italian Army infantry during World War I from 1915 to 1918 and that he had "not yet" applied for US citizenship.[60] The statements concerning his Army service and the steamship on which he came to America appear truthful. The year 1915 through 1918 were the exact years during which Italy fought in World War I and subjected all able-bodied men of Natale's age to military conscription. "Over 400,000 Sicilians— equivalent to more than the whole population of Palermo—were drafted."[61] A crew member manifest of the SS *Logan* available on Ancestry.com listing "Calia, Antonio" as an "attendant" indicates that the *Logan's* port of embarkation from Italy in 1920 was Trieste in extreme Northern Italy, near its current border with Slovenia. Trieste was precisely in the area where the Italian Army fought in the Great War. Natale was certainly a fighter, unafraid of blood and guns, the type of man who would not have attempted to evade the Italian draft. Fighting as an Italian infantryman in the mountainous, topographically impenetrable Trieste theater of war would have involved him in "four Italian offensives in 1915, all staged in the same area, all monotonously ineffective, all mournfully wasteful of blood and bravery [and waged against]...southern Slav, Hungarian, and Tyrolese troops...[who] had no love for Italians... For a few worthless pieces of soil, the Italians...paid with the blood of a quarter-million soldiers, dead and wounded, during the four battles... Years went by, but that was the war for Italy. Its armies, trying to do the impossible, wasted away. The bleeding and brooding by millions of men swelled the resentment that brought postwar fascism to flower."[62] Demobilization of Italian troops like Natale was a cumbersome and delayed process, lasting from 1919 through 1921.[63]

If, as seems likely, Natale experienced the horrors of World War I combat, he would have been exposed to the agony his grandson Greg Guinta described in a college essay written almost seventy years later: "Under constant artillery bombardment, the most solid nerves cannot resist abandonment to fear...[and] the terrible effects of shellfire... '[M]en squashed, cut in two, or divided from top to bottom, blown into showers by an ordinary shell, bellies turned inside out and scattered anyhow, skulls forced bodily into the chest as if by a blow with a club...' Horror scenes were commonplace,... One of the most profound sociological revelations of World War I was how men of all nations adjusted themselves to, and then accepted over such a long duration, the mutilations, the indignities, the repeated displays of incompetence by the leaders,... The impersonal nature of the violence in World War I had a terrible effect on men of all countries. The men began to believe that war is perhaps the nature of the world in essence... [They became a] generation 'grown up to find all Gods dead, all faiths in men shaken'... A tough cynicism grew out of all soldiers that would surely last the rest of their lives."[64]

No family member interviewed has ever related any recollection of Natale mentioning military service in World War I. Why not? Were his war experiences the final hardener of Natale's young character, teaching him that Godless violence and mayhem were the true nature of man? Why flee and enter America under someone else's name? Was he AWOL (absent without leave)? Why not return home to Castelvetrano where, as eldest Giunta son, he figured to follow his father's footsteps into a lucrative *gabelloto* position and avoid any repercussions from desertion? Why misspell his own name on the registration form? Why give an erroneous birth year? For now, what is certain is that Natale emigrated alone. In 1900, he would have been twelve years old, too young for a treacherous solo journey to America. Since we know from his obituary, death certificate, and other circumstances that he first arrived in New Orleans in 1922 and that New Orleans was not his initial place of residence in America, it seems likely that he came to America as a hardened veteran Italian World War I infantryman sometime around 1920. What is also certain is that once he left Sicily, Natale Giunta of Castelvetrano—later Natale Guinta of New Orleans—never returned for any reason: not to visit; not to sightsee; not for the funerals or illnesses of his father, mother or siblings; not to reminisce.

"It was like he put it all behind him once he left Sicily," Mom said. *Omerta,* the Sicilian Code of Silence, applied even about himself to his loved ones.

CHAPTER 5

MEZZOGIORNO, THE SICILIAN DIASPORA

On another indeterminate date just before the end of the nineteenth century, probably in 1898 if Gaetano's obituary is believable, Gaetano and Angelina DiGiovanni decided to leave Western Sicily, uproot their young family and move to the promised land, America. Like Natale Giunta of Castelvetrano, who would later become Natale Giunta of America, the DiGiovannis had become swept up in the *Mezzogiorno*, the "massive emigration" from the southern part of Italy that occurred between 1871 and 1915.

During that time, "over 13.5 million emigrants left the country for European and overseas destinations."[65] The causes were many, particularly in that southernmost of Italian regions, Sicily. One cause was a massive increase in Italian population growth nationwide, resulting from a rapid fall in death rates coupled simultaneously with an increased birth rate. Other causes were more endemic to the South, especially isolated and comparatively primitive Western Sicily. "In the years that followed the establishment of the new Kingdom [of Italy in] (1861), [the newly 'unified' nation] showed a growing dualism, a disparity in social and economic conditions that separated the industrial north from the agricultural south... The south had experienced centuries of economic and political domination under foreign conquerors. In addition, it had poor soil, lack of irrigation, recurrent

49

droughts, massive deforestation, and malaria. Agriculture was still dominated by large estates and absentee landlords... Moreover, the south had a feudal social system and little industry... Government was inefficient and dishonest. The centralizing policies of the new state also contributed to the impoverishment and backwardness of the south;... [Thus], the general factors that caused migration from Italy at the end of the nineteenth century [were] demographic pressure, low wages, the desire for greater social mobility, the stagnation of the economy and...inability to absorb surplus labor, particularly in the south, the agricultural crisis of the 1880s, cheap and more efficient transport... [I]n the *Mezzogiorno*, peasants were fleeing from hunger, malaria, rising taxes, and rising prices. Migration in the south became an act of defiance, a form of class struggle of peasants against landlords."[66]

Gaetano and Angelina DiGiovanni were not among the vast majority of the Sicilian peasantry who were worst afflicted by the societal plagues that sparked the *Mezzogiorno*. As he matured into the firm manhood of his thirties in the final decade of the nineteenth century, Gaetano had continued to make his "cowboy" living, handling cattle as they were liberated from the great estates, acting as middle man between the *gabelloti* and the *carabinieri*, including his father-in-law, plying in the cattle trade that had been organized and perfected by Don Vito Cascio Ferro. He acquired not only cattle but a few goats, sheep, and donkeys. It was during this time that he began to be recognized among the people of his small hometown of San Cipirello as a reliable problem-solver, a man of judgment, and an effective mediator of disputes of all kinds. "[S]uch a mediating function was an extension of a traditional role performed by men of honour [sic], in assisting *paesani* in difficulty."[67] The family's oral lore depiction of Gaetano is consistent with the historical characterization of certain Western Sicilian men of that time who assisted *contadini* (peasants) "'who did not have enough to eat or to pay their rent or to find good doctors for their children.'"[68] These men arranged contracts and kept order, by "provid[ing] protection from all sorts of threats, including the legal authorities,...us[ing] diplomacy rather than force,"[69] since all knew him as a man of respect who "defends his territory,…carries a gun,…shoots straight,…can kill a man if necessary,…enforce his will," so that "he never, or almost never, has the need to shoot."[70] Gaetano's "reward was in the form of favors…, not cash."[71] The peasants would give him slices of goat cheese, lemons pilfered while the *gabelloti* were not looking from the great estates where they performed their day labor, small bits of rag or handmade utensils. It was there and then that his neighbors began to greet him as Don Tano or *Zu* (Uncle) Tano and with salutations like "*bacio le mano* (I kiss your hand)."[72]

Nevertheless, for Gaetano and Angelina, there were reasons more personal than just those that sparked the *Mezzogiorno* for their decision to leave Sicily. Angelina's health was Gaetano's primary concern. Like any good Catholic girl of nineteenth-century Sicily, she became pregnant almost immediately after her marriage. Unfortunately, her elfin stature, the crude conditions that prevailed in San Cipirello and the effects of a disease that would mark her for life made childbearing a risky proposition for Angelina and the children she and Gaetano would conceive. Throughout the course of her young womanhood, Angelina conceived eighteen of Gaetano's children. Miscarriage or death at childbirth claimed the lives of half. For the first nearly twenty years of her marriage, Angelina was almost continually either pregnant or recovering from a miscarriage or childbirth. "She had 18, [but only nine survived]," Nia said. "The rest kicked the bucket… Old Grandma was punctual… I love her."[73] The first to survive was a daughter, Giuseppina ("Josephine" or "Fene"), who was born in San Cipirello on September 29, 1894. The second was a son, the male heir for whom Gaetano had longed, Domenico ("Dominick"), who was born in San Cipirello on February 22, 1896. Angelina, whose piercing dark eyes had first attracted the thunderbolt that struck Gaetano, could see neither one of her children. She had become blind.

"How did Grandma DiGiovanni lose her eye?" my cousin John had asked during Nia's 1988 interview while examining Angelina's 1935 passport, which noted that she was "blind in one eye" and displayed her facial snapshot clearly showing one eye surgically sewn shut.

"She had smallpox in that one eye," Nia said, "Ma-Mamie, you remember Aunt Mary, up until Ma-Mamie was born [in New Orleans in 1905], she couldn't see any of the children. She was blind in both eyes."[74]

Gaetano longed for the kind of medical care that might cure Angelina of her blindness and bring his future children into the world in health and safety. No such medical miracles were available in 1890s Western Sicily, where—by 1898—filth and disease were not the only threats perceived by Gaetano, in his persona as Tano Baiocco.

In 1897–'99, a Mafia war was raging in the *Conca d'Oro*,[75] the golden circle of grain fields, lemon orchards, and olive groves surrounding Palermo. The principal combatants were the Malaspina *cosca* headed by Don Francesco Siino and his supporters and an alliance headed by Don Antonino Giammona of the Passo di Rigano group with the Piana dei Colli and Perpignano families. Killings of rival sub-bosses, wardens, and *cosca* affiliates mounted. When several innocent bystanders were also murdered, Ermanno Sangiorgi, chief of police of Palermo, took action. Sangiorgi had already spent about two years compiling the first "explicit, detailed, and systematic" written reports of "the organizational plan of the eight mafia *cosche* ruling [Palermo's] suburbs and satellite villages…[including] profiles of 218 men of honour [*sic*],…"[76] The so-called "Sangiorgi Report" addressed to Palermo's chief prosecutor still exists in its original form of "485 yellowing handwritten pages" in a restricted file in Italy's Central State Archive in Rome, reference DGPS, aa.gg. rr *Atti speciali* (1898–1940), b.1, f.1[77]… On the night of 27–8 April 1900, Sangiorgi ordered a roundup of *mafiosi* listed in his report… Thirty-three suspects were immediately arrested, as were many more over the coming months."[78]

Perhaps Gaetano was concerned about the threat to his family posed by the violence of the Mafia war. Perhaps he had learned, through the good graces and insider information of his police superintendent father-in-law, that the name of his maternal grandfather, Don Randazzo, and by implication his own identity as Don Randazzo's right-hand man, might be included in the Sangiorgi

Report. Perhaps he was lured by America's promise of opportunity for advancement for a man of his abilities. Perhaps it was the need to seek medical attention for Angelina's blindness. Whatever the reasons or their combination, in 1898,[79] Gaetano uprooted his family from their home in San Cipirello. They made the sixty-kilometer journey through the mountains to Palermo, packed on to the ferry boat to Tunis, from where an oceangoing freighter carried them and other Sicilians fleeing the island to America. Like many of his countrymen, Gaetano had made arrangements with a contract middleman to work as an agricultural laborer in the fields of Eastern Texas in exchange for his family's passage to America.

The agricultural labor track through rural Texas and South Louisiana was a common route for immigrating Sicilians. For example, "[d]uring the 1890s,…Italians settled the Independence [Louisiana] area as laborers and as strawberry farmers,… By 1890, there were between 1,100 and 1,400 immigrants [in Independence], making it [Tangipahoa] Parish's largest Italian settlement."[80] A term "six-month contract to work on a plantation in Louisiana during sugarcane season…for $20.00 a month plus room and board…[and] a $22 ticket in steerage sailing from Palermo to New Orleans… [was] the norm for Italian…immigrants in the South… [T]hey were assigned unskilled tasks of hoeing, cutting…, digging ditches, and other menial chores,…so-called dago jobs… By 1900, Louisiana had the highest number of Italian farm laborers in the United States, about 18,000, mostly Sicilians."[81] Even Giuseppe "Joseph" Morello, "nick-named 'One Finger Jack' by the [US] Secret Service,"[82] a Corleone native, "assumed head of the Black Hand"[83] and later reputed "*capo di capi* ('boss of bosses') of the entire American Mafia"[84] from his New York base in the early 1900s, was for a time "'an agricultural laborer,'…[who] moved to Louisiana in the mid-1890s."[85] A Morello relative named "Ciro Terranova testified in 1910 that when he and his family decamped to Louisiana in the mid-1890s to join Joseph Morello, they knew a 'cousin' who got Morello and Ciros's father… work planting sugar cane… The cousin was likely…a labor agent for Italians wanting work on cotton plantations… The rest of the Morello-Terranova family joined…[him and] [t]hey planted and picked cotton in Texas," before [c]ontracting malaria,...[and] return-ing to New York about 1897."[86] The DiGiovanni family's trek to East Texas was similar to the experiences of Morello and the Tangipahoa Parish contract labor immigrants.

The third and fourth DiGiovanni children, Giacomo ("Jake") and Antonia ("Lena" or "Nia"), were both born in the lumber camp near Nacogdoches, Texas, delivered by midwives[87] in the small DiGiovanni cabin at the camp. Jake was born on September 7, 1902. He was slight of stature, dark in complexion, the Arabic physical image of his maternal grandfather and namesake, the Sicilian police-man, Giacomo Bucaro. The "second" Lena, who became my Nia,

was born on February 10, 1904. Lena was given the name Antonia because "one Lena,...the first Lena, [who was born] in Tunisia, Tunis; she was the smallest," had died in childbirth.[88]

The DiGiovanni place of res-idence in Texas "was just a lumber camp," Nia said. "They cut lum-ber...on the plantation, where they cut...all kinds of wood." Nia's only other recollection of the camp was that her parents "christened four of them [the DiGiovanni children] together...[one son],...the priest put salt in his mouth... They would collect fifteen to twenty kids and then take 'em and christen them all at one time at Nacogdoches...at the Sacred Heart Church... And they christened us in March on the seventh. So my mother, always the good Catholic woman, always cel-ebrated my birthday on the 7th of March. So I used to get two birth-day presents"—she laughed—"and some don't get none."[89] Until she reached Social Security eligibility age in 1969 and broke the news of her true birth date, Nia's children and grandchildren believed that her birthday was in fact March 7, not February 10.

CHAPTER 6

NEW ORLEANS EARLY 1900S

In late 1904 or early 1905, Gaetano moved his family from the lumber camp in East Texas to New Orleans, where the family more than doubled in size. Although Angelina continued to be plagued by miscarriages, the family expanded to nine children when five healthy babies survived as native-born Americans and New Orleanians. Maria ("Mary" or "Ma-Mamie") was born on November 1, 1905. According to Nia and Aunt Lou, Ma-Mamie grew up to become the physical reincarnation of her paternal grandmother, Giuseppina Randazzo DiGiovanni,[90] wife of the original Baiocco. The third son, Fedele ("Sugar" or "Sugie"), was born on July 27, 1907. "In Latin, that means 'faithful,' and you know how faithful he is, huh?" Nia said of the brother who would later become an international seafarer and reputed ladies' man.[91] Lucia ("Lucille" or "Lou"), the firecracker who became Nia's closest friend in old age, was born on March 25, 1909. Vittum ("Vito" or "Walter"), later an incongruous Italian Army conscript soldier in World War II and devoted family man, named for the patron saint of Ciminna, was born on July 2, 1912. Finally, the baby, Francesca ("Frances" or "Nookie"), whose unparalleled beauty later attracted the suave and intellectual Sicilian sophisticate and political rabble-rouser, Carmelo Pedalino, was born on August 17, 1913.

In New Orleans, Angelina's eyes were Gaetano's first order of business. "Poppa brought her to…a specialist. This guy recommended a specialist,…and his name is Dr. Dugan, an eye doctor…

He saved one eye and he wanted to put a glass eye in [the other socket, but] she wouldn't [do it]."[92] Except for those poses in which she turns her profile slightly so that only her restored right eye can be seen, every photograph of Grandma DiGiovanni in the family's possession, all of which were taken since that time, show Angelina's left eye surgically sown shut, the medical handiwork of Dr. Dugan who restored her eyesight, after she refused his recommendation to implant a glass eye. "Until the day she died, she never used glasses and she could thread a needle and crochet and do everything. Yeah. She was [really somethin']... And that same doctor treated...[Nia's son] Joe [Guinta] when he was born. [Joe] had one eye that was kind of puffed, and we took him to Dr. Dugan."[93]

Gaetano easily found work as a longshoreman, unloading the banana boats that thronged the Port of New Orleans from the Caribbean, Central, and South America. New Orleans was then the largest point of disembarkation of imported bananas in the world. For decades, Italian immigrants had monopolized the banana unloading business in New Orleans. In the 1880s, "the wealthy Provenzano family, a politically influential clan not connected to the local Mafia organization...maintained a monopoly of the unloading of fruit ships from South and Central America."[94] A New Orleans crime family, "ruled by the Matranga brothers, Charles and Tony,...[whose] principal activity was extortion, mostly of law-abiding Italians who had emigrated," including banana boat stevedores, attempted "to intimidate the Provenzanos so they would relinquish their control of the docks..."[95] Violence broke out between the two families, and "the Provenzanos sought protection from the New Orleans police, specifically from the police chief, David Hennessey, and Hennessey quickly took up the cause of the Provenzanos against the Matrangas."[96] Near midnight on October 15, 1890, Hennessey was shot four times as he was walking home. Asked as he lay dying, "Who did it?" the chief whispered only, "The dagos."[97] The chief's killing led to the lynching by outraged New Orleans citizens in 1891 of eleven Italians accused of the murder, nine of whom had been tried and acquitted and two of whom were still awaiting trial. For decades afterward, "whenever people wanted to insult Italians [in New Orleans], they would whistle and say, 'Ayyy, who kill-a da chief?'"[98] In addition to a diplomatic crisis between Italy and the United States, the Hennessey murder and lynching also threw control among the Italians of banana stevedoring in New Orleans into confusion, allowing other interested parties to exert influence in the business.

Gaetano did not stay on the backbreaking loading and unloading gangs for long. His maturity, good judgment, air of authority, obvious leadership skills, and reputation in Sicily caught the attention of a younger man of influence and standing. The younger man was an immigrant from Corleone, who would come to rely upon the older, wiser Gaetano as his right-hand man and closest adviser for as long as Gaetano lived in New Orleans. With the younger man's patronage, Gaetano became the man who organized the labor gangs, who said which workers unloaded which boats, who obtained the coveted banana stevedoring jobs for those who needed them, including his own sons. About a century after Gaetano's character first revealed itself in this way on the New Orleans docks, Thursday, April 29, 2010, to be exact, early in my struggle to learn about and understand the character and history of my Sicilians, I stood near Mom at her kitchen stove one late afternoon, as she stewed a rabbit for my brother Steve.

"Steve really likes this rabbit," she said, "especially in the brown gravy."

"Yeah. Who wouldn't? So, Mom, you remember your grandpa from when you were a little girl, don't you?"

"Oh yeah. He was my grandpa. I was ten years old when he died. Nia and Natale sent me to stay with Old Grandma down the street on Tchoupitoulas so she wouldn't be alone."

"So who were some of Grandpa Gaetano's friends?" I asked.

"Well, let's see. There was Mr. Sam, he was about Nia's age, and Mr. Sam's father, Mr. Luke. He was the same age as your grandpa. Yeah, he was my grandpa's best friend, Mr. Luke. Everybody in our house and the neighborhood called him that. They were together a lot. Grandpa used to have Natale take Mr. Luke and Mr. Sam fishing and hunting all the time."

"Mr. Luke," I said, remembering the name from my research. "What was his last name?"

"I don't remember his last name, honey," she said.

She did not need to remember it for my purposes. I already knew him from my research and because her brother, my uncle Joe Guinta, had confirmed the same information in a separate conversation, except that he <u>did</u> remember the last name. Mr. Luke was Leoluca Louis Trombatore, "[b]orn March of 1888," the same year as Natale and twenty years after Gaetano, "in Corleone,"[99] about twenty-four kilometers southeast of Gaetano's hometown. "Trombatore lived in New Orleans for 58 years, first arriving from New York in November 1907," more probably 1905.[100] "An FBI report states that Leoluca 'Mr. Luke' Trombatore was the New Orleans Mafia boss during the 1940s," the end of Gaetano's second stint in New Orleans, "until his death in 1963. That belief connected to [writer David] Chandler's that a 'Leoluca T.' was the 'obscure head of the local *Famiglia*."[101]

Like some of its other work, the 1960s FBI report possibly exaggerated Mr. Luke's standing. The Mafia in Louisiana in the early twentieth century was not a centralized, monolithic structure. Six individual Sicilian immigrants, including Mr. Luke, each with his own interests and operations, have been identified as early 1900s New York crime boss Giuseppe (Joseph—One Finger Jack) "Morello's New Orleans contacts (ca. 1909–1920)," whose names were "revealed…in black hand letters" seized in 1909 raids, either 'written by Morello to New Orleans merchants,' or penned by black-mailers and passed to Morello for resolution" or "from a list of visitors to Morello, and persons to whom he wrote while he was serving time in Atlanta Penitentiary."[102] However, "[t]he New Orleans group tied to the Morellos in New York were [*sic*] conflict-ridden, loosely intertwined, and appeared to have little in common when assessed by the…ventures they individually pursued in New Orleans."[103] For example, an authoritative "list of leading bootleggers in the 1920s… omitted Morello's confederates in New Orleans,"[104] indicating that others in New Orleans controlled bootlegging during Prohibition. In the 1920s, '30s, and beyond, the Louisiana *cosa nostra* was "unlike any other Mafia brotherhood in the United States…, [such as] New York, Chicago, and New England," where "[i]t was a tight ship, in competition with other tight ships…and…men down the chain of command were strictly accountable to the boss and could not found businesses or pull off jobs on their own... In Louisiana,...the brotherhood was much more loosely structured... More a spontaneous grouping of individuals of like mind and inclination, usually but not always tied by bonds of kinship, each with a degree of autonomy, the Louisiana Mafia resembled more the Mafia of Western Sicily from which it sprang..."[105] Silvestro "Silver Dollar Sam" Carolla was one of those like-minded individuals. Author Thomas Hunt has written that Carolla "became affiliated with the regional Mafia organization run by Charles Matranga [of the banana stevedoring family and] participated in bootlegging and narcotics trafficking..., New Orleans fishing, shrimping and dock work rackets [and later] casino and slot machine gambling."[106] As Carolla's career ebbed after his 1947 deportation, "the 'big names' in New Orleans' crime...included...Carlos Marcello, who forged a partnership in the 1940s with New York[]'s Frank Costello...,"[107] with emphasis on gambling, extortion, political influence, and narcotics.[108] "The government believed Carlos Marcello was in control of the family from about 1950 on, but some sources believe another boss worked behind the scenes until Marcello took the helm in the early 1960s."[109]

Perhaps it was the "obscure" Leoluca Trombatore who was "behind the scenes." His principal niche appears to have been labor influence in the banana unloading trade with protection for and tribute from French Quarter merchants. Mr. Luke died in 1963.[110] Thirty-five years later, the particular closeness of the relationship between Mr. Luke and Gaetano DiGiovanni was revealed to Gaetano's grandchildren when his daughter, Antonia (Lena), my grandmother Nia, died in 1998. Through years of visits to the DiGiovanni family mausoleum vault in Lakelawn Metairie Cemetery, on All Saints' Day or Grandma Angelina's birthday, and in the recorded interviews conducted in her old age, Nia noted repeatedly, "My daddy bought that in...1921, when my brother died... I'll be the last one to go in there."[111] She said hers would be the last interment because the vault already held the remains of her oldest brother, Domenico; her father, Gaetano; her mother, Angelina; and her husband, Natale, all of whom have their names with birth and death dates inscribed on the tomb. Nia said that two babies who died at childbirth, Ma-Mamie's oldest, Angie, and Nia's own oldest, Anna, were also interred there[112] although their names are not inscribed, either on the tomb or in the written records of the Metairie Cemetery Association. She repeatedly said, however, that the DiGiovanni family vault had room for one more, and she would be that one.

When Nia died in 1998, Mom dug out her copy of the cemetery vault title, made an appointment at Lakelawn Metairie, and arranged for her brother, Uncle Joe, to meet her at the offices of the historic old cemetery. The twenty-five-acre cemetery was built on an old horse racing track at the western edge of New Orleans. It holds the remains of many significant New Orleans historical figures, including Confederate Civil War generals and soldiers, business tycoons, political and jazz music figures, and assassinated New Orleans Police Chief David Hennessey. The DiGiovanni family vault is located on the cemetery's Avenue B, in the heart of the cemetery section where the remains of deceased Italians were formerly segregated. Jazz great Louis Prima and murdered eight-year-old 1907 Black Hand kidnap victim Walter Lamana, son of "prosperous undertaker" Peter Lamana,[113] are interred nearby. The vaults of the Provenzano and Matranga banana business families are in the same mausoleum wall. A line of several ornate marble mausoleums, built by Italian immigrant societies like the *Societa de San Giuseppe* and the *Societa de Contessa Entellina*, all decorated with ornate statuary, are located across the narrow road from the humble DiGiovanni vault. The cemetery is a beautiful tree-lined, granite, and marble-rowed setting. Uncle Sugie's (Fedele DiGiovanni) daughter Angie told me that when she was a child in the 1940s, the cemetery was the site of Sunday afternoon family picnics.

A day or two after Nia's death in 1998, Mom and Uncle Joe met with a Lakelawn funeral director to make Nia's funeral arrangements. The funeral director was a distinguished man, dressed appropriately in a black suit, starched white shirt and muted tie, with a small and fragrant gardenia bud in his coat's right lapel. He carried a small manila folder of aging documents. He expressed his sympathies, seated himself behind his desk, and calmly presented some surprising news.

"Mr. Guinta, Mrs. Wilkinson," he said, "I am very sorry, but we will not be able to inter your mother in the same vault as her parents, brother, and husband. That particular vault is full and has been permanently sealed."

"What!" Mom said. "There must be some mistake. There should be room for one more."

The funeral director then opened his file and walked Mom and Uncle Joe through its top three pages. The first page was a typed record on Lakelawn's historic "Form 180." The copy I maintain, retrieved from Mom's postmeeting files, reads in its entirety from top left to right: "Metairie Cemetery Association. DiGiovanni, Gaetano. Section 88, Vault 392; Title # 523, 5/12/1921. 23 1/2 × 29 1/2 × 6'9"—$150. **Vault filled—cannot be used for any further interments—1/19/67*** **SEE JUDGEMENT [sic] FILE** Gaetano DiGiovanni—11/7//45—#479. Angelina DiGiovanni—2/11/65. Natale Guinta—1/20/67—#42. ***CLOSED TO FURTHER INTERMENTS***.[114] The director then showed Mom and Uncle Joe the original of the Metairie Cemetery Asociation [sic] title document dated May 12, 1921, a copy of which Mom already had, and he flipped it over to show them the back side of the original document, a copy of which neither Mom nor Uncle Joe had ever seen

before. Hand-scripted in pencil by some long-dead prior funeral director on the back side of the original title was the following notation: **Remains of Mr. Trombatore interred Jan. 25, 1931. Received from New York City metal lined casket.**[115]

An otherwise unidentified Trombatore had been buried in the DiGiovanni family vault in 1931. The vault, in fact, was full. Did anyone other than Gaetano in the family know about this? A few words that Nia had uttered to Mom during the last days of her final hospital stay before she died, which Mom had not understood at the time, came back to her. "You gonna be some surprised when I die," Nia had said. Now Mom understood. She could only chuckle. On the spot, she and Uncle Joe bought a new Lakelawn Metairie mausoleum vault for Nia, in a new wall for the dearly departed, vault Number 427 located some distance from the old site where her parents and husband had been interred. That is why Nia is not buried with her husband. Today, the new vault is full. Nia is happily interred with her children, Joseph Guinta and Ann Guinta Wilkinson, and their spouses, Joseph C. Wilkinson **Sr.** and Patricia Crossen Guinta.

Thus, it was in New Orleans, almost a century earlier, that Gaetano DiGiovanni became an established family man in his late '40s and early '50s. He was "Mr. Luke" Trombatore's older, wiser *consigliori* (counselor) and right-hand man. He had friends and influence in the French Quarter and the important banana stevedoring trade. Like the legendary Don Vito Cascio Ferro, who had himself spent six months in New Orleans during those years,[116] Gaetano cemented his reputation, begun in San Cipirello at the end of the nineteenth century, as a "man of great qualities. There was a natural aura of authority about him: people of all kinds found themselves obeying him and asking for his advice and consent for their projects without knowing why."[117]

CHAPTER 7

LOWER NINTH WARD

MAY 8, 1921

Two men police later identified as Batiste Pecoraro and Giovanni "John" Martello crouched low in the lush spring growth. They were hiding in an Italian immigrant's thickly planted truck garden of vegetables in the 800 block of Tupelo Street in the "back-a-town" neighborhood of New Orleans, now known as the Lower Ninth Ward. It was nearing midnight, and they could hear chirping frogs and crickets and smell the murky stench of the nearby swamp. The two men fidgeted under the weight of their heavy shotguns and the extra ammunition they carried on the thick leather belts they wore across their shoulders. Both were seasoned criminals. Martello was a disgruntled car thief, out for revenge and to further the interests of his boss, a connection of the Mafia chief who had approved and organized both this murder and the bank robbery that was supposed to be happening simultaneously on the other side of nearby Lake Pontchartrain. Martello regretted the unlucky timing that had landed him this assignment. The Northshore bank robbery seemed like the better of the two jobs. Pecoraro was a reliable muscle man. His advantage was familiarity with the back-a-town streets of New Orleans and the peccadilloes of its inhabitants. Pecoraro had no qualms about the job for which he had been selected. This was familiar ground for him, a field in which he was on his way to establishing a lengthy career of arrests.[118] Bank robbery in the wilds of rural Louisiana, outside the familiar darkness of the criminal environs of his slice of the New Orleans Italian community, was not. Martello swatted at a mosquito that had pierced his skin above the oily bandana wrapped around his neck. "Son-a-ma-bitch," he muttered. "Shut up," Pecoraro hissed.

A long Ford touring sedan carrying four people slowly turned onto the 800 block of Tupelo Street, its headlights cutting through the late-night darkness. A swarthy dark-haired young man was at the wheel of his own first car, proudly purchased with the proceeds of his sweat on the banana docks and the extra cash from the bootlegging sideline he had struggled to conceal from his disapproving father. "*Antiquato pensiero* (old-fashioned thinking)," the driver often muttered, when thinking of his father. His passenger alongside him in the front seat of the Ford was also a young man, much like the driver in appearance. The passenger was an automobile mechanic, a dark-skinned, dark-haired young Italian, known by the driver only casually as someone who worked occasionally with his "cousin" Leonardo in one of the other aspects of their sideline. The other passengers were a married couple, snuggled closely together in the back seat. The wife was tired after a long and pleasant Sunday of cruising around the picturesque city in her cousin's fancy Ford, occasionally stopping to window-shop or buy candy or to permit the men to chitchat with some of their cronies on Tulane Avenue. Her weary head rested on her husband's broad chest, and her eyes were closed lightly. Her husband moved his eyes from left to right as his neck shifted quickly in birdlike movements, searching for something that only he expected to see in the Tupelo Street darkness.

The Ford's back seat passengers were Leonardo Cipolla and his wife, a young Bucaro woman whose first name is nowhere reported in the known records. She is identified in the police reports and newspaper articles only as Mrs. Leonardo Cipolla. The front seat passenger was Joseph Gaeto, an automobile mechanic who worked at a small shop on Tulane Avenue run by an older man named Natale Deamore. The driver and proud owner of the Ford was Domenico "Dominick" DiGiovanni, a native of San Cipirello, Sicily, a stevedore on the New Orleans banana docks, and the eldest son of Gaetano and Angelina DiGiovanni. Leonardo's wife was Dominick's cousin on his mother's side.

It was just before midnight on Sunday night, May 8, 1921. Domenico pulled his Ford in front of the Cipolla home at 843 Tupelo Street and stopped to drop off his cousin and her husband. The Cipollas exited the car and walked to the front door of their home. When the couple was just clear of the line of fire between the car and the two assassins crouched in the grass, Pecoraro and Martello rose up from their hiding place, approached the car on its passenger side, and fired their shotguns repeatedly at close range at the two men who remained in its front seat. Domenico DiGiovanni and Joseph Gaeto "had been killed by shotgun blasts to the head... The right side of the vehicle was riddled with buckshot and bullet holes, as was the (nearby) Cipolla home."[119] Both men died quickly in a bloody mess, their bodies slumped in the car's front seat.

Leonardo Cipolla ran into the house, grabbed a pistol, clothes, and cash and rushed away, fleeing hurriedly into the night, through the back door, leaving his wife aghast and crouching at the front door. Momentarily, the young woman lapsed into confusion and terror, but she regained some degree of composure within a minute or two. Realizing she had been abandoned, fearful that more shots would follow, and deathly afraid of the police officers that were sure to be summoned, she grabbed some clothes and wandered off into the night, looking for refuge.

Within hours, there was a knock at the front door of the home of Gaetano and Angelina DiGiovanni. It was not the police. Gaetano's friend Mr. Luke had sent a messenger to deliver the bad news of his eldest son's death. Gaetano frowned a deep frown. For almost a year, since Dominick's arrest at 605 St. Charles Avenue on July 4, 1920, on a bootlegging charge,[120] Gaetano had warned his son away from that business and the group conducting it. "Bad work," he had said. "Stick to the banana business." Now his worst fears had been realized. He lowered his head and walked into the back bedroom to wake up his wife. Angelina wailed when she heard what had happened, then lapsed into intermittent sobbing.

Into her old age, into the late 1950s and early 1960s, long after Gaetano had died and she was living then with a daughter and son-in-law, Angelina Bucaro DiGiovanni grieved the brutal loss of her eldest son. My brother Tom was born during those years on the same birthday as his great-uncle Dominick, February 22. Perhaps that shared birthday explained what appeared to be old Ma-Maw DiGiovanni's special bond with Tom. As an infant, Tom sometimes suffered painful bouts of abdominal colic. When these problems occurred during a visit to see old Ma-Maw DiGiovanni, Angelina would gather the crying young Tom into her arms and retreat to a rocking chair on the porch. She would slowly rock Tom back and forth, shifting him from her shoulder to her chest or down into her lap until she found the position best suited to ease his infant pain. Angelina soothed Tom in Italian, sometimes singing, sometimes humming, sometimes talking slowly, calling him by name until the pain passed and the little boy lay quietly in her arms. Was the name she was calling Tommasino, Tommasino, Tommasino or Domenico, Domenico, Domenico? Her thick Sicilian accent and the quietness of her ministrations made it difficult to tell. It was almost as if she were comforting—not Tom, but the little boy she had carried from San Cipirello through Tunis, across the Atlantic Ocean, through the Texas lumber camp to this deadly place.

CHAPTER 8

THE CIPOLLA-DIGIORGIO LINK

For weeks, the New Orleans newspapers, particularly the city's sensationalist afternoon dailies, *The Item* and *The States*, coupled the Gaeto-DiGiovanni murders with the seemingly related killing of restaurant owner Dallas Calmes during a bank robbery in Independence, Louisiana, on the Northshore of Lake Pontchartrain committed on the same night. The murders were the centerpiece of stories of violence and vendetta perpetrated by organized Italian crime gangs. With police and prosecutors as their sources, the local newspapers consistently linked the three deaths of DiGiovanni, Gaeto, and Calmes and ultimately attributed them to the machinations and internecine conflicts of alleged Mafia chieftains Leonardo Cipolla and Vito DiGiorgio. The news and the faraway origins of many of the suspects were sufficiently national in scope that even *The New York Times* ran a short story linking the New Orleans and Northshore murders. The *Times* reported that "police are working on the theory that their deaths resulted from a disagreement among the members of the band which attempted the robbery."[121] It was the New Orleans newspapers, however, that for weeks beat the drums of Italian mob violence.

The *New Orleans Item* linked the two incidents as the handiwork of a single Italian gang from the outset of its lurid reporting under a banner front-page headline in its May 9, 1921, edition. "[A] volcanic outbreak of violent crime that flared forth first in Tangipahoa parish at 2:00 a.m. Sunday that ran into a double murder in New Orleans at 11:30 p.m. Sunday [has] every available man of the New Orleans police force...now working."[122] After a detailed description of the attempted bank robbery and murder in Independence, the article reported that the link between the two incidents was discovered when two of the suspects apprehended in the Northshore killing "admitted after some hesitation and questioning that [although they] got their mail [at 903 St. Maurice avenue],...it was called for by Leonardo Cipolla of 843 Tupelo street..."[123]

When Assistant District Attorney Thomas Craven and police officers Joseph Horton and Jacob Uhle went to Cipolla's home to investigate, they observed that "the Cipolla house stands in the middle of the block on Tupelo, between Dauphine and Burgundy. A truck garden is on each side. On each corner is another house. Across the street is [another] house...whose truck garden is immediately opposite Cipolla's house. Those four houses are all on the block. The street is a narrow, dirty street, with a deep ditch on each side and a high banquette... [T]wo pickets had been forced from the garden fence on the Burgundy Street side... The man who slew the two evidently crossed [a] garden, and from the high banquette, fired, either behind or in front of the fence. That high banquette gave him an elevation from which he shot down upon the two men in the car, standing to their right and slightly to their rear... [The investigators] saw a Ford standing in the darkness. A flashlight was put on its license number. 'It's the same car we saw on Rampart and Canal,' the patrolmen said."[124] Earlier that day, while searching for a suspect in the Independence murder named Natale Deamore, the same two patrolmen had stopped the same Ford they now saw on Tupelo Street near Deamore's Tulane Avenue auto repair shop. At that time, the Ford had "two men in the front seat, and one in the rear. The men did not give wholly satisfactory answers, but their answers were hardly enough to justify arrest... [At Cipolla's Tupelo Street address], [t]wo men—both riddled with buckshot, both dead—were in the front seat of the car. They were DiGiovanni and Gaeto. Both were shot through head and neck with buckshot, and the side doors of the car were ripped and torn where the heavy slugs had driven through. The men had been seated in the car, looking over their left shoulders at the house. They had been shot from the right side, the slayer, it was believed, standing across the street from the house… In DiGiovanni's side coat pocket was found a .32-caliber Colt six-shooter, fully loaded. Evidently, the man had been slain before he could reach his weapon. Gaeto was unarmed."[125]

The investigators searched the Cipolla house, accompanied by an *Item* reporter. It was "deserted. Boxes of pistol ammunition were scattered about the place. Thousands of labels for liquor bottles were there, mostly cognac. Five barrels of wine were found in the backyard. Telegrams and letters in the house were from points ranging from California through Chicago and New York. Hundreds of checks were found canceled, ranging from $100 to $600, and totaling many thousands of dollars. Clothing cast wildly about the place, overturned furniture and general disorder showed that the house had been deserted in a wild and frantic rush… [The search also found] shotgun cartridges which…are the same as those which slew DiGiovanni and Gaeto…, four automobile license plates…, two [of which] were from stolen cars, [and a] double-barreled shotgun, two gun-cases and hundreds of rounds of pistol ammunition, .32 and .38 caliber. The outfit for manufacturing whiskey and cognac in the house was complete and elaborate. It was supplemented by the contents of a black trunk, addressed by express to [two of the arrested suspects in the Calmes murder]. In that trunk were found hundreds of corks, paper wrappers for bottles, other bottles of cognac flavoring. The trunk had been shipped from Brooklyn to Chicago, thence to New Orleans."[126]

The *Item* reported that the missing Leonardo Cipolla was being sought by the New Orleans police "in a city-wide dragnet."[127] His whereabouts were unknown either to police or to attorney George Gulotta, who had appeared at police headquarters to announce his representation of Cipolla and attempt unsuccessfully to negotiate Cipolla's surrender in exchange for bail. A police memorandum commented on Gulotta's pitch in favor of the proposed arrangement, referring to "the report of a New Orleans lawyer that Cipolla had been seen in the death car on friendly terms, apparently with the two men later slain that same evening, and therefore could not be involved in the killing."[128]

"Police in New Orleans are still endeavoring to work out the tangle of vendetta that led to the two New Orleans slayings so close on the heels of the murderous attempt at a bank robbery in Tangipahoa," the *Item* reported. "Theories are being advanced at headquarters that there is a feud in full swing between rival gangs of bootleggers and Black Hand workers, who attempted what they thought would be an easy and profitable bank robbery as a sideline. Other [police] veterans talked of Southern headquarters here for a national gang of crooks working in many channels,"[129] including "the operations of a large gang of automobile thieves and bootleggers" using the "home of Tony Carrolo [*sic*], 903 St. Maurice Avenue" as its "'clearing house.'"[130]

The *Item* speculated in a separate article about the bigger picture presented by the killings. "Who killed Dominick DiGiovanni and Joseph Gaeto…? What motive was behind the deadly purpose of the man who riddled the bodies of the two with charges of buckshot and slugs that were fired at such close range as to tear through the metal sides of the automobile and bury themselves in the fence in front of Cipolla's house? Was it a gang feud to the death? Was the double slaying linked with the daring attempt to break into the Farmers' & Merchants' Bank at Independence, Tangipahoa Parish, its vaults fat with the wealth of strawberry harvest time?… [Why was it that] two men were murdered while not a neighbor, though hearing the shots, dared to go forth at midnight and investigate? Is there in New Orleans another of those 'crime trusts' of which hectic fiction writers are so fond? Were DiGiovanni and Gaeto slain lest they tell police what they knew? Or did the slayer, finding them at that sparsely populated city block, fear they had come on some underworld vengeance and slay lest he be slain?"[131]

The circumstances of the killings, coupled with his reputation in the New Orleans Italian community, made Leonardo Cipolla the chief suspect as the mastermind of both operations. The Gaeto-DiGiovanni assassination had occurred in front of his house. The killers had not risen up to begin shooting until Cipolla was safely out and away from DiGiovanni's Ford. Cipolla had fled the scene, abandoning his wife, happenstance police always associate with the guilty. The contents of Cipolla's ransacked house indicated criminal activity involving weapons, bootleg liquor, and stolen automobiles. His house contained mail addressed to and sent from some of the participants in the Independence bank robbery and murder. But where was Leonardo Cipolla? And who was Vito DiGiorgio, the second alleged Mafia kingpin whose name began to be linked to the crimes on the stormy day of police activity that followed the murderous night in Independence and the Ninth Ward?

On the first full day after the killings, New Orleans was "[l]ashed by driving rain, etched in sharp relief by jagged flashes of lightning, shaken by tremendous crashes of thunder."[132] The police investigation into what was being characterized as "the triple murder of Independence and New Orleans,...Gangland's latest flareup,"[133] was as active as the weather. To investigators, the evidence was shedding "light...thrown on the personnel and workings of what veteran men at police headquarters assert is one of the biggest gangs of bootleggers and automobile thieves in the South. Definite connection was established between men arrested in Tangipahoa and neighboring parishes after the attempted robbery...of the Farmers' & Merchants' Bank of Independence, when Dallas L. Calmes was slain by the robbers, and the men sought in connection with the murder of Dominick DiGiovanni and Joseph Gaeto, slain on Tupelo street in New Orleans less than twenty-four hours later. For the two crimes had no direct connection, police believe. Either murder was independent of the other. But the links of the chain of evidence bind together the names of men apparently involved in both."[134] The first two men arrested in the Calmes murder and questioned by New Orleans authorities, Andrea Lamantia of Brooklyn and Joseph Rini of Chicago, provided the initial links through mail, telegrams, business cards, and other documents naming them, addressed to the store of New Orleans grocer Tony Carolla but found in the search of Cipolla's home. In the face of this hard evidence, Lamantia and Rini denied the links during their initial questioning.[135]

Leonardo Cipolla was the linchpin. A massive police manhunt to find him was underway. The manhunt exploded into action when Assistant District Attorney Craven received a midnight telephone call from a "source deemed responsible" that "'Cipolla can be found hiding out in a haymow in a barn on one of the farms on the old Story plantation down in St. Bernard, where some friends are keeping him hidden... He's likely to put up a fight or his friends may,' was the telephone warning."[136] New Orleans police loaded up the department's "two big speedsters...with men armed with riot guns and pistols... The long wail of the police siren moaned through the streets. Rain drove in slanting sheets like a vicious spray of machine guns. Thunder crashed and great jagged streaks of lightning flashed across the sky. Down Rampart Street the machines tore like unleashed racers. Out Burgundy, they sped over a pavement of black glass. Then as the Orleans Parish line was crossed, they swirled up a side street," where a St. Bernard Parish deputy sheriff "leap[ed] into trousers and boots; a swift grab at a shotgun [and] the deputy was in the leading machine and with him the local authority for the raid. Once more, the speedsters stretched themselves, and into the midst of the terrific storm they hurtled their roaring way down the long stretch of road that paralleled the levee."[137]

In St. Bernard, "[t]hrough ditches waist deep in muddy water armed [police]men ploughed, as they surrounded house after house, keyed to intensity with expectation of a volley in answer to their summons to open doors in the name of the law."[138] They surrounded the house of Philip Carollo, who "deni[ed] that he knew anything of Cipolla's hiding place," searched his home and barn, "but no Cipolla."[139] The police raiders moved on to the house of Frank and Jake Crifasi. The brothers denied knowing where Cipolla could be found. Police searched their house and adjoining property, where they found a high-stacked pile of hay. Officers dug into the stack with pitchforks and found an automobile, "[c]overed by a protective tarpaulin, A Ford touring car...completely hidden beneath that pile of hay, which had been pitched above it and banked around it to a depth of some three or four feet."[140]

The Crifasi brothers denied knowing who owned the car. "'Some feller I never saw before left it there a couple of weeks ago while he went blackberrying. He never called for it,'" Jake Crifasi told the assistant district attorney. Asked why it was covered in tarpaulin and hidden under the hay, Jake answered, "'That's one of my tarpaulins. He took it off my wagon... I had to put my hay somewhere.'"[141] When investigators checked the car's license plate and engine numbers, they found "[o]n the records of police headquarters that car is listed as belonging to V. DiGiorgio of 2301 Dauphine [street]," who was "believed to be in California, and that a letter from him was found at Cipolla's house, in front of which" Dominick DiGiovanni and Joseph Gaeto had been assassinated.[142]

Vito DiGiorgio, whose World War I draft registration card shows the same 2301 Dauphine Street address, "was possibly the first Mafia chieftain of Los Angeles,"[143] but his organized crime roots were in New Orleans. In June 1908, the store of New Orleans grocer Joseph Serio was bombed. Serio had received Black Hand extortion letters "penned by Joseph Caronia, an alias used by DiGiorgio."[144] New Orleans police "arrested one of the rising young Black Hand leaders, Vito DiGiorgio,"[145] along with alleged accomplices Vincenzo Chiapetta and two Cipolla brothers named Stabile and Vincenzo.[146] Ultimately, DiGiorgio was released because of insufficient evidence,[147] and "[t]he case against DiGiorgio was dropped."[148] On November 5, 1909, reputed New York Mafia "boss of all bosses," Joseph Morello wrote a letter to Vincenzo Moreci, considered to be "the boss of at least a faction in the New Orleans underworld," asking Moreci to "give greetings" to Vito DiGiorgio.[149] In 1914, DiGiorgio bought a New Orleans grocery and saloon from Henry Sciambra. Henry had inherited the business from his brother, Anthony, who had been shot and killed two years earlier while asleep in his bed.[150] In May 1916, DiGiorgio was wounded and a companion was killed in the yard of DiGiorgio's saloon by a gunman whom police theorized was acting in vendetta for the killing of another Italian saloonkeeper, Philip Segretto, about 12 hours earlier.[151] New York boss Joseph Morello wrote letters to DiGiorgio in 1917 and 1920, in which Morello referred to DiGiorgio as "friend" and "cousin."[152] In 1920 or '21, while maintaining his New Orleans residence, DiGiorgio relocated to Los Angeles, where he "may have been the first boss of a united Los Angeles Mafia."[153]

It was a car registered to DiGiorgio that police found hidden under the St. Bernard Parish haystack in their search for Cipolla. It was DiGiorgio who had a criminal history of associating with men named Cipolla. It was Cipolla whose house contained license plates from stolen cars and other evidence of a large-scale bootlegging and stolen car ring. It was Natale Deamore who had connections to both DiGiorgio and Cipolla through his auto repair shop on Tulane Avenue.

Police knew that "[o]n the afternoon of Friday, May 6, 1921," a little less than seventy-two hours before Dominick DiGiovanni was assassinated, "a black Hudson Super-Six rolled out of a Tulane Avenue repair shop in New Orleans."[154] The repair shop was owned by one of the car's occupants, Natale Deamore. It was the same repair shop where Joseph Gaeto was employed and where police officers saw Dominick DiGiovanni and Leonardo Cipolla stop and converse with Deamore just hours before Dominick and Gaeto were killed in front of Cipolla's house. The Hudson's six occupants ("the Tangi 6") were on their way across Lake Pontchartrain to Tangipahoa Parish, where all six would later be arrested, charged, convicted, and hanged for the murder of Dallas Calmes in Independence, Louisiana, on the same night that Dominick DiGiovanni was killed. The driver of the car was Joseph Bocchio, an Italian living in New Orleans, "where he was once arrested and released while living with the DiGiorgio family."[155] In addition to Deamore, the other passengers were Joseph Giglio, Joseph Rini, Andrea Lamantia, and Rosario "Roy" Leona. On April 21, 1924, Leona confessed that he was the actual shooter whose gunfire had killed Dallas Calmes. Leona blamed Vito DiGiorgio for enticing him to join in the crime. "Roy explained that Vito DiGiorgio had told him and Giglio about the opportunity to rob a bank in Independence without harming anyone... 'The only [man] outside [of the six] who had anything to do with this was DiGiorgio with his talk about easy money, easy money, easy money.'"[156]

CHAPTER 9

CIPOLLA CAPTURED

New Orleans police were "[s]eething with unsuppressed rage and font invective" as they were "straining every energy in a roundup seeking Cipolla's arrest," promising a "grilling awaiting Cipolla that will require all the chilled-steel nerve ever known on police record if it is successfully withstood."[157] Police had followed up their initial foray into St. Bernard Parish that uncovered the car registered to DiGiorgio buried in a haystack with more "wild night rides" in search of Cipolla.[158] "While these searches failed to unearth the hunted man, they resulted in the arrests of other men who are charged... with being members of a large gang of automobile thieves and bootleggers who...made the homes of Cipolla...and Tony Carollo, 903 Maurice avenue, their headquarters."[159] Police said the evidence they were gathering was uncovering "one of the biggest gangs of the lawless in the South, [with] Cipolla in their view as the brains of the New Orleans organization, against which they report they have evidence of automobile theft, bank robbery, holdup jobs, and wholesale illicit liquor dealing."[160]

One chase into St. Bernard occurred "a few hours before Cipolla was captured," after police "received information...that Cipolla was hiding in a barn behind the general merchandise store of Louis Caruso at Corinne, near Violet... The place was surrounded and searched, but no trace of Cipolla was found."[161] A short time later, "[s]teady surveillance" of the office of Cipolla's lawyer, George Gulotta, by a

75

private detective agency working with city police led to the fugitive's capture.[162] Officers observed Giacomo Bucaro, Joseph Andranga, and Dr. Christopher Russo pull up in a car that they parked in front of the Strand Theater, exit, and walk to Gulotta's nearby Hennen Building law office.[163] Bucaro was the operator of a grocery at the corner of Clio and Magnolia Streets, himself born in Ciminna. He was the cousin of Angelina Bucaro DiGiovanni, and later the father of future New Orleans Municipal Court Judge Andrew Bucaro.[164] Dr. Russo was "head of the Italian Presbyterian Mission on Franklin Street."[165] Andranga was "said by the police to have used the aliases of DiMaggio and DiGiorgio… [He was] a barber by trade, but made his living by peddling groceries on the street and by working in the grocery of his sister, Elizabeth Andranga [also known as Elizabeth DiGiorgio]… [P]olice expressed the belief that Andranga is a member of Cipolla's alleged gang of bootleggers and automobile thieves,… [who] was arrested in New York in 1909 on the charge of sending a 'Black Hand' letter; was convicted and sentenced to five years in Sing Sing."[166] Dr. Russo and Andranga were later ordered by police to appear for questioning at headquarters, and Andranga's sister was later found to have delivered to Gulotta a check in the amount of $2,000 given to her by Cipolla as his attorney's fee and "the price of arranging Cipolla's release on bond… Cipolla's check for $2,000… was processed by Miss E. DiGiorgio, proprietress of an Italian corner grocery at St. Maurice Avenue and Chartres Street. Miss DiGiorgio, who said her real name was Miss Elizabeth Andranga but her 'business name' was DiGiorgio, said in police headquarters…that she cashed the check for Cipolla as a personal favor."[167]

"Detectives were sent to the grocery of Bucaro, where they were informed that Bucaro and his wife had gone to the wake of Dominick DiGiovanni, being held at the parlors of the Lamana Undertaking Company."[168] A short while later, Assistant District Attorney Craven and two detectives returned to Bucaro's grocery. "Entering the grocery, they found Bucaro's daughters, one about twelve years old and the sister, fifteen, in charge. The officers asked permission to go upstairs. Permission was refused by the girls. As the officers advanced to the door leading to the stairs, the girls threw themselves in front of the door and held the knob. They were taken away from the door by the officers, who started up the stairs. Arriving at the second floor, which was in pitch darkness, the officers using a search light found a number of vacant rooms. Finally, they came to a door which [*sic*] was locked. Detective Cassard knocked on the locked door. The voice of Cipolla asked, 'Who's there?' It was then that Detective Cassard, who often had impersonated female characters as a member of the Police Minstrels, answered in his best feminine voice, 'It's me, honey.' At this, Cipolla threw back the bolt and opened the door on a crack. As he did so, the three officers threw their weight against the door, causing it to fly open, and throwing Cipolla to the floor. The three officers sprung upon the sprawling man and pinioned his arms. Within a foot of where Cipolla fell, a new pistol was found, as were six extra cartridges."[169]

The upstairs room in the Bucaro corner grocery where Cipolla was found was "tiny, tight-shuttered, unlit and indescribably filthy... On the floor beside the bed lay the gnawed remnants of a loaf of coarse bread, a half-eaten raw and unpeeled cucumber, [and] a plate of untouched spaghetti."[170] Cipolla himself was "harried,... crouched,...[b]ristly with black, unshaven beard, his face drawn in deep lines, his eyes shifting like a cornered wolf's."[171]

Cipolla was "taken to the Seventh Precinct police station at Napoleon avenue and Magazine street" where he was grilled "from 10:30 p.m., half an hour after his arrest, until three o'clock Thursday morning" by Craven and two detectives.[172] A newspaper reporter who observed the questioning described the captured Cipolla: "Lines on his face, deep-graven, told of the strain of the past few days. At times, he was openly defiant, sneering and countering with sarcastic retorts... Never did he weaken, however. His only sign of nervousness was a grimy once-white handkerchief with which he continuously mopped the palms of his hands between sessions of twisting the cloth between his stubby fingers. He spoke in broken English at times, professing utter inability to understand simple questions."[173]

Cipolla identified himself as thirty-eight years old, married with no children, a native of Palermo, Sicily. Cipolla said he "'came to America when I was twenty-one, lived in Brooklyn until I came to

New Orleans about four years ago [1917].'"[174] He was initially "sullen and refused to answer questions," then he gave a statement in response to Craven's persistent questioning, "absolv[ing] himself of all guilt" in the murders and "declaring that the same men who killed Gaeto and DiGiovanni made an attempt on the life of himself and his wife."[175]

"'You say you are innocent of any connection with that murder?'" Craven asked. "'Sure, I'm innocent.' 'Why were you hiding, then?' 'I was-a-na hidin'.'"[176] Throughout the questioning, District Attorney Craven was frustrated by Cipolla's apparent deceptions and many self-contradictions. "In one breath, said Mr. Craven, Cipolla would answer a question in the affirmative, and in the next breath, answer in the negative. When this was called to his attention, Cipolla only smiled, and maintained silence until prodded with another question."[177]

Cipolla said that "at about five o'clock Sunday afternoon, Gaeto and DiGiovanni took himself and Mrs. Cipolla out in the automobile, driving to City Park and out on Metairie Ridge… 'After riding around…, we stopped at Rampart and Canal streets at six o'clock Sunday evening, where I got out of the automobile, after Gaeto and DiGiovanni said they would pick me up about a half-hour later… We returned to my home about eleven o'clock Sunday night,…and myself and my wife got out of the automobile. We were about to open the gate to my home when I heard a shot. I first thought it was an automobile tire. I turned around in time to see the flash of the second shot. I didn't stop to look at Gaeto or DiGiovanni in the automobile. I ran through my house in the backyard, jumped over the fence into Burgundy Street. Then I ran to Dauphine Street, where I caught a [street]car and went to the home of Dr. Christopher Russo. I sat on Dr. Russo's steps until four o'clock Monday morning, when I decided to wake him up… Dr. Russo called the police station, but he was told the captain was busy.'" Cipolla said he then went to Gulotta's law office but did not see him, and Gulotta later "'sent word that he believed I would be released on $15,000 bail if I surrendered.'" He said he then "'went to the grocery of my cousin, Bucaro, Monday morning, and remained there up to the time I was found.'"[178]

Cipolla said that the stop at Canal and Rampart Streets was so he and his wife could "'buy-a da candy.'" He said that when the shots were fired in front of his house, "'I wasn't in da car. When those shots fire, I lay down in the grass.'" He thought two shots were fired. "'They go boom! Boom! like dis.' He clapped his hands… 'It sounds like da long gun… Then I lay down in the grass.'" He admitted that he knew Tony and Philip Carolla but denied seeing them on the night of the killings. He denied that he was hiding in Giacomo Bucaro's grocery store. "'I ain't hiding. I ain't afraid. I walk out on the streets. I don't hide. I neva' kill nobody.'"[179]

Cipolla admitted that he knew some of the suspects arrested for the bank robbery and murder in Independence, including Lamantia, Giglia, and Ms. DiGiorgio and Andranga for "two or three years… pretty well," stating that a $2,000 check he had given to Ms. DiGiorgio "paid the DiGiorgio store bill and repaid a loan he had made there."[180] He admitted that he knew Gaeto and Natale Deamore and that Gaeto was an auto mechanic who worked for Deamore but denied that he stopped during his Sunday drive in front of Deamore's Tulane Avenue Auto repair shop.[181] Police officers Horton and Uhle were then brought into the interview room, and they positively identified Cipolla as the man they saw in the car with Gaeto and DiGiovanni when it stopped in front of Deamore's garage,[182] both by his appearance and by "the same broken English" he had spoken at the Tulane Avenue auto shop.[183] Cipolla said that the night of the killings was "the first night DiGiovanni had driven him to his home"[184] and that the license plates from stolen cars found in the search of his house had been "drop-pa in da road in front of my house,…all wrap in paper and tied with string. I pick 'em up. Don' wanna see 'em go to waste, thas-sa all. Some fella pass and throw 'em away."[185] He claimed that the ten barrels of wine and ten-gallon whiskey still found in his house were "for my personal use… I make a leetle whisky for myself in that still in case-a da sickness. I guess every man do that, huh? That's-a no crime. You get-a every man what make-a da wine and da whiskey, you get-a everybody.'"[186] As to his wife's whereabouts, "'My wife, I don't see since those boys is shot.'" [187]

"'So you just ran away and left your wife to be shot for all you know?'" Craven asked incredulously. "'Uh-huh,'" Cipolla replied.[188]

Cipolla's "cousin," Giacomo "Jake" or "Jack" Bucaro, was also interrogated that night. He was a "great, gross, obese figure of a man, blabby faced [and] furtive eyed,…in bright orange and purple silk shirt, unwashed, unshaven, with little shifting eyes,…whose fat fingers twisted nervously as his eyes shot about the room."[189] He was arrested the same night that Cipolla was apprehended and charged with harboring a fugitive. Police records contained three pending charges against Bucaro for receiving stolen property, including "three sets of costly stolen table silver hidden in a feather mattress of his bedroom" uncovered when Cipolla was arrested.[190] Bucaro at first denied knowing Cipolla. When Cipolla was brought by police into the same room, "unblushing at his former denials, Bucaro admitted that Cipolla was his cousin and that he had hidden in the Bucaro grocery… Tripped in statement after statement that conflicted with the story of Cipolla and other witnesses, Bucaro after flashes of insolence [said], 'Aw right, if you say so. Sure, you're da boss. What you say gotta go, I guess,'" and then was marched off to a separate cell.[191]

CHAPTER 10

FRIDAY THE 13TH

Cipolla and Bucaro did not remain incarcerated in the precinct station for long. "Receiving warning that the friends of Leonardo Cipolla held in connection with the assassination of Joseph Gaeto and Dominick DiGiovanni would attempt to forcibly deliver him from the station…, police rushed the suspect to the parish jail in St. Bernard Thursday evening and threw a guard around the station."[192] No such attempted breakout occurred.

Assistant District Attorney Craven announced that his "investigation of the assassination of Gaeto and DiGiovanni was not completed [and] no charge was made against Cipolla…, [who continued to be held for questioning. Instead], believing him to be the 'brains' of the gang of bandits who attempted to rob the Farmers' and Merchants' Bank and who murdered Dallas L. Calmes in Independence [that same night], Tangipahoa authorities…issued a warrant for the arrest of Leonardo Cipolla, charging him with conspiracy to rob the bank."[193] Martin Williams, Southern manager of the Burns Detective Agency, saw Cipolla as an even bigger crime fish. "'I believe that the New Orleans police have got their hands on the brains and some of the shock troops of the crime organization that in the past three months has robbed a score of a small town and country banks in Louisiana and Mississippi' under the protection of the Burns agency,…[including] gangs of automobile bandits [that] have flared strongly in Southern crime annals in recent months. The loot aggregates somewhere around $50,000."[194] Cipolla's attorney, George Gulotta, visited Cipolla at the St. Bernard jail and advised him "'to keep silent'" during a "conversation...in swift Italian."[195]

Meantime, much was happening on Friday, May 13, 1921. "[Y]et another Italian was rounded up on the charge of harboring a criminal. He is Battisto Pecarro [*sic*], 34, of 2428 Washington Avenue... While police were searching for Joseph Andragna, convicted black hander..., reported involved in Cipolla's affairs," they tracked him to Pecoraro's house, where Andragna had spent the night.[196] Dominick DiGiovanni was being waked in preparation for his funeral and interment in Metairie Cemetery.[197] Nine Italians, not including Leonardo Cipolla, but including New Orleans auto repair shop owner Natale Deamore, whom Dominick had visited on the night of his murder, were indicted by the Tangipahoa Parish grand jury, charged with the murder of Dallas Calmes.[198] "Leonardo Cipolla was taken from the St. Bernard Parish jail...to the scene of the assassination of Joseph Gaeto and Dominick DiGiovanni in front of Cipolla's home at 843 Tupelo Street. Cipolla enacted the movements he alleges he made following the firing of the shots which killed Gaeto and DiGiovanni."[199]

Cipolla "was given full freedom of action" in the reenactment of his actions during the killing. "The [police] superintendent's car was parked exactly where the police found the death car. Cipolla stepped out of the car and walked to his fence. He did not take the normal entrance through the gate. He chose instead the big automobile gate in the fence. He had to reach over the fence and lift a heavy wooden bar to unfasten the big gate." Police Superintendent Guy Molony, Assistant District Attorney Craven, and other police officers observed nearby and used the flash of an electric flashlight to simulate the murderer's shots. Cipolla "called for the shot. The electric torch flashed. Cipolla stood a moment, and repeating his words on the night of the crime: 'Wassa matta, boys? Why you make the auto explode like dat? Jesus Christ. Somebody shoot.' He threw himself on the ground. But his drop to the ground was after all the shooting had ended. That much Cipolla conceded. And there was the telltale hole the buckshot made through the fence where he stood."[200]

Prosecutor Craven opined that through the reenactment "Cipolla shattered much of his own defense... Had he stood in that position when that murderous volley blazed into the night, Cipolla would have been shot in the stomach, Mr. Craven reports."[201]

Cipolla remained a suspect in both the DiGiovanni and the Calmes murders. After completing the reenactment, Cipolla "was taken to the Second Precinct police station. While warrants have been issued by the Tangipahoa authorities for the arrest of Leonardo Cipolla [and two others] charging them with conspiracy to rob the Farmers and Merchants Bank, these charges were not placed before the Tangipahoa grand jury Friday. It was reported that the grand jury probably will reconvene Saturday or Monday to investigate the charges against Cipolla... It is not believed that Attorney George Gulotta will make any attempt to have Leonardo Cipolla, held in connection with the assassination of Joseph Gaeto and Dominick DiGiovanni in front of Cipolla's home, released on a writ of habeas corpus."[202] Cipolla was reported "still protesting his innocence, still claiming he is the intended victim who miraculously escaped."[203] His legal problems were compounded when federal authorities issued a detainer, subject to a $5,000 bond, to hold him on bootlegging charges based on the ten-gallon copper whiskey still and 350 gallons of ten percent alcohol wine found at this house after the murders.[204]

By this time, auto garage operator Natale Deamore, in custody in Tangipahoa Parish and indicted for the Dallas Calmes murder, whose Tulane Avenue shop was the scene where police officers observed Cipolla and Dominick during their joyride on the night of the killings, was beginning to squawk. He was the centerpiece of a new police theory: "The assassination of Dominick DiGiovanni and Joseph Gaeto...were revenge murders in retaliation for a 'double-cross' in a stolen automobile transaction" with Deamore's Tulane Avenue garage as "one of the underworld clearinghouses for stolen automobiles... [Police sources said Deamore] is almost ready to 'kick in' with the whole story. For D[e]amore was also slated to be slain, according to the latest developments the police have run down. In fact, D[e]amore's absence in Tangipahoa with the bank bandits who slew Dallas L. Calmes as he thwarted their raid was all that saved his life. Now D[e]amore is the first of the gang to weaken, confess he was on the raid, and identify his companions in crime. And D[e]amore, it was learned, is ready to talk. He knows, it is understood, who killed DiGiovanni and Gaeto. D[e]amore...has weakened in morale steadily since his arrest. His full confession is expected to clear the murder angle of the whole case of all the last shreds of mystery that surround it."[205]

CHAPTER 11

VENDETTA AND THE "GOOD ELEMENT"[206]

In May 1921, New Orleans police, a sliver of the New Orleans news-paper community and representatives of the vast majority of honest New Orleans Italian-Americans who lived ordinary, hardworking lives without involvement in criminal activity of any kind, all attempted in their own ways to put the horrific murders of Dominick DiGiovanni, Joseph Gaeto, and Dallas Calmes in some sort of overall historical and societal perspective. They framed it in terms of vendetta, which in the old Western Sicilian countryside sense was ritualized revenge, an expression of the "mixture of violent passion and… pride…, a primitive notion of honour [sic], a rudimentary code of chivalry," theatrically displayed in Pietro Mascagni's 1890 opera, *Cavalleria Rusticana* (rustic chivalry), which "runs through Francis Ford Coppola's [film] *The Godfather Part III*."[207]

The *New Orleans States* ran a front-page Sunday edition article recounting New Orleans' long history of revenge murders in the city's Italian immigrant community. It placed the Gaeto and DiGiovanni murders at the center of "the Italian vendetta menace."[208] The *States* described the Gaeto-DiGiovanni murders as the culmination of a "new era of bloodshed," behind which was "the hand of the vendetta" dating back at least thirty years in New Orleans.[209] The vendetta stemmed from "the fact that there are always two or more

85

factions [of organized crime gangs in the Italian community] in a city the size of New Orleans... The Italian feuds in this city may be traced back thirty years when the two factions—the Provenzanos and the Matrangas—fought each other bitterly" over control of the banana boat unloading business, culminating in the killing of Police Chief David Hennessey.[210] "Later, the names of DiChristina, Moreci, Matranga and Segretto were coupled as leaders of one faction, while the Giaconnas, DiMartini, and the Pepitones were said to be identified with another faction bitterly antagonistic to the first... It was hard to say to which faction belonged Vicento [Vito] DiGeorgio [sic], grocer, of Dauphine and Marigny streets, who was shot and dangerously wounded [in 1914]..., but police never doubted it was a vendetta case."[211] "[W]ill vengeance be visited upon the authors of the assassination of Joseph Gaeto and Dominick DiGiovanni...[and enter] New Orleans' long history of the work of the blood-thirsty vendetta? Has the vendetta of this city taken on new life? And will there be a sequel or many of them to the bloody tragedies of the last few days?... [A] new order of things [has sprouted] among the younger generation of Italians, [and] [p]rohibition and the evolution [of] automobile traffic are believed to be...the evolution of the latest vendetta... So that today, they say, hundreds of liquor runners and auto thieves are daily operating in the city."[212] The Gaeto-DiGiovanni murders were evidence of these phenomena.

Leaders of the New Orleans Italian community were divided on what to do. Some issued frantic calls for action. Others calmly denied any great problem. Condo Puglisi, editor of *L' Italia Americano*, decried that "the Italian criminal is again on the front page. What a hateful animal... It is a tale for tears, especially for those Italians who, as good citizens, are always endeavoring to go ahead side by side with human progress and activities."[213] The editor intimated that the vestiges of Western Sicilian *omerta* and fear of reprisal in the good element of the immigrant community were partly to blame. "A handful of criminals [is] protected by the silence of many...Italians [who], instead of publicly saying what they know or what they saw, have held their tongues for fear of vengeance. This silence has not only protected the criminals but has also fostered them to perpetrate other crimes. The police cannot discover the culprit unless he be assisted by the public, and it is every honest citizen's duty to help the police in his search. The Italians should learn to be frank and open-hearted with the police and not to mind the criminal's threats."[214] He accused the courts of treating Italian criminals leniently. "In the past, whenever an Italian criminal was caught by police, by hook or by crook, generally speaking, after a few days or weeks [he] was set at liberty."[215] Puglisi feared that without dramatic action, the same would happen again. He publicly urged other leaders of the Italian-American community, including a dozen by name, "to call a mass meeting of Italians in order to organize a Committee of Protection which would work together with our police department…to bring…to justice and punish…their degenerate countrymen."[216]

Other Italian-American leaders rejected editor Puglisi's call for action, exhibiting calm confidence in the authorities and denial of any massive Italian crime problem. "[I]s there any necessity for the Italians, the good element I am alluding to, to unite into a great mass meeting for the purpose of assisting in weeding out…Italian criminals…? [asked] Frank Cabibi, one of the best-known Italians of New Orleans… Our city and state are not infested with a band of criminals, such as the editor describes."[217] Cabibi denied that the "good element" of Italians was terrorized or uncooperative with authorities, remembering the community's cooperation in 1907 in locating the body of kidnapped and murdered seven-year-old Walter Lamana, during a period when "our city was being flooded with Black Hand letters threatening…peaceful Italians."[218] Cabibi's opinion was that a mass meeting of the type urged by Puglisi "would have nothing good to accomplish… The good element of the Italians have [sic] complete confidence in the law, authorities, and the courts of our state, and they feel certain that when an Italian criminal, or a criminal of any nationality, is brought before the courts, if found guilty, [he] will receive his just due."[219]

CHAPTER 12

THE MISSING WIFE

The labyrinth of clues was causing Assistant District Attorney Craven's head to spin with theories. He told the press that "Joseph Rini, one of the nine men indicted by the Tangipahoa grand jury for the murder of Dallas Calmes..., sent word to [him] that he is ready to talk. Rini is said to have been a gunman from the north and has been under suspicion of having been hired to kill Joseph Gaeto and Dominick DiGiovanni in New Orleans. Mr. Craven is confident his interview with Rini will throw new light on the mystery which [*sic*] has been puzzling New Orleans authorities. The fact that Rini sent an urgent call for the assistant district attorney is believed to mean that he has something new to bear. Mr. Craven also said he has a definite tip which he is sure will lead to the arrest of the slayers of Gaeto and DiGiovanni. He said he intends to see two persons...who have promised to throw new light on the situation. He said he was not ready to divulge the names of these persons. Maurice Rochan, a Negro, said to have been taken to the Flint-Everidge hospital by Dominick DiGiovanni and Joseph Gaeto on the night of their murder in an automobile in front of the home of Leonardo Cipolla in Tupelo Street, will be questioned...by the police. Octave Lacaz, a Negro of 907 Bartholomew Street,...told [police] he went to the home of Rochan next door to the Cipolla house to visit Rochan who was sick. He said he tried to make arrangements to have the man sent to the hospital. When the two bodies were found, a Negro woman in the crowd told Lacaz those are the same men who took Rochan to the hospital."[220] The key information Craven thought he needed, the key clues he thought could be provided from the key witness, had not yet been located. That key witness was Mrs. Leonardo Cipolla.

The New Orleans police superintendent announced that he had "received information which might lead to the arrest of Cipolla's wife within the next twenty-four hours. The police believe the woman knows of the killing and they want her as a material witness... [Two] detectives...were detailed to run down the tip which the head of the police department received."[221] The detectives immediately "went out to search for her,...expecting...to arrest her...at any minute."[222] Their information was based on "clues said to have been furnished by two Negroes which they hoped would lead them to Mrs. Cipolla. The police said the two Negroes were John Everidge, Egania and Burgundy streets, employed by F. G. Pommes, a cattle buyer, and Octavia Lacabe, 907 Bartholomew Street [probably the same Octave Lacaz who claimed knowledge of Mrs. Cipolla's whereabouts]. Mr. Pommes told the police Everidge had said he knew where Mrs. Cipolla was hiding and that Lacabe also possessed the information."[223]

Throughout the hunt for Leonardo Cipolla, throughout his arrest and grilling and the collection of physical evidence, throughout the roundup of other suspects and supposed confederates, the only remaining eyewitness to the killings remained missing and largely anonymous. She was known to the newspaper reading public only by association with her husband. A week after the murders, it had been reported that "police are still searching for Mrs. Cipolla, wife of the accused, as a witness in the investigation."[224] It was the only way in which she was ever identified in the newspapers or by the police. But what was her name, her Christian name (*nomu Cristiani*), the name her parents gave her at birth in Western Sicily (*nomu di battiu*)? She must have had some identity apart from Mrs. Leonardo Cipolla, the formal name attached to her by reason of her marriage. How was she called by the people who loved her? No official record, police report, obituary, or newspaper article located to date reveals her first or maiden name.

Gaetano DiGiovanni knew her name. She was his wife's niece, the daughter of one of Angelina's siblings or cousins, but which one? Applying the rule of naming employed by Western Sicilian parents near the turn of the nineteenth to the twentieth century, her name must have been Arcangela, Andrea, Angela, or Antonia Bucaro. Gaetano knew. He also knew her location.

On the day after the police net tightened around his niece, Gaetano paid a visit to the municipal authorities who were investigating his son's murder. The newspaper reported on the visit but misidentified Gaetano's first name and revealed only one of the reasons for the meetings. "Dominick [*sic*] DiGiovanni, father of one of the men killed in an automobile in front of the home of Cipolla,...called on Superintendent Molony for his son's automobile, which is riddled with bullets. He also asked to see Assistant District Attorney Craven. The automobile will be used in the court as evidence and will not be released until after the trial."[225] Gaetano's actual purposes were more complex. *La machina* (the machine, the car) meant little to him. He wanted to size up these two *pezzanovanti*, Police Chief Molony and Craven, measure their worthiness of respect, and reach his own conclusions from whatever they said about the truth of who was responsible for his son's killing. By this time, Gaetano also had possession of the missing witness, Mrs. Leonardo Cipolla, Dominick's cousin, Angelina Bucaro DiGiovanni's niece, who was then safely ensconced in Gaetano's own home, under the watch of his wife Angelina's one good eye. Gaetano wanted to decide for himself whether his niece could be safely turned over to these authorities, whether some deal for the girl's protection might be struck, or if he should take some other action in the best interests of the young woman and his *famiglia*. His decision became apparent a few days later.

"Haggard and worn and apparently in a highly nervous condition, Mrs. Leonardo Cipolla was found at 8 o'clock Tuesday night in bed in the home of her uncle, Dominick [Gaetano] DiGiovanni, 642 Erato street, father of one of the men whom her husband is charged with assassinating in front of the Cipolla home... Mrs. Cipolla, in answer to questions put by Assistant District Attorney Craven, told a harrowing tale of wandering aimlessly about the city in a dazed condition for the past three weeks, with scarcely any food. She related how she finally made her way to 'a place back of the cemetery near Metairie ridge,' from where she asserted, she sent word to her uncle, Dominick [Gaetano] DiGiovanni, to come for her. While in the main Mrs. Cipolla corroborated the story told by her husband as to their movements immediately following the firing of the shots that killed Joseph Gaeto and Dominick DiGiovanni Jr. [*sic*], she blasted one detail in the husband's recital that Assistant District Attorney Craven considered of extreme importance. When Leonardo Cipolla was captured two weeks ago and his home searched, police alleged they found four exploded shotgun shells in the yard. Cipolla explained the presence of the shells by saying that he had used them in firing at a mad dog that ran by his house the day of the murder of Gaeto and DiGiovanni. Mrs. Cipolla asserted…that she was home with her husband all that day and that she did not remember his firing the shotgun at any dog. She also contradicted other statements made by her husband… She claimed she could speak no English, so Mr. Craven questioned her through an interpreter… Mrs. Cipolla declared that she was taken to 642 Erato street by her uncle DiGiovanni. He took her there, she said, in an automobile back of the cemetery near Metairie Ridge… Craven announced that he would request Coroner O'Hara to examine Mrs. Cipolla, [who] was allowed to remain at the DiGiovanni home,…[and] that he did not believe any charge will be made against her… It was at 5 o'clock the afternoon of May 8, said Mrs. Cipolla, that she and her husband met Dominick DiGiovanni, and he took them riding in his automobile. She said they picked up Gaeto some place on Canal street, but she did not remember exactly where. After riding around,…she continued, they drove to the DiGiovanni home at 642 Erato street, where they remained some time…[before] they drove to Canal and Rampart streets, where she and her husband got out of the car to look at shop windows. In his statement to Mr. Craven, Cipolla said he and his wife got out of the car at Canal and Rampart streets to buy candy. Mrs. Cipolla…asserted that her husband bought no candy. She and her husband again met DiGiovanni and Gaeto and got in the automobile again… After riding around some more, they drove to the Cipolla home, arriving there at 11 p.m. Just as she and her husband had left the automobile...and were about to enter the gate of their home, the shots were fired... 'I fell to the ground,' said Mrs. Cipolla, 'and fainted. When I came to, I ran—I don't know where. I didn't know anybody was killed, I was nearly crazy, and I don't know how many shots were fired. I can't remember where I went—I just walked and walked. I don't know where I got anything to eat—I don't believe I got much to eat. I remember that Monday night I was some place back of the cemetery near Metairie Ridge. I believe it was a stable. I got an old woman that I didn't know to go to my uncle and tell him I was sick. He came after me in an automobile and took me to his house.'"[226] She denied having seen attorney Gulotta.[227]

Gaetano "corroborated the woman's statement as to how she notified him, but he also said he did not know where he had found her, except that it 'was around Metairie Ridge.' Assistant District Attorney Craven and Police Superintendent Molony declared that they placed absolutely no credence in Mrs. Cipolla's recital, both declaring that they did not believe Mrs. Cipolla was in the automobile in which Gaeto and DiGiovanni were slain."[228] Craven announced that he would question Mrs. Cipolla again the following day "in an effort to get further information. He believes Mrs. Cipolla knows more about the murder plot than she has told...[and that] statements made by the woman...contradict many previously made to the police by her husband."[229] The subsequent interview included taking her to the scene of the murders so she could reenact the crime, since "[g]rave discrepancies have already developed between her story and that of her husband. They have been given no opportunity to compare notes and their parallel stories will be closely checked... when Mrs. Cipolla goes over the ground once more," with her story being translated by the police department Italian interpreter since "[s]he speaks no English."[230]

CHAPTER 13

CHARGED

On Saturday, May 14, 1921, "John Mortello [*sic*] [actually Martello], said to be a brother-in-law of Joseph [actually Giacomo] Bucaro, was arrested...and taken to police headquarters to be questioned in connection with the assassination...of Dominick DiGiovanni and Joseph Gaeto... According to the police, they have received information that John Montetto [*sic*] [actually Martello] left an automobile said by the police to be stolen at Natale Deamore's garage in Tulane avenue, and that Deamore and Gaeto, his assistant, sold the car and told Martello that the police had seized it... [B]efore the murder Cipolla and Gaeto drove up to Deamore's garage in an automobile owned by DiGiovanni and Gaeto got out and knocked on the door... Later, it is presumed that DiGiovanni encountered the men and got in the car. **He may have been an innocent victim**, according to the police."[231] At the same time, Baptiste Pecoraro was also arrested for questioning concerning the murders, which police were now "satisfied...was the result of a vendetta" in which DiGiovanni had been "**slain by mistake**..., mistaken by the assassins for Natale Deamore," Gaeto's employer.[232]

Meanwhile, Leonardo Cipolla "again was taken to the scene of the crime and there questioned by [Assistant District Attorney] Craven with regard to the finding in his yard of four empty shotgun shells. Cipolla stated that Sunday noon before the killing a mad dog had come along the street and that he fired four shells at the dog. After discharging the gun, he declared, he immediately cleaned it. Police have received no report of a mad dog being in the street that day or any of the neighbors hearing a gun discharged."[233] Craven immediately told reporters that Cipolla would be charged with murder.

On the following day, the newspapers reported that murder charges would be formally pursued against all three men, Cipolla, Martello, and Pecoraro. "Cipolla is the man to whom suspicion points strongest, in the opinion of police... Cipolla engineered a plot to lure Joseph Gaeto and Natale Deamore,...garage operator, to their deaths. Martello and his brother-in-law, Pecararo, close friends of Cipolla, are said to have had a quarrel with Natale Deamore over an alleged stolen automobile left in Deamore's garage."[234] Craven believed that the car stolen by Martello and Pecoraro "was sold by Gaeto and Deamore, who kept the money and then told Martello and Pecararo that the police had confiscated the car. This alleged 'double-cross'...was the motive for the murder of Gaeto and the alleged plotted murder of Deamore. Cipolla...was the 'brains' of the large gang of alleged automobile thieves and bootleggers and shared in the division of all of the loot. It was Cipolla's part...to lure Gaeto and Deamore to Cipolla's home...while Martello and Pecararo... were 'planted' across the street armed with sawed-off shotguns... Cipolla borrowed the automobile of DiGiovanni, said to be Cipolla's cousin by marriage, and to have lured Gaeto into it... Cipolla with Gaeto in it drove to the home of Natale Deamore...to get Deamore into the car. Deamore was not at home,...as he was with the gang who are alleged to have attempted to rob the bank in Independence and murdered Dallas Calmes... DiGiovanni...got into the car by accident."[235] "It is now believed that DiGiovanni was slain by mistake and that Natale Deamore...was the man marked for death with Gaeto... Cipolla it is believed did not wish to have DiGiovanni killed, but fearing the men who lay in wait in front of his house would believe he had double-crossed them, Cipolla found himself in a position where he had to...carry out the program or invite disaster upon himself. And so DiGiovanni, if this theory holds good, was the victim of circumstances."[236] Deamore had avoided assassination on Tupelo Street only because he was with the gang on the Northshore robbing the Independence bank and murdering Dallas Calmes. Dominick died in Deamore's place.

On May 18, 1921, Cipolla, Martello, and Pecoraro were taken before Judge Alex O'Donnell for arraignment on murder charges in Second City Criminal Court. They pleaded not guilty and were initially remanded to Orleans Parish Prison without bail.[237] They did not remain in jail for long. "On June 4 [1921], Cipolla was released from the Parish Prison on a $10,000 bond arranged by George J. Gulotta, his attorney."[238] Cipolla fled immediately and was never seen in New Orleans again. He was formally indicted and charged with the double murders by a New Orleans grand jury on June 7, 1921.[239] "On the issuance of the indictment...a capias was issued for Cipolla and his immediate arrest without bond was ordered."[240] He was never apprehended. With Cipolla's disappearance, the case against Martello and Pecoraro collapsed, or perhaps the authorities simply lost interest, and they were released. The story of the double murders, the assassination of the eldest son of Gaetano and Angelina DiGiovanni, which had been front-page news for almost a month, disappeared from the newspapers and the public consciousness. They were forgotten as thoroughly as Leonardo Cipolla himself had disappeared. Editor Cono Puglisi's fears were realized. Prominent Italian community leader Frank Cabibi's confidence in the authorities proved unfounded. No one was ever tried for Uncle Dominick's murder.

CHAPTER 14

MISTAKE 1921

From time to time, on All Saints' Day, or Angelina's or Gaetano's birthdays, or the interment dates of other relatives, surviving members of the DiGiovanni or Guinta families would visit the burial vault in the old Italian section of Lakelawn Metairie Cemetery. A young first-time visitor would notice the inscribed birth and death dates of Uncle Dominick, born February 22, 1896, died May 8, 1921, at only twenty-five years old.

"Poor Uncle Dominick," the youngster would say. "How'd he die so young?"

"Ohhh," would come the long moan from one of the elders. "It was a terrible accident, a big mistake. He was in the wrong place at the wrong time."

The family story had always been that Dominick's death had been a mistake; that he had been an innocent bystander, simply in the wrong place at the wrong time. It certainly was a plausible story. Its roots were in a "scenario created by [Assistant District Attorney] Craven and the police"[241] that Cipolla had known about the murders both in Independence and his own front yard, with DiGiorgio masterminding the Independence caper and connected to the Tupelo Street murders through his dealings with Natale Deamore. According to this theory: "Probably in late April [1921], two of Cipolla's men brought a stolen car to Deamore and Gaeto for repairs. Natale [Deamore], who supposedly operated Cipolla's clearinghouse

96

for stolen vehicles, decided to sell the car and keep the money... As a result, Gaeto and Deamore were marked for death. In the meantime, Leona and Deamore had developed with Vito DiGiorgio a scheme to rob a bank in Independence... DiGiorgio recruited outside Mafia men, such as Rini, Lamantia, Giglio, and Leona, to execute the robbery. Then on Sunday night, Cipolla, who was fully aware of the Independence plans, borrowed DiGiovanni's car. Planning to avenge Deamore and Gaeto's betrayal, he wanted to lure Gaeto into the car for a ride to Deamore's [garage on Tulane Avenue]. Once both men were in the car, he was to take them to a prearranged spot to murder them. The only thing Cipolla did not count on was DiGiovanni's insistence on riding along. When Cipolla arrived at the garage, he did not find Deamore at home. Leonardo was in a predicament. He feared taking Gaeto and DiGiovanni to his house, where the killing was to occur. However, if he did not, the city's other *mafiosi* [DiGiorgio, for example] would believe that he had betrayed them. Feeling he had no choice, Leonardo ordered DiGiovanni to take them to his home," where Gaeto and DiGiovanni were murdered by Cipolla's men.[242]

Thus, some of "[t]he authorities agreed...that the killing of DiGiovanni was in the way of a mistake. Gaeto, indeed, was marked for death. What the assassins expected...was that Gaeto would be accompanied in the automobile by [Natale Deamore]; it was their intention to dispatch these two. Instead..., Gaeto invited DiGiovanni to ride with him, with the results related."[243] Lending credence to this theory was the pre-hanging public confession of Dallas Calmes' killer, Rosario Leona. When asked by a reporter, "'What did Cipolla, Gaeto and DiGiovanni have to do with this thing [the Calmes murder in Independence]?' Leona stared blankly for a few minutes. 'They didn't have nothing to do with it,' he answered finally. 'That shooting was something else I don't know anything about. It just happened that same night—that's all."[244]

Gaetano DiGiovanni knew that the killing of his son could never be considered a "mistake." In his nineteenth-century Western Sicilian experience, culture, and mindset, men did not make such mistakes. The responsibility of the actual gunmen was minimal.

To Gaetano, Martello and Pecoraro were merely hired hands, professionals instructed by higher-ups to perform an assigned task. It was the bigger shots who were truly culpable. If DiGiorgio and/or Cipolla had been so stupid as to get Gaetano's son involved in something that was intended for someone else, they were responsible for his killing. The civil authorities and newspapers who were exhibiting what Gaetano considered only passing interest in determining who was responsible for Domenico's murder had fingered Cipolla as the ultimately responsible mastermind. Gaetano knew better. As to who bore the greatest responsibility for his son's murder, Gaetano's verdict was similar to the judgment reached by the fictional Don Vito Corleone concerning the death of his own eldest son in Mario Puzo's novel *The Godfather*. In assessing who was most culpable for the murder of Santino "Sonny" Corleone on the New Jersey Turnpike, *The Godfather* concluded, "Tattaglia is a pimp. He could never have outfought Santino… It's enough to know that Barzini <u>had a hand in it</u>."[245] In Domenico's case, Cipolla was just a rum-runner, a car thief, hapless middle-manager of a "mistake" he was not smart enough to fix before the worst happened to his own cousin-in-law, Dominick. To Gaetano DiGiovanni, Vito DiGiorgio was the ultimately responsible big shot, the real boss of these violent squads of bootleggers, stolen automobile dealers, armed bank robbers, and murderers with whom his Domenico had become involved. It was DiGiorgio to whom a cut of these activities flowed. It was DiGiorgio whose Northshore robbery scheme had lured Natale Deamore away from his Tulane Avenue chop shop and into Tangipahoa Parish instead of where he rightly belonged on the night Domenico was killed: the front seat of the death car parked in Cipolla's driveway, sitting next to Joseph Gaeto.

It would not be an accurate assessment of Gaetano's background and character to say that he seethed as he contemplated what must be done. His thought processes were calm and calculating. His eldest son had been assassinated. The fact was that Domenico had been intentionally killed, perhaps mistakenly but certainly not accidentally. This was an affront to both the standing and security of Gaetano and his family. In the Western Sicily in which Gaetano had been born and come to manhood, an "honourable [*sic*]…gentleman is 'the man who, out of a refined moral sensitivity, does not believe that the laws…are sufficient to protect his honour [*sic*], and imposes on himself the rigid observance of special rules which are called the laws of chivalry'; honour [*sic*] is determined from outside, *all' Italiana*; it is defined as 'the esteem and consideration which an honest person has been able to gain in public opinion through his actions,'… Offenses are graduated in a scale of intensity like earthquakes or typhoons. The most serious, fourth degree, are those 'which touch the family.'"[246] Domenico's murder had been an offense of this most serious kind.

Certainly, the New Orleans police, the district attorney, the state of Louisiana could not be trusted for justice. The authorities seemed more interested in some bigger, alien American picture and not in bringing to justice those responsible for his son's death. "The police were inclined to think that the blotting-out of the lives of Gaeto and [Dominick] DiGiovanni, which involved no loss to the community, inaugurated a new era in Mafia activity in New Orleans. In this development, the main interest was rum-running and automobile stealing. Just how the two victims fitted into that scheme of things none can say; whether they were shot by competitors, who took this effectual way of eliminating them from a profitable industry; or were something like innocent bystanders; or had been guilty of some infraction of the Mafia laws, the punishment for which was invariably death. At any rate, about 1921, there had arisen among the younger generation of Italians in New Orleans a new criminal brotherhood."[247]

Gaetano knew that some of the men who had killed his son, permitted it to happen, or planned and plotted the murder had already been released on bond and subsequently disappeared. Gaetano knew that the bigger culprits, more responsible than the trigger men themselves, would never be apprehended through the ordinary abilities and means of the civil authorities. In Gaetano's late-nineteenth-century Western Sicilian mind, "society, the law, and the State have feeble powers. He must defend himself…he must be…his own strategic expert,…his own lawyer, policeman, and judge. In short, his security depends not on the combined exertions of his countrymen to which he should add his own but mostly on his individual capacities and native shrewdness… He…can occupy in society only whichever position he can conquer and defend with his personal authority. His authority depends on many factors, his capacity, his talents, energy, determination, but ultimately on his ability to intimidate his enemies and, if need should arise, to destroy them."[248] In Gaetano's Palermo Province hinterlands, which had been transported with him and others to 1921 New Orleans, "[t]he recourse to violence prevalent in [his] part of Sicily and expressed in…shooting and homicide was taken for granted and accepted rather than questioned. The use of violence was encouraged and justified, though people were never aimlessly harmed or killed: violence was proscribed in those situations where people sought to get their claims to honour [sic] and power ultimately recognized."[249] By definition, the men responsible for killing his beloved eldest son, the son for whom he had such high hopes, whom he had brought as a small boy out of Western Sicily through North Africa and into America, were his enemies.

In its first report of the double murder, *The Times-Picayune* had quoted the grim but accurate forecast of a veteran New Orleans police captain of Italian extraction. "Further assassinations as the result of the killing of Joseph Gaeto and Dominick DiGiovanni… are feared by Acting Police Superintendent [Thomas] Capo, who has had long experiences with the vendetta in New Orleans… Captain Capo asserted he saw the probable falling out of a band of automobile bandits and bootleggers whose operations in New Orleans and surrounding country have been extensive. 'Vengeance will be taken,' said Captain Capo. 'It may come swiftly, or the friends of Gaeto and DiGiovanni may proceed cautiously and wait—but it will come.'"[250]

Gaetano DiGiovanni knew what must be done. "[H]onour [sic] has been offended,…vendetta is a right."[251] Yet it must not be done too quickly. He recalled the old Sicilian proverb: "Revenge is a dish best served cold." With the prescience that he alone recognized as his special gift, Gaetano foresaw it done within a year.

CHAPTER 15

NEW ORLEANS-ST. LOUIS-CHICAGO 1922

Who can know for certain how justice for the New Orleans murder of Domenico DiGiovanni was obtained? Does it matter whether the correct Cipolla among the three or four with whom DiGiorgio associated was the Cipolla who paid the price? Is it not enough to know that the requirements of Sicilian vendetta were fulfilled? Perhaps it happened this way.

A man in a northbound railroad car sat quietly in his seat, which rocked gently from left to right, keeping time with the swaying of the car itself. It was a soothing rhythm, one to which he had become accustomed through his own years as an immigrant railroad worker in America. He had been summoned to New Orleans, a place he had never previously visited, at the direction of a boss he had never met. He was on his way to Kansas City to meet another man he had never met, a man who would travel with him to St. Louis, an alliance territory of the Kansas City mob's organized crime jurisdiction, to carry out Part 1 of his two-part assignment.

According to the "1960s-era memoirs and interviews" of "Mafioso Nicola 'Zio Cola' Gentile,…when he transferred his Mafia membership to Kansas City, Missouri," in 1921, Kansas City was a place "where Paolo DiGiovanni ruled. (Because [Paolo] DiGiovanni died in 1929 he did not receive the fame and notoriety of his younger brothers, Pietro 'Sugarhouse Pete" and Joseph ['Scarface' DiGiovanni], both of whom garnered national attention during the Kefauver Committee hearings in 1950–1951)."[252] "The DiGiovanni's were old Mafiosi from Sicily that [*sic*] derived their earnings from extortion rackets based in the local Italian neighborhoods."[253] All three were "Sicilian-born, the founding fathers of the organization, who settled in Kansas City's North End in the early 1900s. Labeled 'Mustache Petes' by younger mobsters, they adhered to the culture and protocols of the Old World Sicilian Mafia… In what was known as the Black Hand era, they formed criminal factions that extorted fellow immigrant countrymen. The competing North End factions came together in the late 1920s as the result of Prohibition, and a single Outfit was born."[254] Together, the DiGiovanni brothers forged a close alliance between the Kansas City and St. Louis mobs. "The Kansas City family has a strong historic link to St. Louis. However, the Kansas City organization grew far more powerful than its cousin on the eastern side of Missouri. Its influence could be felt as far south as Texas."[255] One Missouri narcotics agent who testified before the 1950s Kefauver Committee of the U.S. Congress viewed the St. Louis mob as "a branch office" of the Kansas City organization's drug operations.[256]

Was the correct Cipolla killed in the vendetta to avenge the murder of Dominick DiGiovanni? And when did he die? Some of the sketchy published reports hint that sometime during May 1922, Leonardo Cipolla was assassinated in St. Louis. Little is known of the exact circumstances of Cipolla's death. With unnamed police as the principal source of its story, the New Orleans *Times-Picayune* perfunctorily stated about one year after Cipolla's flight from New Orleans, it was "reported that he had been murdered in St. Louis."[257] One journalist has concluded that a different Cipolla in fact had been killed. "The press apparently confused Leonardo Cipolla with Joseph Cipolla, a young member of the Egan's Rats Gang of St. Louis, who was murdered on Dec. 28, 1921. Leonardo Cipolla died in Brooklyn on July 7, 1943."[258] However, neither that author's text nor his footnoted conclusion cites any references to documentation or other evidence to support it, including no explanation of why or how the press would have waited to mention or mistaken the December 1921 murder of Joseph in May 1922. Another "unconfirmed" listing of Mafia members includes a simple columned chart entry: "Cipolla-Leonardo. 1884–19**43**. Palermo, Sic. 1920–'40s. Brooklyn Ex N.O."[259] Other reports identify the victim as Leonardo. "Once Cipolla obtained his freedom" on the bond obtained by his attorney on June 4, 1921, "he disappeared from New Orleans. A year later, it would be reported that he had been murdered in St. Louis."[260] Word of Leonardo Cipolla's killing in St. Louis was reported again two years later, on May 10, 1924, the third anniversary of Dominick's death and the day after six men—four of whom had ties to Cipolla—were hanged in Amite, Louisiana, for the killing of Independence grocer Dallas Calmes. "Cipolla was held on a murder charge, indicted by the Orleans parish grand jury [for the killing of Gaeto and DiGiovanni], but by special arrangement with District Attorney Marr was released on a bond of $10,000. He vanished, and later, police in New Orleans heard that he had been killed in an Italian vendetta in St. Louis."[261]

A few days after the New Orleans report of Cipolla's reputed killing, at the end of the first week of May 1922, a train from St. Louis reached Chicago, and a man stepped from the passenger coach in which he had made the short journey. In Rockford, Illinois, a suburb located 107 miles northeast of Chicago, lived another branch of the DiGiovanni family, including two of Gaetano's brothers, Giuseppe and Dominick,[262] a sister, Josephine, who had married Albert Provenzano, and various nieces and nephews.

The Chicago-New Orleans Italian connection was not unusual. Less than two weeks earlier, on April 30, 1922, "[t]he body of an unidentified Italian believed to be an Orleanian or one who recently was in New Orleans was found with two bullet wounds in the back in a basement in Chicago… The Italian, according to the Chicago police, was the victim of the vendetta… The slain Italian was about five feet seven inches tall, slight build, and about twenty-seven years old, he wore about $500 of gaudy rings, watch and chain, and a chain amulet on his wrist. He was dressed in a gray suit, green hat, and yellow shoes. A laundry ticket and $20 were found on the body, which was still warm when found by the police."[263]

The man who stepped from the train was in Chicago because Vito "DiGiorgio was in Chicago."[264] It was almost precisely one year since Dominick DiGiovanni had been gunned down in New Orleans. DiGiorgio had told his wife, who resided at 1015 Chartres Street in New Orleans, that he and his friend, James Cascio, had "left for Chicago last Sunday [May 7] saying he had an important business engagement in that city."[265] "On the morning of May 13, 1922, DiGiorgio, [Giovanni 'Big Jim'] LoCascio [sic] and an unidentified man entered a combined barbershop and poolroom at 956 Larabee Street near Oak Street in the Little Italy section of Chicago. The three men approached a pool table, but DiGiorgio commented, 'I might as well get shaved.' He sat in barber John Loiacano's chair for a shave while LoCascio [sic] and the third man played pool. Two young Italian men entered the business. One of the men walked quietly over to DiGiorgio's chair and put a revolver close to the relaxing crime boss's ear. The other moved into the poolroom and pointed a revolver at LoCascio [sic]. Shots rang out. DiGiorgio was struck by six slugs in his head and upper arms. LoCascio [sic] was hit three times. Both died instantly. The shooters ran out through a side door to Oak Street, as employees and patrons fled or took cover. The killings made national news."[266]

They also made local news in New Orleans. "The names of Vito DiGiorgio and James Cascio, New Orleans Italians, who were shot to death Saturday morning in an Italian barbershop in Chicago by two unidentified assassins, have been mentioned prominently with several black hand vendetta killings in this city during the last seven years," wrote *The Times-Picayune* on the day after the killings. "The shooting in Chicago, the police believe, was the continuation of a feud that started in New Orleans as far back as 1914... The... last time the name of DiGiorgio was mentioned in connection with a vendetta shooting was last May [almost exactly one year earlier] when Joseph Gaeto and Dominick DiGiovanni were found murdered in an automobile in front of the home of Leonardo Cipolla on Tupelo Street, who after remaining in hiding for a week was captured and charged with the crime. Because the presumption of guilt was not great District Attorney Marr released him on a $5,000 [sic] bond.

Since his release, Cipolla left the city and is reported to have been murdered in St. Louis. While the investigation of the double killing was being conducted the police are said to have been searching for DiGiorgio, who was reported to know something of the killing."[267]

Police in four cities—St. Louis, Chicago, Kansas City, and New Orleans—were stymied, or perhaps simply disinterested, in their investigations of the murders, reputedly of Leonardo Cipolla and definitely of Vito DiGiorgio. The victims and their deaths appeared related, by their temporal proximity; by their connection to the Gaeto-DiGiovanni assassinations, which had just reached their one-year anniversary; by the style and method of their execution; by the evident vengeful intent with which the killings were committed. No suspects were ever arrested or prosecuted.

As to DiGiorgio's murder, "A coroner's inquest, which went on from May 15 to May 31, [1922], closed the case without resolving it…"[268] Opinions vary among chroniclers about the motive for DiGiorgio's assassination. One historian concluded that the reason "was as murky as DiGiorgio's life in the Mafia had been."[269] Another speculated that "[i]t is possible" that DiGiorgio's death was connected to a feud reflected in "gangland murders" out West coinciding with DiGiorgio's arrival and brief ascendency in Los Angeles.[270]

Others contemplating DiGiorgio's end from a New Orleans perspective were unanimous in their view. "New Orleans police speculated that DiGiorgio's death was somehow connected with southern Louisiana quarrels…"[271] One prominent journalist noted that "although [DiGiorgio] was a New Orleans product, he met his end in Chicago, apparently at the hands of a gunman sent to that city especially for the purpose… Although the [DiGiorgio] shooting took place a thousand miles away, it was really a New Orleans crime. There can be no question but that someone was dispatched from the southern city with a mandate from the Mafia to put DiGiorgio out of the way, and apparently followed the doomed man…to Chicago,…until that luckless day when DiGiorgio decided that he needed a shave."[272] About two years after DiGiorgio's assassination, commentary on his killing was publicly registered by another interesting source, Rosario "Roy" Leona, confessed killer of Dallas Calmes, the grocer in

Independence, Louisiana, murdered on the same night as Dominick DiGiovanni by men police linked to Cipolla and DiGiorgio. Of DiGiorgio's death, Leona said of his former sponsor, DiGiorgio: "I am glad they killed him—glad. They ought to have killed him before."[273]

A similar sentiment was overheard in 1965 by DiGiovanni family mourners at the Lamana-Panno-Fallo funeral home in New Orleans during the wake of the family matriarch, Angelina Bucaro DiGiovanni. A small group of Bucaro and DiGiovanni men was gathered in a corner, whispering to each other. They were recounting the great tragedy of Angelina's life, the killing of her eldest son Domenico in 1921. New Orleans Municipal Court Judge Andrew G. Bucaro was in the huddle. He was the son of Giacomo Bucaro, who had harbored Leonardo Cipolla in his grocery store in 1921. He was the great-nephew of Giacomo Bucaro, the late-nineteenth-century police chief of Ciminna. His middle initial "G" stood for Giacomo. The judge was a family success story, a man of integrity, prominence, and standing. Born in New Orleans on January 21, 1923, he earned his undergraduate and law degrees from Tulane University and served with distinction as a lieutenant in the United States Navy aboard an amphibious surface ship in the Italian and Southern French campaigns during World War II.

As a judge, "He strongly advocated the decriminalization of minor drug violations and medical intervention for defendants as an alternative to incarceration,"[274] thoughtful, progressive views that are fairly commonplace these days but were controversial reformist ideas when Judge Bucaro voiced them. Appointed to the New Orleans Municipal Court by Louisiana Governor Robert Kennon in 1955, he was subsequently elected, then repeatedly reelected unopposed, serving continuously until he retired in 1977. In 1967, the judge made national news when he was quoted in a *Life* magazine series about *La Cosa Nostra* ("this thing of ours"), organized crime in the form of the Sicilian-American Mafia. In the *Life* article, Judge Bucaro "freely discusses his friendship with [reputed New Orleans Mafia Kingpin Carlos] Marcello, an old pal and a remote relative by marriage. He admits that he attends frequent parties at Churchill Farms [the Marcello estate on the West Bank of Jefferson Parish], but says his visits have nothing to do with judicial discretion. 'We don't discuss cases,' he says, 'we just barbecue goats on a spit. There is nothing sinister about our relationship. Carlos Marcello needs a fix in the municipal court as much as Rockefeller needs to steal pennies.'"[275]

At his aunt Angelina's wake, concerning his cousin Dominick's reportedly mistaken murder in 1921, Judge Bucaro was reputedly overheard to whisper in conclusion of the hushed conversation among the DiGiovanni-Bucaro men, "The mistake was corrected."

CHAPTER 16

RETURN TO SICILY 1922

On July 22, 1922, less than three months after DiGiorgio was murdered and Cipolla was reportedly killed, Gaetano DiGiovanni pulled up his family by their New Orleans roots and returned all that he could control to Sicily. Two married daughters stayed behind. A few years earlier, eldest daughter Giuseppina (Josephine, "Fene") had married Philip Ferraro and settled in old St. Bernard Parish, where she bought a few cows and goats. Fene retreated into the seclusion and separation from the rest of the family for which she later was called "Fene the Recluse" by some of her siblings. Maria (Mary, "Ma-Mamie"), exhibiting the same kind of rebelliousness against a father's wishes that her mother, then fourteen-year-old Angelina Bucaro, had displayed in Ciminna, Sicily, more than thirty years earlier, eloped on the night before her family left town. Rather than go to Sicily, she married Frank Towle, a man from New Hampshire, who was called "Yanks" ever after by Ma-Mamie's Sicilian family or "Uncle Yanks" by youngsters like myself. "We don't know nothin' about them [Towles]," Aunt Lou said. "New Hampshire. Her husband was from New Hampshire." Nia added, "Frank Towle. And I can tell you when [Ma-Mamie] got married. She eloped [right] before we were gonna leave for Italy, on the twenty-first day of July, because we left on the twenty-second…1922."[276]

When asked by her grandson John Guinta why the DiGiovannis pulled up stakes to leave New Orleans and return to Sicily in 1922,

Nia said, "My father took us to Italy on a visit. After we were there, my [grand]mother [Antonia Petrano Bucaro] had a stroke… We approximately were there two years and then Grandma, old Grandma, had a stroke, and my mother wouldn't put her in an institution, because my mother was her only [daughter], and my uncle Frank, her only living [children], and they weren't gonna put her in an institution,… and so we stayed there seven years, expecting Grandma to either die or get better, or wait [until] the money ran out. She wanted to wait… We couldn't stay any longer. You know, seven years, and money, with all the kids, and my grandma, my daddy was paying for all this stuff."[277] Mom once asked Nia why they stayed in Sicily for seven years if Grandma had been so sick when they arrived. "She lingered," Nia said.

Of course, Gaetano knew that vendetta was a moral obligation, a right among Western Sicilians, whether in New Orleans or in Palermo Province. In New Orleans alone, "[i]n the Third Police Precinct, for example, in the region around the intersection of St. Philip and Chartres Streets [in the heavily Italian-populated French Quarter] there were, between 1913 and 1927, seventeen murders which were, in all probability, due to the vendetta" waged among competing Italian factions.[278] Gaetano knew that DiGiorgio and believed that Cipolla were now dead. He had three younger sons, Jake, Sugie, and Walter, who could be targets of further vendetta. Based in part on family lore and in part on circumstantial evidence, it appears that Gaetano returned his family to Sicily in 1922 for safety reasons.

In New Orleans, the family boarded the S. S. Guillermo Pesht, sailed to New York, then proceeded to Rome. "It wasn't such a hot-lookin' [ship]…twenty-five days it took them" to travel from New Orleans to Italy in 1922, Nia recalled.[279] They disembarked in Rome, went south by train to the tip of the Italian boot, ferried to Palermo, then further south overland to San Cipirello.

CHAPTER 17

NEW ORLEANS
RIVERFRONT 1923

Anthony Tumarello was decidedly among the "good element" of New Orleans Italians whom newspaper editor Condo Puglisi had implored in 1921 to take action against the small slice of the local immigrant community whose lawlessness had resulted in the murder of Domenico DiGiovanni. I imagine that a nineteen- or twenty-year-old Tumarello was a native of someplace like Campobello di Mazara in Trapani Province, Salaparuta or Chiusa Sclafani in Palermo Province, Western Sicily. He probably arrived in New Orleans around 1899 aboard one of the giant freighters from Palermo, penniless and alone, just another of the thousands of landless Sicilians, without prospects at home, swept up in the *Mezzogiorno* at the dawn of the new century. Perhaps he became one of the strong-backed, broad-shouldered young men whom Gaetano DiGiovanni selected for work among the labor gangs of his fellow Italians unloading bananas from the cargo ships in the city's busy port, principally at and around the Thalia or Erato Streets banana wharves. That work may have resulted in his first meeting with his future father-in-law, an older stevedore named Salvatore Pelligrini.

One late afternoon, right after his shift had ended, Tumarello may have spotted Pellegrini walking along the edges of the river's batture, where the sand and driftwood from the rushing current met the ends and undersides of the cypress planks of the unloading docks. Pelligrini's arms may have been laden with green bananas and a smattering of lemons, plucked where they had fallen to the ground or were floating in the shallows of the river's edge, stray extras or rejects from the bounty of the unloading effort.

"*Paisano*," the older man may have shouted to Tumarello. "Lend me those strong young arms of yours." The request would have been made in a fatherly fashion, a combination of earnest delight and command. Tumarello obliged. The older man immediately stuffed his pockets with some of the bananas and lemons from his own overburdened arms. He probably reached into the deep pockets of his pants legs and pulled out two folded burlap sacks, which he opened to their most expansive shapes, then turned immediately to fill them with more of the abandoned unripe fruit.

"*Grazi*, young friend," Pelligrini might have said. "Now you come with me to my home for a meal and some good conversation." Tumarello accepted silently, and the two men began to walk away from the riverbank and into the French Quarter, past the old square and into its residential section, where large groups of recent Italian immigrants had concentrated their homes, most of them rented from the old French Creole families who still owned the buildings. Along the way, Tumarello listened, astonished, as Pelligrini described his plans for the scavenged fruit.

For months, Pelligrini had been making his afterwork collections and storing the fruit temporarily in baskets on the back stoop of his home, where he lived with his only daughter. As he aged, Pelligrini had to know that the backbreaking labor on the banana boats was sure to take him in death long before his beloved daughter and that he must ensure the girl's future. So he began to collect his abandoned fruit, marveling to himself at the great waste in perfectly good food that these rich American shipowners and produce importers, in their vast wealth, so exorbitantly let slip into the river's batture and currents. Whenever he collected enough, he washed his produce, loaded up an oversized wheelbarrow that he had refurbished from a construction site discard and painted garishly in the old Sicilian style, and pushed it through the neighborhood. He would cry out his list of that day's inventory—"I got bananas, I got lemons and oranges, tomatoes"—whatever had fallen off the wharves in the preceding days, selling his wares to the American Sector housewives or their Black housekeepers at prices that astonished Pelligrini. He was saving the nickels, dimes, and occasional dollars that he made this way in a secret hiding place known only to himself.

"One day soon," he may have confided proudly to Tumarello, "I have enough money to open my own little store. Then, no more docks for me."

From that evening forward, Tumarello found himself more and more in the company of Pelligrini and his daughter. Nature took its course, prodded at every turn by the gentle encouragement and quiet determination of Salvatore Pelligrini. Within months, the daughter became Mrs. Anthony Tumarello, and Anthony had become his father-in-law's partner in a small store, specializing in the sale and home delivery of the freshest of fruits and vegetables. As the 1900s passed into the 1910s and early 1920s, Tumarello children were born, all of whom were given American first names. The enterprise grew into "S. Pelligrini, Wholesale Produce and Vegetables," with three New Orleans locations: 1118 Decatur Street, the French Market, and 1119 Gallatin Street. They no longer relied on discarded fruit from the city's wharves to stock their inventory. They cultivated relationships with the Italian truck farmers from nearby Kenner and Algiers and with the chiefs of the stevedoring gangs, who would sometimes make arrangements to sell some of the importers' surplusage for their own profit. Pelligrini always bought low, sold higher, and profited accordingly.

When Salvatore Pelligrini died, he was among the most respected and successful Italian immigrant merchants in New Orleans. Anthony Tumarello took control of the family business, leaving its name intact as a tribute to the father-in-law who had laid the groundwork for his own standing and success. Anthony became a patriarch in his own right. With the same pride and astonishment of so many others like himself, he was able to marvel at the stark difference between what he had found in America, a place where wealth, home, and security could be made for oneself from a man's own sweat and industriousness, and what he had left in Sicily, where no such thing would have been possible and whose heartaches and injustices Anthony had almost forgotten. Surely, Anthony Tumarello believed in America.

It, therefore, came as a jolting reminder of the darkness he thought he had left behind in Sicily when in the late summer of 1923, he received an unmistakably threatening letter: "If you don't meet us at the corner of Decatur and St. Philip Streets tomorrow afternoon, your store will be dynamited and your wife will be killed. The same fate is yours if you betray us and go to the police. *La Mano Nera*."

Anthony knew the name. *La Mano Nera* (the Black Hand) was a systematic blackmailing technique brought to early-twentieth-century America by immigrants from Sicily. The Black Hand was "one method of parting a susceptible Italian immigrant from his money,... the extortion of the Italian-born via threats of harm to persons and/ or property if their demands were unmet... [A] Black Hand episode began with the sending of several letters. [Though always unsigned, the letters often bore an] emblem utilized to frighten victims."[280] Sometimes the emblem was hand-drawn skull and crossbones; more often, the letters were marked with a crude drawing of an open hand, palm side up, colored with black ink or dark pencil.[281]

How real was the Black Hand phenomenon in early-twentieth-century America? Was its extent inflated? Was it related to organized crime activity, including the Mafia? Historians hotly debate these questions. "Black Hand crimes defined the southern Italian immigrant experience so far as the public was concerned. The stigma of the Black Hand was applied 'to the Italian community's criminal problem and sometimes to Italians in general... The Black Hand label was applied to most unsolved 'Italian-on-Italian' crimes... Because of newspaper publicity, vendetta killings and almost every other crime in the Italian community were soon attributed to the Black Hand.'"[282]

Although some evidence of ritual and criminal organization has been associated with Black Hand activities, "case studies show a weak association between Mafia membership and Black Hand racketeering. Sicilians did mount Black Hand forays, but almost always acted on an individual basis and did so before joining an organized crime family... However, several instances were identified of men who would later join and even lead [Mafia] families being involved in the Black Hand prior to their Mafia membership. [One of these men], Joseph DiGiovanni, subsequently of the Kansas City 'outfit's' elite, was arrested in July 1915, with several associates, for sending a Black Hand letter."[283] Giuseppe "Piddu" Morello, a member of the Corleone Mafia who—like Gaetano DiGiovanni—had worked as an agricultural laborer and picked cotton in South Louisiana and Texas upon coming to America in the late 1890s, later reputed to be "*capo di capi* [boss of bosses] of the entire American Mafia," head of the "First Family" of New York organized crime, "was the assumed head of the Black Hand."[284] Nevertheless, Black Hand crimes were also a pop culture "criminal fashion" of early-twentieth-century America. "Professional gangs apart, jealous neighbors, commercial rivals, hard-up workers, and pranksters also sent 'Black Hand' letters... [O]rdinarily, the recipient of a 'Black Hand' missive paid, and said nothing."[285]

Who or what was the source of the Black Hand threat to Anthony Tumarello? It made no difference to the prosperous New Orleans grocer. When the first letter was followed in short order by similarly threatening sequels, Tumarello's anxiety multiplied. The tone and content of the letters were distinctly Sicilian, and Tumarello was fully aware of the capabilities and seriousness of his *paisani*. He knew that he could not simply continue to ignore the threats. The initial course of action he decided upon was peculiarly American.

CHAPTER 18

IRISH CHANNEL
OCTOBER 9, 1923

By Tuesday night, October 9, Anthony Tumarello had decided to do what any law-abiding American might do under similar circumstances. He went to the police. He walked into the Seventh Precinct station of the New Orleans police department located not far from the Tumarello home on Annunciation Street, only four blocks from the Mississippi River in a neighborhood known then and now as the Irish Channel. Tumarello told the desk sergeant that he was afraid to walk to his home alone because a man who had threatened to kill him was lying in wait for him. The police sergeant was told that Tumarello and some of his neighbors had seen the man for three weeks looking for him in the neighborhood of Religious and Nuns Streets, along the Irish Channel riverfront.

The desk sergeant eyed Tumarello skeptically. "These dagos," he thought derisively to himself, "always at each other's throats." Nevertheless, a murder on the streets of his own precinct, especially after he had been told it might occur, even if it was just another "wop-on-wop" crime, was not something the sergeant wanted to see written about himself in the newspapers.

"Dendinger," the desk sergeant shouted out the name of one of his patrolmen who was just coming on for the night shift. "Walk this poor fella home. He's on your beat."

Patrolman Louis Dendinger was a relative youngster on the Seventh District force: midtwenties; trim; sinewy in build; the son of a family of German immigrants who had settled alongside their fellow Irish and Italian immigrant families and their Black neighbors in the working-class Irish Channel neighborhood. He was decked out in the loose-fitting navy-blue uniform of the New Orleans police department, wearing the odd, rounded, standard-issue hat of the cop on the beat, half derby and half helmet. He sported a trim dark mustache. A long billy club dangled from his left hip; a police revolver was holstered on his right. Dendinger turned sharply from the big book all cops signed at the start of their shifts when he heard his sergeant's command, and he hustled eagerly to Tumarello's side. "Ready," he said to the grocer crisply. "Lead the way."

Tumarello and Dendinger stepped through the door and down the brick steps of the Seventh District station, onto the cobble-stoned Annunciation Street sidewalk. They walked side by side, parallel to the downriver path of the nearby Mississippi River, heading toward Tumarello's home at 1930 Annunciation Street, only a few doors from its intersection with St. Mary Street.

After a couple of blocks, they spotted their suspect, standing in the shadows a few blocks ahead, at the corner of Annunciation and St. Mary Streets. The man was shorter but thicker in build than the patrolman, broad and powerful through the chest, shoulders, and hips, dressed in the rough clothing of a laborer. A floppy, cloth peasant's cap of the type commonly worn by Sicilian immigrants of the time covered the thin, auburn hair that framed his mostly bald head. The man's muscular right arm was bent at the elbow. He cradled a threatening dark object in the palm and fingers of his beefy right hand. It was a loaded pistol.

"That's him," Tumarello said to the patrolman, and he raised his right arm to point a bony finger in the man's direction. Patrolman Dendinger instinctively reached to his hip to pull his own revolver and simultaneously barked in his commanding policeman's voice, "Hey, you."

The man bolted immediately, running south from Annunciation Street onto St. Mary Street, heading for the perceived safety of Tchoupitoulas Street and its riverfront wharves. Patrolman Dendinger gave chase. The gunman's gait was oddly deliberate, more a gamboling trot than out-and-out flight. After only a block and a half, the younger, trimmer police officer was gaining ground, and the stouter suspect calmly—and in plain sight of his pursuer—tossed his pistol into the high grass of a small vacant lot that he passed as he ran. The faster police officer continued his chase until he caught up with the man from behind at the corner of St. Mary and Religious Streets, only three blocks from the corner where he had first spotted the suspect. The fleeing gunman, now disarmed, sensing capture but oddly unconcerned, slowed to a stop, turned toward the policeman, and raised his hands in surrender.

"You dago bastard," Patrolman Dendinger spit out the words as he caught up to the man, only slightly winded. Dendinger raised his right hand, intending to pistol whip the man with a backhanded swipe of the gun's grip across the temple, standard practice for New Orleans beat cops executing a 1920s street arrest. Something unnerving in the suspect's grim countenance and glinting blue-gray eyes caused Dendinger's raised hand to freeze. He thought better of delivering the blow. "Son of a bitch," Dendinger hissed, and instead of striking the suspect across his brow, he spun him slowly around and cuffed his hands in the heavy iron bracelets he carried on his belt. "You're under arrest, you guinea bastard. You're going to the station. My gun's drawn on you now. Run again, and I'll shoot you down."

Officer Dendinger placed his left palm on the man's back and shoved him forward, retracing the steps of the chase. "Follow me to the station so you can identify this fella and we can put him in jail," the patrolman said to Tumarello as the cuffed suspect passed the grocer on their walk back to the station. For a fleeting moment, a victorious smile flashed upon Tumarello's face, his tormentor at last in the hands of the rightful authorities. Surely, the sweet justice that was the promise of his adopted homeland's court system would now be his. But then the suspect raised his head, and his blue-eyed stare met the eyes of Anthony Tumarello, Americanized native of Western Sicily. Tumarello saw in the man's grim countenance and glinting bluish eyes a familiar expression of unconcerned calculation that he recalled from his youth. A cold and sobering fear wiped the brief smile from the grocer's face. Obediently, Tumarello followed the policeman and his collar to the Seventh Precinct station, but Tumarello's look and feeling of vindication had disappeared into the heavy New Orleans air.

The alleged extortionist, gunman, and agent of the Black Hand, chased down, arrested, and now in custody of the New Orleans police, was my grandfather, Natale Guinta.[286]

CHAPTER 19

LA MANO NERO (THE BLACK HAND)

The morning newspaper sensationalized the incident as best it could. It was reported separately on three different pages of section 1 of the October 11, 1923 edition of *The Times-Picayune*. It was front-page news as an item in the "Gist of the News," a tease of single-sentence summaries of the day's top stories that ran daily in the bottom left-hand corner of page 1: "Police believed they had uncovered a 'black hand' plot in the arrest of a man accused of lying-in wait with a deadly weapon," the "Gist" reported. The arrest and charge were also listed with eighteen others in a separate column on page 7: "Criminal District Court. Affidavits Filed…Natale Giunta [*sic*], 813 Hospital Street; lying in wait armed with a deadly weapon with intent to commit murder." Finally, the main story, with no byline and only four paragraphs long, ran at the top right-hand corner of page 9 under the headline "Police Suspect Black Hand Plot—Man Arrested, Accused of Lying in Wait with Weapon." *The Times-Picayune* story misspelled the names of the victim, the alleged perpetrator, and the arresting officer. It also incorrectly reported the suspect's age and the victim's home address. "Police believe they uncovered a 'Black Hand' plot with the arrest Tuesday night of Natalle Guinto [*sic*], thirty-two years old, 813 Hospital Street, who is alleged to have threatened to take the life of Anthony Tumerallo [*sic*], 462 St. Mary Street. After Guinto's arrest, charged with lying in wait, armed with a deadly weapon, with intent to commit murder, police were unable to get information from either their prisoner or Tumerallo [*sic*]. They believed the latter is afraid to tell why his life is alleged to have been threatened for fear of vengeance from other sources."

Natale accepted it all with equanimity, either confident of or disinterested in the ultimate outcome of his arrest. He had been marched at the point of Patrolman Dendinger's cocked sidearm from the scene of the arrest to the Seventh Precinct police station, where he was booked. He spent only a few days in a cell before he was released on bond. He had accomplished his relatively swift release shortly after a phone call and a brief conversation between the desk sergeant and an unknown voice at the other end of the line.

And why should equanimity not be the reaction that might be expected from Natale, a man who—until much older age—seemed capable of only two states of mind: rage and equanimity. Perhaps both had prompted him to leave the relatively privileged life of a Sicilian *gabelloto*'s eldest son and emigrate to America: a combi-nation of some unknown, never told act of rage committed in his Castelvetrano home town or a World War I battlefield, coupled with studied disgruntlement with the slowness of his release from Army service near Trieste after the Great War's end, followed by a cool-headed determination to transplant permanently to America. His exact path from his Trapani Province birthplace to his 1923 attempt to terrorize or kill Anthony Tumarello in New Orleans, however, can only be sketched through the scant hints known by his family about this period of his life.

After his arrival in America from Trieste under an assumed name after World War I, Natale slowly made his way from New York down the Atlantic seaboard, working as a railroad laborer. Sometime around 1920–'21, he found a temporary home in Tampa, Florida. "My Daddy told me he liked Tampa because he could live close to the water," Uncle Joe told me on a rare occasion when he talked to me about his father, even in the most meager detail.

If Natale liked Tampa, why leave it for the hard scrabble river town life of Italian immigrant 1920s New Orleans? Was his reason opportunity, restlessness, a summons from some authority he recognized as higher than himself? According to Natale's 1967 obituary in *The Times-Picayune*, he arrived in New Orleans in 1922 and made it his home for the next forty-five years.[287] His death certificate confirms that he had been a resident of New Orleans for forty-five years before he died on January 18, 1967,[288] placing him in New Orleans in early 1922. Initially, his occupation, as reflected in the official police report of his arrest in the Tumarello affair, was "laborer." His place of residence, however, and the circumstances of his arrest, speedy release on bond, and the subsequent course of his criminal case proceedings indicate other pursuits and sources of support. The police arrest report listed his French Quarter home address as 813 Hospital Street, subsequently twice renamed; first as Governor Nichols Street for one-armed Confederate and Post-Reconstruction Louisiana Governor Francis T. Nichols, and then again in 2021 for Lolis Edward Elie, 1960s civil rights activist and lawyer.[289] The 800 block of Hospital Street was a notoriously dangerous 1920s New Orleans street address, located in the near vicinity, only six blocks from the heart of what the New Orleans newspapers then called the "Circle of Death." This label had been coined by "[a]n imaginative newspaper writer…to describe an area thirty feet in diameter on St. Philip Street, near Decatur. It was a good name, justified by the fact that…in the region around the intersection of St. Philip and Chartres Streets, there were between 1913 and 1927, seventeen [17] murders which were, in all probability, due to the vendetta" among "Sicilians in New Orleans…distributed between two groups, between which a state of more or less open war existed."[290] The names of the victims and their assassins in and near the Circle of Death reveal the ethnic character of the neighborhood: Genova, Luciano, Giovanni, Pepitone, DiMartino, Genna, Cancenu, Segretto, Barocco, Dartello, Caliva, and Venezia.

The official records of Natale's 1923 arrest and prosecution indicate that his life and associations were consistent with the character of the neighborhood in which he resided. The October 9, 1923, arrest report states that Natale was arrested at 7:35 p.m. About three hours later, his bond was set as a $750 personal surety and property bond signed both by Natale and by Salvatore Calaserone, who pledged "movable and immovable property located at 1225 Chartres Street and all other property located in the Parish of Orleans." The bond obligation guaranteed that Natale would "personally appear before the Honorable the Criminal District Court for the Parish of Orleans…and shall not depart thence without the leave of said court, and shall keep the peace in the meantime…"[291] The Chartres Street address, located two blocks from the dead center of the Circle of Death, is now the stylish Le Richelieu, an upscale French Quarter boutique hotel. It was and is only one block from the historic Beauregard-Keyes House, 1113 Chartres Street, once the home of Confederate General P. G. T. Beauregard, conqueror of Fort Sumter in 1861. Later, it was the site in 1909 of the triple-killing of Giovanni and Antonio Baracca and Giuseppe Luchessi, apparently in a vendetta shootout with Corrado and Pietro Giacona.[292] It took a few days for Natale's property bond paperwork to be completed and filed. According to Natale's statement to the police on another matter about a year later, he spent five days in the Orleans Parish Prison before he was released.[293]

Natale was initially charged on October 10, 1923, by an affidavit executed by Anthony Tumarello. He was accused of violation of Act 26 of the Louisiana Legislature of 1892 in that he "did…willfully and unlawfully and feloniously lie in and wait arm[ed] with a deadly [weapon], to wit a pistol, with intent to commit murder…" In addition to Tumarello, the charging affidavit listed the State's witnesses as Charles Miller, 464 St. Mary Street; F. Gandolfi, 444 St. Mary Street; C. Erickson, 1820 Religious Street; and Officer Dendinger. The affidavit was followed by a formal bill of information, filed on October 17, 1923, by Assistant District Attorney Frederick B. Freeland, asserting the same charge. The proceeding was assigned Case No. 17796 and allotted to Section A of the Orleans Parish Criminal District Court.

Natale's reaction to the formal charges appears to have been unconcerned nonchalance. The clerk of court's handwritten minute entries of the criminal proceedings show that the initial arraignment was scheduled for November 23, 1923. Natale failed to appear. It was rescheduled before the court on November 28, 1923. When Natale again failed to appear, the court issued an attachment for his arrest, returnable two days later on November 30, 1923. This time, Natale was present although the court's records do not reflect whether he appeared voluntarily or under arrest. He entered a not guilty plea, and his trial was set for January 23, 1924. Despite his two failures to appear as ordered and the seriousness of the charged offense, Natale remained free on his $750 property bond. No trial occurred on January 23, 1924. Instead, the clerk's court minutes reflect that the trial was "cont. [continued] without day" by the State.

At about that same time, Anthony Tumarello began to receive overtures, some verbal, some silent, varying in subtlety, but all aimed at persuading him to a particular course of action. One day in late January 1924, while attending to the affairs of his Gallatin Street store, he overheard two customers from the neighborhood speaking in Italian in louder voices than necessary. They were extolling the virtues of Natale Guinta as the no-nonsense strong man sent by a caring uncle to put an end to the rudeness and disrespect the neighborhood ladies had recently experienced from the mouths of a couple of shiftless rowdies. A week or two later, while working at his French Market location, Tumarello noticed two burly young men, dressed in the dingy clothing of banana dock stevedores and leaning against a wooden crate of oranges. They seemed to be watching his every move. "Go ask those two what they want," Tumarello ordered one of his employees, a young clerk he had only recently hired to tend to the produce and customers at his French Market store. The young clerk eyed the two loiterers warily, then turned toward Anthony, untied his produce clerk's apron, and handed it to his boss. "No thanks," he said, obviously fearful. "Go ask them yourself. I quit." Throughout the spring of 1924, Tumarello thought he saw the two young toughs lingering around his stores, never addressing him, never overtly gesturing toward him or threatening him in any way, only watching and whispering between themselves.

On March 24, 1924, the Orleans Parish Criminal District Court minute clerk in Section A made another handwritten entry in the record of Natale's case: "Cont. [continued] by defendant without day."

The delays in the case against his assailant, the gossip of the neighborhood women, and the silent surveillance of the two anonymous toughs all heightened Anthony Tumarello's anxiety. Although the American Sector housewives and their maids continued to buy from him, business from his Italian customers began to fall off. Perhaps the epiphany that Tumarello experienced happened this way:

As April became May in 1924, Anthony quietly voiced his concerns to two of the banana boat stevedore gang leaders from whom he occasionally bought fruit directly from the boats at the river wharves or along the New Basin Canal. The men were Giovanni Armorici and Giuseppe Simone. They had come to visit Tumarello at his French Market location to advise him regretfully that until "this trouble" with Natale Guinta was resolved, they would no longer be able to sell him fruit from the docks. Tumarello considered them friends. The advice they provided to Tumarello was sensible, calm, and thoroughly grounded in the realities of the lives of honest Sicilian merchants and workmen living in New Orleans at that time.

"*Que disturbo*," Armorici said. "What trouble. What a misunderstanding."

Simone agreed. "My friend," he placed a firm hand on Tumarello's shoulder. "These American police and courts, these American lawyers, they care nothing about you or your well-being. Behind your back they call you 'dago' and 'wop.' They still say, 'Who killa da chief.'[294] "An honest man like yourself cannot expect help from such as these. What misunderstanding. No one has been hurt. No one is in jail. Yet your business suffers. Your health suffers with worry. You must put this all behind you, my friend. Put an end to these troubles and get on with your good life and family."

"Let us arrange for you to meet with our *patrono*," said Armorici. "He is the man who recommends to us honest *paisani* to unload the bananas from our boats on the docks. The small fee we give him for this service is the very picture of reasonableness. He makes sure we have no trouble with our men or with the *pezzonovanti* of the fruit and ship companies who sometimes try to tell us how to run our unloading work. He is a man of reason and understanding, of influence and wisdom. He is a friend worth having. Please meet with our friend, 'Mr. Luke,' Don Leoluca Trombatore."

Tumarello did not know the name. For a fleeting moment, he feared the implications of what Armorici and Simone had suggested. It was men like Trombatore, a silent influencer of the banana docks, whom Tumarello thought he had left behind when he left Sicily. Yet he now also feared that his trust in the American authorities had been misplaced. He was exhausted by the court delays in the Guinta prosecution, by the drop in his business, by the recurring sight of the two silent toughs who appeared to be shadowing him. An epiphany began to bloom in his practical businessman's mind, an epiphany that ultimately changed his immediate business fortunes in New Orleans for the better. He agreed to the meeting with Mr. Luke.

It was Armorici who arranged the meeting and accompanied Tumarello to Don Luca's plain and unmarked French Quarter office. At Armorici's suggestion, Anthony had packed a giant basket of beautiful fruit, the best of the oranges, lemons, bananas, and melons from Tumarello's stores, all to present as a token of hoped-for friendship, counsel, and assistance.

Mr. Luke proved himself everything that Simone and Armorici had promised. He was warm and welcoming. He accepted the gift of Tumarello's fruit basket with delight and sincere thanks. "I was very sorry to hear about your difficulties from our friend here," Mr. Luke said, nodding toward Armorici. "Tell me about your troubles." Mr. Luke listened intently, saying nothing, nodding understandably, as Tumarello told the story of his stalking by Natale Guinta and its aftermath. When Tumarello finished, Mr. Luke raised his hands and rested them on his chest, pressing the tips of the five fingers of his left hand against their counterparts on his right. His bearing and sincerity, the aura of authority and wisdom that emanated from the pores of Mr. Luke's skin, the simplicity of his speech and surroundings, worked a hypnotic trance on Tumarello's formerly troubled mind. The grocer felt perfectly comfortable in whatever Mr. Luke was about to advise. He resolved to accept it.

Mr. Luke contemplated the situation briefly, then uttered his conclusion and advice. "Ah, Natale," he said. "A good man, but a difficult man as well, a man not to be trifled with." Mr. Luke's solution was a simple letter, which he was sure would solve Tumarello's difficulties, revive his business to its former vibrancy and bring peace to his mind and family.

The letter, a copy of which is preserved in the official court records and now in my personal files, was typed on the formal printed stationery of "S. Pellegrini, Wholesale Fruits, Produce and Vegetables," with the addresses of three proud New Orleans locations. It was dated June 9, 1924, and addressed to "Hon. Thos. Cravin" [*sic*], District Attorney," misspelling his last name. It was the same Thomas Craven who had investigated the murder of Domenico DiGiovanni three years earlier with such poor prosecutorial results. "Dear Mr. Cravin," the letter began. "This case against Mr. Natale Junta [*sic*] was only a slight misunderstanding between him and myself, it did not amount to anything except a few words between us, we have made friend [*sic*] since and wish of you to drop all charges pending against him. Thanking you kindly, I am, Yours Truly, A. Tumarello."[295] In addition to Tumarello's signature, the letter was signed by "G. Armorici" and "G. P. Simone" beneath the handwritten word "Witness."

When he received the letter, Assistant District Attorney Craven could only shake his head and mutter to himself. His experience with Italian-on-Italian crime was substantial, including the investigation of the Gaeto-DiGiovanni double murder only three years earlier. "These dagos," Craven muttered to himself. He had seen it all before, so many times, in fact, that he almost welcomed the relief from tedious trial work that such letters brought to his office. Who was it, he wondered to himself, who had persuaded an honest merchant like Tumarello to abandon Craven's justice system and return to the kind of approach that must have been the way of doing things in that place Craven knew so little about, Sicily or Italy or wherever these guineas had originated? Giacona, Carollo, Segretto, Marcello, Trombatore? Craven knew all of their names. They were all the same. He decided that he would seize the opportunity presented by Tumarello's letter to take a little walk, to get out of his office and stroll over to the nearby criminal district courthouse. Although the summer solstice had not yet arrived, the New Orleans weather had already become so hot and sticky that Craven's indoor work was almost intolerable. The short stroll to the courthouse offered at least the chance of some small breeze from the river or the misting of a cooling rain shower as a respite from the stuffiness of his assistant district attorney's office. At the conclusion of his short walk, once inside the clerk's office, he retrieved the official arraignment sheet from the record of Natale Guinta's case file. With a flourish of his pen, he scrawled across the cover sheet in his own tall script, "NP dismiss, Thomas Craven, ADA." The minute clerk followed Craven's signature with his own final entry in the court's official record of Case No. 17996, *State of Louisiana v. Natale Guinta*: "June 10, 1924, Nolle Prosequi," and signed his name and title, "Chas. Mercadel, Min. Clk.," indicating final dismissal of the charges.[296]

Natale's reaction to the news that the charge against him had been dropped was probably studied nonchalance. He had expected nothing less, to whatever extent he had expectations of any sort about the case.

The only photograph in the family records of Natale Guinta during the 1920s provides insight into what his attitude and comportment might have been at the conclusion of this episode. It is a posed, formal photo-portrait, taken in what appears to be the staging area of a professional photographer's studio. Natale is standing, perfectly erect, next to a small, round-topped wooden table. An ornate vase filled with fully blooming roses, daisies, and carnations sits atop a knitted cotton doily. In the background is a painted canvas wall covering, draped over a row of sturdy exposed brick. Natale is dressed—not in the rough-hewn clothing one might expect of a person whose occupation has officially been reported as "laborer" on a recent arrest report—but in an exquisitely tailored, light-colored summer suit, white shirt, and dark tie. The waist of his sharply creased trousers rises high above his navel. His two-button suit coat is open at the waist, revealing an ornate belt buckle clasping the leather strap around his midsection and a long, linked fob holding what appears to be a diamond-shaped railroad worker's timepiece dangling from a pants pocket. The end of a long, pointed metal object—perhaps a pen but giving more the appearance of the handle of a small sheathed knife protrudes from the chest pocket of his coat. A golden stick pin presses the starched collar of his shirt together behind the half Windsor knot of his black, too-short necktie. His left arm dangles straight down at his side. Natale's right arm is bent at the elbow, exposing a muscular bulge at the bicep, and his bulky right hand deftly holds an unlit cigarette between his long index and middle fingers, rising up to the tip of his thumb. Two rings adorn the last two fingers of that same hand; one with a large, sparkling orb on the ring finger; the other a simple gold band on the pinky. Atop his head is a jaunty straw hat, the kind one sees today only on the heads of singers in a barbershop quartet, its flat round brim topped by a flat round crown encased in a broad, dark ribbon band. The hat reveals close-cropped auburn hair on each side of his head, barbered well above the ears with almost no sideburns. His mouth is firm, neither smile nor frown; his nose is broad; his lips are thin; his eyes are wide open and piercingly light-colored beneath his thick eyebrows. His overall appearance exudes sophistication, confidence, and prosperity, a man of strength and standing not to be trifled with. His facial expression indicates a singular but ironic state of mind: equanimity.

CHAPTER 20

SAN CIPIRELLO REDUX

When the DiGiovannis returned to Sicily in 1922, only one of Gaetano's siblings, his younger brother Mateo, remained in San Cipirello. *Zu* Mateo may be the unnamed man pictured in one of the snapshots in the family archives. Scribbled on its back is the inscription "uncle with goat." Seeing the photo prompted me one day to ask cousin Paolo what the DiGiovannis did for a living when they returned to San Cipirello in the 1920s. He chuckled, smiled a mischievous grin, and said, "They were shepherds and cheese-makers." Paul then became wistful and said his grandfather Gaetano certainly had been a "man of respect" in the small town during those years, a stature earned in the way described by the historical and sociological chroniclers as involving "ambition, responsibility, family,...a reputation not only for being smart..., but also for being more efficient and even 'fairer' than the state,"[297] all backed by a "capacity to coerce with physical violence and thus invoke fear in others..., closely related to...[being] able to provide access to resources,"[298] like work, advice, mediation, intelligent judgment, goats and cheese.

At the family Christmas Eve dinner at Mom's house in 2010, Mom told me the story of her cousin Angie's trip to Sicily as a tourist sometime in the 1980s. This Angie was Walter's (Vito's) Angie. She and her husband were driving in the countryside outside of San Cipirello when they stopped and pulled to the side of the road to take in the beauty of the olive and lemon groves, acres of golden grain, and grape vineyards of the *Conca d' Oro*. They saw some older men picking grapes in a nearby orchard. Angie's husband, an avid photographer, wanted to take some pictures. Angie approached the men respectfully and asked for their permission to take the photos. "Who do you belong to?" one older man asked warily in Sicilian dialect. "My grandfather was Gaetano DiGiovanni," Angie replied. The weathered old grape harvester gazed back in awe, astonishment, and nostalgic respect. "Ahh, Don Tano Baiocco," the man said deferentially. "Take all the pictures you want. You may have anything I can give you."

Earlier that same year, Paolo DiGiovanni told me a similar story. On one of his many trips back to San Cipirello, Paul ventured out to a small mountain village nearby. An old man spotted him, the odd sight of a stranger in the village. "Who are you?" the old man asked suspiciously. Wary, Paolo replied, "Paolo Baiocco." The old man asked if Paul was related to Don Tano Baiocco DiGiovanni. "Yes," Paolo replied. "He was my grandfather." The old man was moved almost to tears. He escorted Paul to his modest home, fed him lunch, and told him stories about what a fine man Gaetano was, how he always helped people in need, including himself. He explained how, as a young man in the nearby town some sixty years earlier, he had found himself in trouble, accused of stealing a donkey. He had gone to Don Tano Baiocco for advice and assistance. Gaetano listened carefully and quietly, then left the younger man's side and returned within minutes, leading two goats by a rope tied around their necks. "'Take these animals,'" Don Tano told him, pointing upward. "'Go into the mountains. Stay there. Live there. These troubles will pass.'" The shepherd said that he had done as instructed, had married, multiplied, lived peacefully and prosperously. He raised his right arm and moved it left to right. "Now all this has been my life." He thanked Paul and sent him on his way back to San Cipirello. The next day, two huge wheels of goat's cheese arrived at the family home where Paul was staying, with a thank you note in appreciation and respect for all his grandfather had done for the man.

Family lore depicts Gaetano DiGiovanni, in his persona as the 1920s Don Tano Baiocco, as one of those *uomini rispettati* (men of respect) whom anthropologist Anton Blok chronicled in his lengthy studies and residence in Palermo Province. Don Tano and his family lived in the town itself, in a modest home on a side street that abutted a sheer mountainside, a steep rise that the locals called "DiGiovanni Mountain." The doorway was adorned with a horseshoe, hung upside down in the Sicilian way of good luck, but not just for good luck: the horseshoe also signified Don Tano's expertise in horsemanship as a means of engaging in his business activities. Their closest friends were the Todaro family, who lived across the street. As Blok observed, "In the much smaller and isolated village[s]…, the peasants were granted fewer power chances. In various ways and in different degrees, they were drawn into and constrained by the power domains of the landlords and their retainers… People were dependent upon kinsmen, friends, and powerful protectors for sheer physical survival. To right wrongs, to settle conflicts, and to solve problems of various sorts, they could hardly rely on the police and law courts. The very fact that they only rarely appealed to State institutions for protection and to settle wrongs reinforced the power domains of local private magnates… [A] person who had a reputation for violence and who eschewed recourse to public authorities commanded respect. They were quite literally the most respected, the most honourable [sic], the most powerful, and very often the most wealthy men of the community. Others less skilled in the realm of violence turned to them for mediation and protection."[299]

"We never wanted for anything," my mother once said in responding to my attempts to explain to her what my research was teaching me about her grandfather, Don Tano Baiocco. "But if my grandpa was the big shot you say he was, how come he never seemed to have two nickels to rub together when it came to money?" What was the basis for Gaetano's standing? From what source did he draw the livestock, jobs, and influence that he so freely bestowed on the less fortunate of his community who came to him for help?

An extensively researched and heavily footnoted reference book, meticulously based upon documents in the annals of the public archives of the Province of Palermo, the village of San Cipirello and its larger neighbor, San Giuseppe Jato, written and compiled by Gioacchino Nania, a San Giuseppe Jato native, states that in the 1920s Gaetano DiGiovanni, *fu* Domenico (son of Domenico), was affiliated with the Mafia as the *gabelloto* of *La Torre dei Fiori* (the Tower of Flowers),[300] one of the area's large landed estates. The book's author gleaned this information from sworn declarations listing known *Mafiosi* prepared by members of the local agricultural cooperative, which they sent to Cesare Mori, the newly assigned Fascist Police Chief of Sicily in 1926.[301] Nania's publisher describes the work as "a manual, supported with impressive evidence, of the depth and incredible breadth of the Mafia" and its socioeconomic and political influence in San Giuseppe Jato and its small satellite community of San Cipirello.[302] Quoting a 1926 report by Balsano Bocco found in the records of the college at Palermo, Nania writes, "'If there was one community in Sicily where the Mafia was omnipotent, it was probably San Giuseppe Jato,'"[303] with its closely related and dependent smaller neighbor San Cipirello.

Nania describes the years 1918–'25 as "*Anni Dei Grande Arrichichimenti* (the Years of Great Enrichment)" among *Mafiosi* in San Giuseppe Jato and San Cipirello.[304] Nania offers the sworn testimony of local peasants in the Archives of the State of Palermo[305] concerning Santo Termine, "*Sindaco e capo Mafia di* San Giuseppe Jato (mayor and chief of the San Giuseppe Jato Mafia),"[306] as an example of the sudden acquisition of wealth accumulated by *Mafiosi* during these years. "Until a few years ago,…Santo Termine worked for the most part in the countryside and lived in absolute poverty," testified Salvatore Canella in a statement to the *carabinieri* dated October 12, 1926.[307] Similarly, Pasquale DiGiovanni [family relation, if any, unknown] testified on August 6, 1926, that "until a few years ago, before his marriage, Santo Termine lived in great economic constraints. He possessed one small horse and had no means to buy straw and [was]…a dependent of Pietro Cannella [family relation, if any, to the Cannella women who married the DiGiovanni sons unknown]. I remember that such was his poverty that he had no bread and I had to give him some to eat."[308] By 1926, however, Santo Termine had risen to become Mafia chief, mayor, and confidante of the noble Beccadelli family, princes of the rural Comporeale and Misilmiri regions southwest of Palermo.[309] "In San Cipirello, the [Mafia] leaders were Vito Todaro, the Pardo brothers, Francesco Leone, the Todaro brothers [Giuseppe. Batista and Gaetano]…and Filippo Randazzo."[310]

The family oral history paints Gaetano in San Cipirello in the 1920s as a country *gabelloto-Mafiosi* in the old-school style of the fictional Don Bucilla, described by author Mario Puzo in his historical novel *The Sicilian*. "He was a short but broad man, his body powerful from a lifetime of hard work… [H]e had a reputation for honesty, that he was a modest man though he could have turned his power into riches. He was a throwback to the old Mafia chiefs who fought not for riches but for respect and honor."[311] In San Cipirello and later upon his return to New Orleans, Gaetano lived and earned the expressions and salutations his descendants remember from those days and were reminded of by the older residents of the Palermo Province villages when they returned to visit and sightsee years later. "Better a friend on the street than an account in a bank," Gaetano would often advise his children and grandchildren. Or as his constituents would greet him in the streets and in the countryside, "*Bacio la mano* [I kiss your hand], Don Tano."

In stark juxtaposition with the sympathetic family oral history, Nania's historical portrait of the role of Mafia-affiliated *gabelloti* in 1920s San Giuseppe Jato and San Cipirello is quite different. Nania quotes from the 1926 sworn declaration of Giuseppe Cimino, president of the San Cipirello component of a nascent agricultural cooperative, *Cooperativo Pio X*, to describe the harsh relationship between working peasants and the *gabelloti*: "The cooperative arose with a well-defined purpose, that of freeing the peasants from the servitude to which they had to submit because the Mafia of San Giuseppe Jato and San Cipirello were *gabelloti* of all the fiefs close to these commu-

nities and imposed burdensome pacts on the peasants for the cultiva-
tion of land. The cooperative proposed to rent fiefs by selling part of
the land to its members at the same price for which the cooperative
bought the fiefs. The *gabelloti* class that identified with the Mafia
saw that the cooperative offered the owners rent prices far superior to
that charged by the *gabelloti* and that they produced scarcity in their
labor force because farmers preferred to work directly the land rented
instead of subsisting on the pacts imposed on them by the *gabelloti*.
The Mafia opposed the cooperative arrangement. [Giulio] Virga, the
proponent of the [agricultural cooperative] movement, was subjected
to a number of crimes in hopes that he would be intimidated and
would end up withdrawing from the direction of the *Cooperativos
Pio X* of San Cipirello and that of *Giosue' Borsi* of San Giuseppe Jato.
At the same time, the Mafia took to targeting the peasant members
of these cooperatives who became the systematic victims of a series
of robberies that were committed against their animals and along the
roads that lead to the fiefs kept for rent by the cooperatives on the
same lands that the peasants worked in such a way as to force the
peasants to abandon cultivating the land to avoid further reprisals…
The one who was made most a symbol of the persecution of the
Mafia was Virga, who suffered damages to his vineyard in the district,
the burglary of his shop in San Giuseppe Jato with huge damage, and
a beating outside a church by Vito Todaro and others. It was known
inside the cooperative that the Mafia would not stop,…until Virga
stopped all opposition to the economic activity of the *gabelloti*."[312]

Nania reports that Virga offered his own testimony to the Fascist
authorities that same year: "Since I have resided in San Giuseppe Jato
and San Cipirello since 1903, my activity has principally been as
the organizer of the agricultural cooperative in the interest and the
well-being of the farmers and peasants. This task has been full of
difficulties,…especially against the organized crime that surrounds
us in every way…and at all times. I refer to the violence and bullying
employed by the members and affiliates of the Mafia and even in
the community police, as elsewhere, and with whom the *gabelloti*
are definitely acquainted… I always have fought openly the crimi-
nality of the Mafia, which I have always considered the ruin of these

counties...[and] which fuels the violence and the bullying exercised
in the countryside to the detriment of honest and peaceful peasants;
that all serious crimes, especially of blood, were committed by the
Mafia, and is sure to go unpunished through the protection that it
boasts through the political personalities... [It is] a painful situation
in which these hardworking people are constrained."[313] According
to Virga, chief among the crimes committed by the Mafia against
the peasants was the old tactic of livestock rustling. In this instance,
however, the thieves did not steal from the landed estates of the
nobles. Instead, they stole the "four-legged animals" of the *contadini*,
then forced the peasants to pay "large sums for the ransom of the
animals."[314]

Which of these types of Mafia-affiliated *gabelloto* was Gaetano
DiGiovanni? The Don Bucilla version of family lore: much-re-
spected mediator, wise counselor, and deliverer of justice for otherwise unprotected peasants who could not trust the State authorities?
Or the intimidating, violence-prone, protector of the established
economic order generally depicted in the historical archives? Some
of both? Final judgment must rest with God, influenced perhaps
by the prayers and faith of Don Tano's wife, the devout Angelina
Bucaro DiGiovanni, and the infinite mercy and understanding of
the Almighty.

In any event, never one to let a prominent father, a small village
setting, or challenging times stand in her way of having a good time,
Gaetano's daughter Lucia (Lucille, Lou) recalled that she took full
advantage during her teen-aged years in San Cipirello of the facts that
she was a *gabelloto*'s daughter and that her uncle Frank "Francesco"
Bucaro was a railroad executive. She took frequent joy rides on the
train. "We used to ride first class," she recalled. "I used to ride with all
the English tourists in the tourist section, and they wanted to know
what all the trees were, the artichokes. Them damn people didn't
know what the shit artichokes were. Well, that's the truth. They...
wanted to know what the artichokes were. I said, 'They artichoke
bushes.' [One tourist] asked, 'What's that?' I said, 'Well, you eat 'em.
It's a vegetable.'"[315]

Don Tano's older daughter Antonia (Lena, Nia), on the other hand, had some melancholy memories of her days as a young woman in 1920s San Cipirello. "The people were so poor, you know. And because we came from America, they thought we were millionaires. We always had plenty of cheese in our house because they used to make cheese, you know, sheep, goat cheese, all of it. And my mama would cut up big chunks and give those out like candy... My father made all his children careful... [Others] wasted their good American money for trips. My sister-in-law is one of them... Oh, it was rough... People were starving."[316]

In Sicily, as mere teenagers in the 1920s, the American-born Lena and Lucille managed to avoid marriage while their brothers were swiftly scooped up by a family of gorgeous San Cipirello natives. As much of the family remained in Sicily into the 1930s, however, their youngest sister, Francesca (Nookie), became the romantic object of local politico and orator, Carmelo Pedalino. "I could-a married one too, if I wanted to," Lucille said of her flirtatious young womanhood in San Cipirello. "But I never would... Take the barber...oh, the barber was good-lookin'"[317]

As for the brothers, "after the boys were there, these three girls trapped the three of them in Italy," Nia said.[318] "Aww, wait a minute," Lou responded, "they got trapped because they wanted to be trapped."[319] The three girls were two sisters and their first cousin. "That's the trouble," Nia said. "They might as well all be sisters."[320]

Sugie (Fedele) married Philippa (Philippina) Riccobono. "That was class, Riccobono," Nia opined. By "class," I suppose that Nia was referring to the social standing of the Riccobono family as identified by Nania's research identifying brothers Erasmo and Pasquale Riccobono as the Mafia-affiliated *gabelloti* of the *Pietralunga* estate.[321] "I gotta show you a picture of her when she was young, how beautiful she was," Nia said.[322] At about the same time in the early 1930s, "Two sisters married two brothers," Aunt Lou said. "Yeah, they stole Grandma's sons," Nia added.[323] The sisters were the dissimilar daughters of Paolo and Giuseppina Vaccaronotti Cannella. Their father, Paolo Cannella, "was a man of modest means,...an agriculturist, a farmer...[who] raised goats, grains, citrus, and in later years... tomatoes."[324]

Walter (Vituum, Vito) married Vincenza (Agiutsa, Giuzza, or Giutsa) Cannella, a delightful and sweet peasant woman. Giuzza was the soul of fidelity and support, sticking by Walter's side through the Depression, the Fascists, his work on both sides with two separate armies in World War II—briefly as a conscript soldier of the Italian Fascists and later an interpreter for the occupying Americans—and their final but separate cross-Atlantic voyages to America, where they settled into long and comfortable family life in the Algiers section of the New Orleans West Bank.

Giacomo (Jake) married Giuzza's less agreeable, less-liked (at least by the DiGiovannis), but spectacularly gorgeous sister, Antonina (Nanina) Cannella. "She was a flipper... She was a hellcat. And I liked her. I really did... We played cards. Oh, she was a beautiful woman, beautiful. Her hair was beautiful... I'd come to Kenner just to play [cards] with them...," Nia said.[325] "She had beautiful skin... She had a gorgeous complexion... She was a pretty woman," Uncle Joe's wife, my Godmother Aunt Patricia (Nonnie) added in admiration, almost enviously.[326] "And my mother loved her to death," Nia said in one breath, laughing and dripping sarcasm while later admitting that Angelina Bucaro DiGiovanni "couldn't stand this daughter-in-law."[327] It later became obvious that, except for Nia, few in the DiGiovanni family—even her husband Jake himself—could abide Nanina for long, and vice versa.

Shortly after their marriage, when Jake had followed his father out of Sicily while the women remained behind in San Cipirello, evidence of tempestuousness and disharmony in the marriage began to emerge. When Jake's sisters "asked him to send us a wedding picture of himself, he cut his wife's picture out to send [only] himself in this letter," Nia said laughing, "so we knew something was wrong."[328] Nia saved some of Uncle Jake's sliced wedding photos and showed them to me one day during a visit to her house in the 1980s. There was Uncle Jake, slim, dark, debonair in the classic groom's black tuxedo with no bride on his arm or otherwise depicted in the severed photos. In the late 1930s or early 1940s, while Nanina remained in Sicily but

Angelina, Jake, Nia, and Lou had returned to New Orleans, Nia said that Nanina "wrote,…she wanted to know why she wasn't getting letters [from Jake]. And someone brought a—mailed a letter from New Orleans telling her that he [Jake] was running around, that he must have a girl, and 'I want to know if it's true.'"[329] Nia said her mother "comes to me one morning. 'Lena,' she said,…'get your pen and your pencils…and you gonna write exactly what I tell you to write…and in Italian, you hear, in good letters.' So I got the pen and pencils. My husband said that she was standing behind me, you know, to understand, you know, Italian. She says, 'Dear Daughter-in-Law. I'm so sorry to hear about your troubles. But you knew that my son had a wooden dick, so you shouldn't have married him.'"[330] Nia howled with laughter. "I said, 'Ma, I can't say that.' She said, 'Yes, you can.' [When Nia refused to write it], she goes to Miss Victorino's, [who] says, 'sure, I write it for you.'… She wrote it in Kenner and she showed it to all of us, the sisters, you know, and she was right there. So we were all worried then."[331] The tumultuous marriage of Jake and Nanina ended in permanent separation, though never in formal divorce.

Nia recalled an epic "fight" between Jake and Nanina during an incident that occurred as the family greeted Nanina at the dock when Nanina finally came from Sicily to New Orleans, accompanied by her two children, Angie and Dominick, in 1947 or '48 to rejoin Jake. Nanina greeted him, not with a kiss but by immediately "criticiz[ing] her husband's coat."[332] Nia explained. "Now in Italy during the war, everybody is selling clothes, selling things, you know, to give the things you couldn't use, you could give them to [your relatives in Sicily. Nanina] was in Palermo selling them. When she gets off the boat, she's got a fur coat on that would make [you choke]. And so my poor brother [Jake], it was Carnival, he says 'we got a parade tonight and it's starting, it's a little chilly'…, and he comes with this [old] coat, and I had the tailor mend it,…but you could tell it was mended. [Nanina] says, 'I'm not going to the parade with you wearing that coat… Look, it's not even [fit for]…the goat shavers… If you come to my wake,'" Nanina later told Jake, "'I'll lift my foot up and kick you in the face.'"[333] Nanina ultimately did not quite carry out her threat. Uncle Jake died in 1966, only eleven months after his mother's death[334] and more than two decades before Nanina's own death in Los Angeles where her daughter Angie was living. "And sure enough," Nia said, "the woman [Nanina] did come to the wake [Jake's] and threw a [fit]."[335] Despite her bombastic earlier threats, however, Nanina did not appear at Jake's funeral wearing a red dress, nor did she kick his corpse laid out in the open coffin in the face.

Of the four DiGiovanni siblings who married while in Sicily, the youngest—Francesca (Nookie)—made the highest-profile union in 1933. Her husband, Carmelo Pedalino, was the grandson of Sicilian nobility. Carmelo's father, Cataldo Pedalino, was reputedly the illegitimate son of a Sicilian count, perhaps a Beccadelli of Comporeale and Misilmiri, or a Bourbon nobleman of Trapani Province, and his mother was the count's maid. The count did not legally acknowledge Cataldo or give the boy his name, so Cataldo took the name of a small town near Palermo. Since the count and his wife were childless, they reared and educated young Cataldo.

Cataldo's son Carmelo was born in San Giuseppe Jato in Palermo Province, just outside San Cipirello.[336] Carmelo's parents saw to it that the count's grandson and all of their children were well-educated. Carmelo became a college-degreed agricultural engineer.[337] According to Nia, Carmelo began "scheming for [her youngest sister Nookie] at school, you know, at the college."[338] Nia also accused her sister Lucille (Lou) of bringing her younger sister Nookie to Carmelo's attention when Lou began a flirtation with Carmelo's brother, Giuseppe Pedalino. "It's your fault," Nia said to Lou. "Why you didn't run away with him [Giuseppe]? You flirted with him all the time. You did. You did. You're guilty... Up on the mountaintop... with a bottle of..." Lou admitted her flirtatiousness. "'I figured if I was in love with him [Giuseppe],...yeah, because I was the first [to attract a young Pedalino male]...'"[339] Nookie's union with Carmelo was a success in many ways. The couple produced eleven children all of whom ultimately settled in the United States and grew through marriage and procreation into a sprawling and successful American brood. The Pedalino marriage also at times posed difficulties. Into the 1950s and beyond, Carmelo's political activities in Sicily, including his varying stints as an activist and high-profile Communist and Socialist government official, raised obstacles to Gaetano's vision of reuniting his entire family in the safety and prosperity of the United States.

CHAPTER 21

FRENCHMEN STREET 1924

Only four months after the Black Hand scheme and the stalking with intent to kill charges against him were dismissed, Natale Guinta again found himself in conflict with the police. This time, it was either an attempt by Natale and his brother-in-law, Vincent Napolitano, to intimidate police officers who threatened their Prohibition Era wine-making business or a shakedown by graft-seeking police to protect the winemakers from prosecution, depending upon whose contested version of the events are believed.

On October 6, 1924, three New Orleans policemen, "half of... [a] crack raiding squad, were suspended pending further investigation of charges of accepting bribes. Patrolmen Theodore Peters, Joseph Maes, and Edward Kavanagh...stand accused of accepting $300 from Vincent Napolitano, 2337 Frenchmen street, for 'protection' when the patrolmen found several barrels of wine at his home... 'This is not the first rumor I have heard like this concerning these men, [Police] Capt. Inspector [Theodore] Ray said, 'but I never have been able to substantiate the rumors or get enough evidence to bring a concrete charge. If such a thing is going on it will be stopped immediately, if I have to go on every raid personally to put an end to it.'"[340] Police Superintendent Guy R. Molony suspended the officers immediately and declared that the matter would be thoroughly investigated and the men "brought to trial before him when the evidence on both sides have been prepared... The policemen vigorously denied the charges…and said they believed Napolitano brought the allegations out of spite, citing an alleged incident in which they 'gave him the laugh'…after his place was raided by police from the Fifth Precinct."[341]

Napolitano told the police captain that "he, Natale Guinta, 1176 Constance street, and a man he knew only as Joe were sitting in the basement under Napolitano's house, when the three officers, in plain clothes, entered his yard. He said he had four barrels and a demijohn of wine and eleven barrels of mash. The officers, he said, demanded to know what he was doing, and finally, after considerable talk, Kavanagh said, 'Maybe we can fix it up.' Napolitano asked if $100 would do…and they replied it was not enough. He offered $200…and a conference between Kavanagh and Peters took place for a few minutes, after which he was informed by Peters that 'it would take $300 to fix it up.' Napolitano did not have the money…but called his daughter Annie Napolitano, twenty years old, to bring the cash box out of the house… [H]is daughter turned the box over and counted out $200, which was all there was in the box. The officers insisted on $300…and he tried to borrow it from Guinta [who] did not have the money with him, but gave him a check. He explained that Guinta could not write or speak English and that [Napolitano's] son Joseph, fourteen years old, wrote the check, and Guinta signed it. Napolitano said he and the three policemen and Guinta came to town to cash the check, but the banks were closed, and they were unable to cash it elsewhere then. He told the officers to meet him at Ursuline and Decatur streets at seven o'clock that night and he would have the money. They met him…and the four got into the police car and drove to Gallatin street, between Hospital and Barracks, where Napolitano handed Peters two $100 bills and another hundred in tens and twenties. 'I had thirty-two cents left,' he told Captain Ray, 'and had to buy food for my family for Sunday. I told that to Peters, and he gave me $10 back.'"[342]

Five days later, despite this alleged payment, four other police officers "went to Napolitano's home, and finding several barrels of wine, arrested him" on Prohibition charges. When Napolitano told these officers that "the police had been there before, and that he had

conducted the second raid upon the Napolitano establishment... denied Napolitano's story that he had been told of the bribe money passed to the three previous visitors and had informed the victim he 'was a fool' for paying money to the police."[350]

"The defense called twenty-one-character witnesses, including business and professional men of all kinds, and twelve of these appeared and gave the three policemen a clean bill of health over varying numbers of years." [351] Kavanagh's war service record and police academy training certificate were introduced into evidence. All three officers testified in their own defense consistently with each other and with their initial statements about the affair. Although they admitted making no report to their captain on their visit to the Napolitano house, they flatly denied demanding or taking any money.

When the evidence concluded, Superintendent Molony "declared a recess of five minutes, during which he walked from the side hallway of the police headquarters offices, which was blocked off and used as a courtroom, and into his own private office. When he emerged, he resumed his seat before a small table and told the three men to stand. 'Patrolman Peters, Patrolman Maes, and Patrolman Kavanagh, I find you guilty on two counts, conduct unbecoming to an officer and corruption in office, and dismiss you from the force.'"[352]

The officers' defense attorney immediately announced that he would "appeal to the Board of Police Commissioners... If the board upholds the verdict of the superintendent, it is considered probable that an appeal will be made to the courts."[353]

No appeal became necessary because the officers' trial in criminal court on the same bribery charges proceeded promptly on December 18, 1924. It ended with a resounding verdict in favor of the police and against what clearly was perceived to be organized crime interests. "After but ten minutes of deliberation and before a crowd of spectators that was packed with notorious members of the city's underworld, a jury in the criminal district court last night put an end to one of the most sensational cases New Orleans has known in years when it acquitted three former crack policemen of charges of accepting graft."[354] The jury heard the same testimony from the same witnesses who had testified before the police superintendent, with the additional admission by Vincent Napolitano that he "had used several names since coming to the United States approximately fourteen years ago."[355] The "us versus them" theme of the police officers' defense resonated with the jury. Defense attorney Doyle "in his speech to the jury created a sensation in the courtroom when he walked to the railing and singled out one spectator—a man whose lottery shop had been raided by the three men on trial and shouted, 'Run this man out of the courtroom and you'll hear nothing of police graft. It is this man and his ilk who are responsible for these charges and nothing would please them better than to see the men responsible for their grief behind prison bars.' Mr. Doyle also told the jury that money had come 'from unknown sources,' intimating the underworld, 'to help prosecute the three men.'"[356]

CHAPTER 22

DON TANO BAIOCCO VERSUS
IL PREFETTO DI FERRO

In the annals of Sicily's long history of crime and crime-fighting, Cesare Mori is perhaps its most famous policeman. In 1920s Sicily, he was the Fascist regime's scourge of the Mafia, what Western Sicilian *carabinieri* of the time described as a "'vast association for criminal purposes (*associazione a delinquere*),'...which involved well over 150 *mafiosi* from seven different villages and towns...along the western border of the provinces of Palermo and Agrigento. The offenses attributed to it included homicides, cattle, and sheep rustling, and various forms of extortion..., with a division of its territory into smaller sectors... The alleged...chief (*capo*) of the association was Vito Cascio Ferro from Palermo, residing for many years in Bisaquino."[357] Policeman Cesare Mori became known as *Il Prefetto di Ferro*, the Iron Prefect. He was such a prominent figure in Sicily in the 1920s that Nia twice mentioned him by name in her audiotaped interviews recounting her father's flight from Sicily, return to the United States, and ultimate extraction of his family from Fascist captivity. Judged against the backdrop of historical fact, Nia's truncated recollection of the events that were the beginning of the end of the DiGiovanni family's second Sicilian sojourn is remarkably accurate.

Like the original Giacomo Bucaro's adopted son, John Boncorrea, Cesare Mori began life as a foundling in a small town

147

near Milan. "For a bright boy from nowhere, with no contacts, in late-nineteenth-century Italy, the army and police were among the few places to make a career...," especially for a young man of demonstrable "driving ambition and courage."[358] In 1903, policeman Mori was assigned to Castelvetrano, Sicily, the hometown of Natale Guinta. "From this point onward, his life was entwined with the history of the mafia."[359] By World War I, Mori was deputy police chief of Trapani and became "relentless in the fight against rustlers who infested the countryside..."[360]

Mori's greatest and lasting fame came after his belated embrace of Fascism. "The Fascist movement (*Partito Nazionale Fascista*) was founded in Milan in March 1919 by journalist and combat veteran Benito Mussolini."[361] As a career policeman whose focus was law and order, not politics, Mori initially cracked down on the street violence perpetrated by the black-shirted gangs of Mussolini's supporters, treating it like any other criminal activity. "After Fascism took power in 1922," however, "Mori came to terms with Fascism,... made known his admiration for Mussolini" and lobbied for advancement in the Fascist police force.[362] "In May 1924, Mussolini went to Sicily for the first time... In the province of Trapani, the *Duce* heard about Cesare Mori's achievements..., and about how serious the mafia problem was there... A deputation of veterans told him that...the mafia was the main reason for Fascism's failure to take root on the island."[363] In August 1925, a local election campaign was being waged in Sicily, "the last before democracy disappeared,... the last hurrah for the old political dignitaries of Sicily... Among them was Vittorio Emanuele Orlando, a former prime minister and the most powerful Sicilian politician of the old order, whose power base was in a heavily Mafia-infested area."[364] Orlando had been the Italian prime minister at the conclusion of World War I and, along with America's Woodrow Wilson, Britain's David Lloyd George, and France's Georges Clemenceau, one of "the Big Four" who negotiated the disastrous Treaty of Versailles.[365] Shortly before the 1925 vote in Sicily, Orlando made a speech decrying the Fascists' "proclaimed intent to combat the mafia. Orlando said, 'If by Mafia, they mean having an exaggerated sense of honour [sic]; if they mean being furiously intolerant of bullying and injustice, and showing the generosity of spirit needed to stand up to the strong and be understanding towards the weak; if they mean having loyalty to your friends that is stronger than anything, stronger even than death;…then I say to you that what they are talking about are the distinguishing traits of the Sicilian soul. And so, I declare myself a *mafioso* and I am proud to be one!'"[366]

Nia's recollection of these events depicts her father, Gaetano DiGiovanni, as an outspoken Orlando supporter. "Yeah, the Black Shirts… Fascism developed, and my daddy had to open his big mouth about democracy and all that crap… When Mussolini was there [in Sicily], Poppa went to the social club, his social club, [and] started talking during the election, talking about democracy and 'don't y'all vote Fascist,' and all of that, and people at that time are telling how they own government, you know, and he opened his big mouth… He says, 'Listen, the best way to vote is to vote Democratic.' They got in a lot of trouble. That's when he went to town and Tunisia."[367]

The "lot of trouble" in which Gaetano found himself was Mori's mission, assigned to him by *Il Duce*, to wipe out the Mafia. "On 23 October 1925, Mori became prefect of Palermo with full powers to attack the mafia and with it the [Fascist] regime's political enemies."[368] He began by soliciting and receiving sworn statements from individuals aggrieved by the Mafia, including leaders of the agricultural cooperatives, and systematically drawing up lists of Mafia leaders and their *gabelloti* affiliates.[369] Mori "created an interprovincial police force, an autonomous and highly mobile instrument directly under his personal control… All persons under suspicion were arrested en masse."[370] In San Cipirello and San Giuseppe Jato, "the [agricultural] cooperatives sent [Mori] a list of the territories of Mafia retainers."[371] The list included familiar names: the Riccobono brothers, Erasmo and Pasquale (Sugie DiGiovanni's wife, Aunt Philippina's family name, "that was class," Nia said) as *gabelloti* of the *Pietralunga* estate; the DiGiovannis' neighbor, Vito Todaro, as Mafia *capo* of San Cipirello; Calogero and Santo Randazzo (Gaetano's mother's maiden name), as the 1920s Mafia-affiliated *gabelloti* of *Feudi Montaperto*; and Gaetano DiGiovanni himself as Mafia-affiliated *gabelloto* of *Torre dei*

Fiore.[372] In May 1926, Mori's first roundups occurred in Bisaquino, Corleone, Contessa Entellina, Aderno, Fioravante, and Burgio,[373] all towns within scant kilometers of San Cipirello. Among those arrested was Don Vito Cascio Ferro, who was tried on an old murder charge, convicted, and put in prison, where he died in 1942.[374] In all, "some eleven thousand people were arrested, five thousand of them in the province of Palermo alone."[375] "Mori conducted these operations all over western Sicily, and it took him two years to complete them. In this way, hundreds and hundreds of *mafiosi* were rounded up, tried, and imprisoned for many years."[376] Two of Gaetano's sons, Giacomo (Jake) and Fedele (Sugie), were swept up in the Iron Prefect's dragnet and imprisoned for a short time until their American citizenship was established. "We used to say that's when Jake and Sugie 'went off to college,'" a few of the first cousins told me.

However, "[n]ot all *mafiosi* fared badly under Fascism. Official American sources estimate that five hundred of them escaped Mori's clutches by emigrating to the USA."[377] Gaetano DiGiovanni was one of the five hundred. He hurriedly fled Mori's flurry of mass arrests, leaving his family behind in San Cipirello, abandoning his wife and daughters to be taken hostage by the Fascists, who hoped to coerce the fugitive's return by threats to his family. "[H]e went back to Palermo," Nia said, "then he…and a few others, they went straight to Tunisia. Then they went to his grandfather's house,…[where] he stayed with this kid that left and his grandfather…named like my daddy, Gaetano and DiGiovanni,…and, uh, from there, they stayed to see a bullfight. How you like that? Yeah, he's at the bull fight. He was somethin'."[378] From Tunisia, Gaetano sailed to Canada, then entered the United States through Detroit and back down by train to New Orleans, where he arrived in April 1928.[379]

Nia described the roundup from which her father fled and its hostage-taking aftermath. "They started arresting everybody… Our people, they arrested…and held hostages, just to get the men to come back… That's why, you know, they sent a quick message to me, give up the other DiGiovannis…[380] So they take the families as hostages… We were the first, me and Lou, Grandma and the youngest kids, [including Francesca (Nookie). The Fascists] said, 'sure enough, they'll show up for the babies,' but they never did...[381] They went in big trucks. It took them to prison, some of us, we went to the Benedictine Convent,...the Benedictine nuns' convent. That's the best convent in Italy. Those nuns lived good there too... They [the Fascists] try to get you to mention names, and they try to do that no matter what. It was Lou and I and Grandma and Nookie. We were, you know, American citizens, and they treated us as citizens, but [they held us for] a few months... That's why I never wanted to go back... [They want you to] accuse a brother, fink on your family, neighbors against neighbors, just for what?... They took all the money away from the rich and give it to the poor. That's why they were kind-a, you know, thinking they would get the land and it would be rightfully theirs. It was awful. I hope it never happens here... In Italy, it was a Fascist-Nazi thing. Nobody talked. They still don't talk, you know. So the few of us who could help anybody would keep 'em up in the hayloft—had a little time to get them out. But my Daddy lost all...of his bunch."[382]

Because they were American citizens, "we weren't really mistreated," Nia said. "But they had, uh, one woman I knew from the same village, she was pregnant now too. They asked her where her husband was. And then the what-cha-ma-call-em starts. And she said, 'I haven't seen him in over six months.' They said, 'Then where did you get that letter?' I spoke better English. I said, 'you son of a bitch,' you know, I didn't even understand, so right away they pushed us, pushed me out, you know. I had no business being in there... She didn't say nothin'. She held up her hand. And she...mentioned some places in Palermo, the houses... Then they started getting rough. But nobody gave themselves up because they were hostages."[383]

Asked how they escaped from the Fascists to return to New Orleans, Nia was blasé. "[T]his fella was named Mori, he was head of the whole Fascists... [W]hile we [were] on the hill [held in the convent],...[even] before we were in there, a cousin of mine had notified the American authorities, the Customs... Oh, they discharged us. After my daddy gets to America, he writes a big telegram to the *policia*, to the head of...Mori his name was, and says..., 'I have arrived in America, doing fine. If you need money, please so and so,' and that was it… So he sent the money…and they let us all go at one time. We all went, just my sister and I, us and what-cha-call-'em, then we left from there to go, but they didn't mistreat anybody, you know, not that much people."[384]

"On 23 June 1929, after more than three-and-a-half years as police prefect of Palermo, Cesare Mori received a brief telegram from *Il Duce* instructing Mori that his job was finished. In a farewell speech to the Fascist Federation of Palermo, Mori [unabashedly said of himself]: '[T]here remains the man, the citizen Mori, the Fascist Mori, the fighter Mori,…living and vital. Today he takes his path towards the horizon that is open to all men…of goodwill. I have my star. I watch it faithfully because it shines, and will continue to shine, along the path of work and duty.'"[385]

Safely back in America, Gaetano DiGiovanni could have said the same of himself. Cesare Mori died in 1942.[386] Gaetano DiGiovanni outlived him by three years.

CHAPTER 23

ATLANTIC CROSSING 1929

In late 1928, before the Iron Prefect had so ceremoniously departed the scene, Gaetano began the long process of sending money back to Sicily to bring his family home to New Orleans, a few—sometimes one—at a time. His daughters Antonia (Lena, Nia) and Lucia (Lou) were first, traveling from San Cipirello through Palermo to Naples to depart by steamship. Their American passports were stamped "valid for immediate return to the United States" at the US consulate in Palermo on January 7, 1929. Nia's passport states that she is being "accompanied by [her] minor sister Lucia." The passport contains the photos of two beautiful young women, black-haired, brown-eyed, dark-frocked. Their faces bear identical thin-lipped, straight-lined, close-mouthed not-quite-smiles, the same expressions painted by da Vinci on the face of his classic *Mona Lisa*. Nia, almost twenty-five years old, the adult, signed her name in strong script "Antonia DiGiovanni." Lou signed hers in a shakier, younger scrawl "Lucia DiGiovanni."

"You see, we had American passports...because we were American citizens... We came on the first maiden [voyage of], uh, [something *di] Roma*," Nia said.[387] Lucille was seventeen. "Because I was a minor," Lou said, "she [Nia] was my chaperone. I had to share clothes with her..." Nia added, "We had one pair of socks, but two pairs of feet."[388]

Lucille was not Nia's only charge on the transatlantic voyage. The passengers included two children, Luciatina and Giuseppe Tariavia,[389] who had been left behind in Italy with their grandparents when their parents immigrated to America because the children had been too ill to travel. "The Travelers Aid asked if we would take care of two babies," Nia said, "so their parents could get them [in New York]. When they left, when the family left, the babies had sore eyes and they couldn't take them. The grandparents kept them. Now they were cured, and they were looking for somebody to take these two kids. What-cha gonna do? I said, 'Sure we'll take them.' Now these two, they got little valises… Grandma must have told them, 'Don't ever leave your valises, no matter where you go.' If we went to dinner, those valises were with us. If they slept, they had to put them between them so they'd be safe. And the little boy would say, 'la valicias, la valicias!' The valises. One was about four, and one was about seven. The cutest children, smart. And then we always sat at the front, you see, and we used to get a kick out of these kids. [The little boy would ask me], 'You got your valise?' I told him, 'No. Don't rub it in, that's enough.'"[390]

Nia described the ocean voyage as a rough crossing. "See the weather was so bad, and everybody was falling out of their bunks, and they had a baby born during that time, a baby, and they had this little stinker… And the [Tariavia children] had their little valises. Their grandmother there [had told them], '…la valicias, Hold on tight to your valises.' And whenever they would go [out of their room], they took their valises, and [would] not leave them."[391]

"We got back in 1929. That's when we got back… It took twelve days to get there," Nia recalled, noting that the twelve-day trip was half the time it had taken to travel from New York to Italy seven years earlier in 1922. They had left Italy on January 29, 1929, and were unprepared for the bitter cold winter weather when they arrived in New York in February. "We waited for people in New York to come find us to get off... It was covered, we had to come through the snow..., and we weren't equipped for cold weather... We had those light wool coats... We were freezing. Our relatives were there...waiting for us. It was a grand commotion." Lou added, "I wanted to find me...a Cognac... [W]e were freezing."[392]

"And the [Tariavia] children," Nia said, "when they saw their father, I thought one of them was gonna jump over the railing. We had to hold on to them... You couldn't blame them... Their father, you ought-a see that thing, who came for those two kids. We thought it was a parade, that family, waitin' for them babies. They had overcoats [for them]."[393]

From New York, Nia and Lou returned to New Orleans by train, arriving home just before Mardi Gras.[394] "You know who we traveled with?" Aunt Lou added. "You remember Mrs. Which-a-Call-It? She had a whole two cars. We used to call them Pullmans, and she had one car full of all kinds of birds she brought from Italy."[395] Lou's description intimates that perhaps their traveling companion was the wealthy and well-known Effie Whitaker, the "Parrot Lady of Palermo," whom author John Dickie described in his history. The Whitaker family "belonged to the leading English business dynasty in Sicily. (Palermo's British community had put down strong roots when His Majesty's Forces had occupied the island during the Napoleonic wars.) Whitakers were involved in the Marsala wine business..., [were] invited to London for Queen Victoria's state funeral in 1901...[and] founded a charity for abandoned infants, an animal welfare society, and the Palermo Football and Cricket Club... Effie [Whitaker] cultivated an eccentric image. She toured Palermo in her carriage with a parrot on her shoulder. It was fed with sunflower seeds from a silver box, and a silver trowel was kept ready for its droppings... Effie's parrot was allowed to fly free during [tennis] games [played on the Whitaker garden's three lawn tennis courts]. It was during one such match that Ignazio Florio's teenage brother Vincenzo, not sharing the English sentimentality about animals, shot the pampered bird out of a tree."[396] Effie "the Parrot Lady" was the mother of "ten-year-old Audrey Whitaker [who] was kidnapped by *mafiosi* under the command of the Noto brothers" in 1897 but released and "back home within days" after family scion "Joss Whitaker…paid…the huge ransom…immediately and denied that the whole episode had even happened."[397]

When they were settled with their father into their renewed situations in New Orleans, the lives of Nia and Aunt Lou initially went in different directions. Lucille did not remain in New Orleans for long after her return from Sicily. "When I come from Italy, my aunt come down to see us."[398] It was Aunt Mary Pumilia DiGiovanni, the wife of Gaetano's nephew, Anthony DiGiovanni, son of Gaetano's brother Giuseppe. Aunt Mary lived among a large branch of the DiGiovanni family in the Chicago suburb of Rockford, Illinois. "She wanted to take me back [to Chicagoland], so I went with her. I wind up staying almost a year with her. I didn't want to come back. My Daddy made me come back. My aunt would've had me married already over there."[399]

Lou recalled nothing but rollicking good times about her year in Chicagoland. "It was during the Depression. So my aunt told me, 'You gotta go to work.' I said 'all right.' They got me a job at a stocking place, you know they put packing in men's socks. Tacking. It was all piecework… Every day I would come home from work, [and] all the sisters would say, 'Lucille, how many dozen you make today?' And they liked to die laughing. [Everybody had a] quota. But that's how [Aunt Josephine] got the cancer,…from the cotton. She got that lung cancer from breathing all the lint from the stockings… She died of that. But they were good to me, during Prohibition time, and all this bootlegging [was going on]. Somehow, I had to [occupy] myself makin' socks. They were all bootlegging. I had all the money I wanted. [Lou's cousin] Pete [Provenzano, son of Gaetano's sister, Josephine DiGiovanni Provenzano], used to give me money for a show. I'd say, 'Pete, you gonna treat me tonight?' [He'd say], 'Yeah, Lucy,' they used to call me. 'Yeah, Lucy.' He'd pay for my show. He'd buy me whatever I want. We'd all go. I'd say, 'thank you, Pete.' Then they had a poker game at night. We'd serve coffee, couldn't go no place, and I used to win all of his money... And my paycheck, I didn't spend it. I kept giving each of them like alligator shoes, my cousins and them, that's the truth. [They had] the best of everything." Nia added, "Well, they had the money." Lou explained, "They were making it. They were bootlegging. I think they worked for what's his name, Caputti [*sic*]." "Big Al," Nia said. "Big Al," Lou agreed.[400] Big Al Capone.

While Lucille partied in Chicagoland, Nia's times were not so rollicking back in New Orleans. Mom recounted that Nia once told her she was wooed and fell in love for a brief time with someone Mom recalled only as Mr. Sam. Nia cut it off cold, however, because Mr. Sam was divorced and an American with no Italian vintage, two facts that the felicitous Lena (Nia) knew would not make him a mate acceptable to her parents. Within two years, Nia married Natale Guinta, a man she barely knew, except as the choice of her father. The exact date of their marriage is not quite clear. One record says it occurred on January 31, 1931, before New Orleans First City Court Judge Val J. Stentz. Her brother Sugie (Fedele), sister Lou and a city Board of Health functionary, Jacob Reatz, were the signatory witnesses. Natale's signature bears a dot over the first loop of the vowels of his name so that it looks like the original Giunta.[401] A later issued city certificate says the marriage occurred three days later on February 3, 1931.[402] Nia offered a third possible date. "Yeah, I was married on my birthday," Nia recalled. "Wouldn't you know it."[403]

Perhaps the confusion about the date of the Guintas's marriage was caused by the fact that the civil ceremony at city hall was followed by a church wedding. Lena's mother, Angelina, the devout Catholic woman that she was, insisted that her daughter's marriage must be sanctified through the sacrament of holy matrimony. About the church wedding, Nia once confided in my wife, Sue, the granddaughter-in-law with whom she bonded and came to think of as Nia's own blood: "We were in the back of the church, and my daddy was getting ready to walk me down the aisle. All of a sudden, I saw tears in his eyes. 'What-sa matter, Daddy?' He said, 'Daughter, you do not have to marry this man. If you want to leave, I'll take you away from here right-a now.' What-cha gonna do? I said, 'No, Daddy, I'm gonna do it.' We were really already married under law down at the city hall anyway."

After the ceremony, Gaetano packed the newlyweds off on the northbound train for a honeymoon in Chicago. When Natale and Lena arrived at the Chicago train station, they found that the Rockford branch of the DiGiovanni family had turned out in force to welcome them like visiting royalty. They were treated to a suite at one of the Windy City's finest lakeshore hotels. They were feted nightly with drinks and dinners at Italian restaurants or the homes of their DiGiovanni compadres. The effervescent Lena was treated like a princess. The taciturn and imposing Natale was treated with the formal deference generally accorded *uomini rispettati* (men of respect).

Upon their return to New Orleans, the newlywed Guintas settled into domestic life. It seemed an odd pairing: the ebullient, level-headed and generally delightful Lena (Nia) matched with the unsmiling and tempestuous Natale. The differences in their ages and times of life were significant. Natale was forty-three years old on his wedding day, sixteen years older than Lena. What was his motivation for this relatively late-in-life union after years of solitary and wholly independent bachelorhood? A capacity for romantic love did not seem to be a component of his psychological makeup. Perhaps he had learned the same lesson that had motivated Gaetano's father, the nineteenth-century Domenico DiGiovanni, to abandon his life as a bandit in the Sicilian mountains and marry Giuseppina Randazzo, daughter of one of Western Sicily's nineteenth-century men of respect: "Often, the only way for an ambitious man to succeed is to marry one of the daughters of the men at the top."[404] But what was Natale's ambition? Nia's reasoning for this odd pairing seems more transparent. She and the younger Lucille were the most available remaining unwed daughters of Gaetano and Angelina. At twenty-seven years old, Lena was quickly passing her feminine prime as Sicilians of that era then reckoned it. There can be little doubt that Natale Guinta was the choice of her father, and above all else, Lena was a filial and obedient daughter.

For a short while, the newlyweds rented a place in the back-a-town section of New Orleans, behind the French Quarter, before moving to another rented spot closer to Nia's parents on Tchoupitoulas Street. Like any good Sicilian daughter and wife, Nia was soon pregnant. In 1932, she delivered a son who became Natale's pride, joy, and best friend, my Godfather, Joseph Guinta. But then the next child, their eldest daughter Anna, died only a few days after her birth of a congenital heart defect. Their youngest, my mother Ann, was born in 1935. Natale made his living in those early days of their marriage during the Depression in various ways: as a general laborer, as a dock worker on the banana boats, doing this and that for his father-in-law. Not until 1939, as the Depression eased and World War II loomed, would Natale and Antonia (Lena, Nia) Guinta realize something of the American dream of security in property and business ownership. Before then, in the interim, making a living was something of a struggle.

CHAPTER 24

BOOTLEGGERS

For the thirteen years of its existence, Prohibition was a source of nationwide crime, wealth, violence, public corruption and expense, deceit and hypocrisy, with little of its high-minded goals of temperance, family stability, and cultural morality actually achieved. Like many other slices of American society, cutting across social, ethnic, demographic, and regional boundaries, some of the DiGiovanni family participated in its sweep.

The Nate Goldberg Bootlegging Gang of New Orleans was less an organized criminal enterprise than a loose amalgamation of available men looking to make some ready cash during the Great Depression from a product "which most people want [but] is forbidden them by the *pezzonovanti* [big shots] of the church and the government."[405] "Nate Goldberg, described by federal authorities as a gangster,"[406] was the gang's unquestioned leader and organizer. Goldberg, along with "Merchant D. O'Neal, 4118 General Pershing street, [were] named by federal authorities as ring leaders in [an] alleged rum smuggling conspiracy case for which 104 persons and firms were indicted by a federal grand jury [in New Orleans]..."[407] Goldberg associated a few men with him because they could be trusted and brought useful assets to the operation: a big empty building; trucks to haul crates of liquor; axes and hatchets to open the crates; shotguns and pistols to protect themselves and their product from rivals, hijackers and law enforcement agents; and contacts with able-bodied laborers willing to do the heavy lifting, packing, loading, and distribution.

On Friday, March 18, 1932, twenty-one members of the gang, including ringleaders Goldberg and O'Neal, congregated for a weekend of receiving, transporting, uncrating, and distributing heavy wooden crates containing more than $100,000 worth of Canadian Gold Label whiskey.[408] The source of the whiskey was an "alleged international rum smuggling ring," with "most of the liquor…bought from the Consolidated Exporters Corporation Ltd., of Vancouver, BC [British Columbia, Canada], and diverted to New Orleans by way of Belize… O'Neal…was the representative of the Consolidated and other distilleries from which thousands of dollars' worth of liquor was purchased."[409] In addition to Goldberg and O'Neal, other members of the gang involved in the operation included Fedele ("Sugie") DiGiovanni; his brothers-in-law, Natale Guinta and Frank ("Yanks") Towle; and a few extended family members of the DiGiovannis' across-the-street neighbors from San Cipirello days, Guy and Salvadore Todaro.

The operation began late Friday night, March 18, with the leaders and gang members who owned trucks, including Sugie DiGiovanni, picking up the men who would provide the labor, like Yanks and Natale. They went to a "point on the banks of a river or lake…, a concentration point…being used by Goldberg, O'Neal, and others near Covington," [Louisiana], as a "liquor depot."[410] At the Northshore depot, the men "loaded trucks that were then driven back to New Orleans," specifically to "an abandoned bakery at 2331 North Rampart street," owned or leased by one of the gang members, "Vincent Lentini, who lived in quarters above the bakery."[411] The cargo consisted of dozens of big, unopened wooden crates, which "bore no marking, other than 'Fragile, handle with care.'"[412]

Federal agents had been tipped off about the operation by "an informer called Duplessis."[413] Some agents were dispatched to the Northshore depot for surveillance purposes, but "[b]y the time the agents arrived at the Covington site, they found none of the alleged conspirators, nor any of the liquor."[414] Along the way from Covington to Rampart Street, however, one of the gang's vehicles, "a two-ton truck,…stalled at Esplanade avenue and Dupre street, and from which…[a]gents trailed two coupes which made three trips to and from the stalled truck…[to] the bakery."[415]

Inside the bakery early Saturday morning, the men leaned their shotguns against the crates, grabbed hatchets from bags that had been brought by their henchmen, and began to unload the bottles of whiskey. Their unloading and opening of the crates' cargo did not last long. "At or about 3 a.m."[416] on Saturday morning the nineteenth, "[f]our prohibition agents with drawn guns"[417] barged into the bakery. "[A]gents found hundreds of veneer boxes with four cases of liquor neatly packed in each, covered over with sawdust."[418] They also found a five-ton Studebaker truck parked in the driveway, "[a] distinct odor of whiskey,…a number of sacks the size and appearance of whiskey sacks,…leaning against the rear wall, a double-barreled shotgun which was loaded,…a broken sack of 'Gold Label' whiskey which [sic] had evidently been dropped, and whiskey flowing on the pavement,…[and] a keg or two of three penny nails, single nails, and also rolls of steel tape wire."[419] A few of the men tried to run, but agents apprehended them immediately and placed all nineteen of the men then in the building under arrest. The agents shouted that all contents of the bakery were then and there seized. At first, Goldberg "attempted to resist the officers."[420] "Goldberg dived for his overcoat pocket; he grabbed his overcoat to take his gun out."[421] When the officers told him they were prohibition agents, Goldberg "is said by the agents to have raised his hands and commented, 'you should have told us that first. I thought maybe you were hijackers or that you wanted to take someone for a ride.'"[422] An agent took a loaded .38 pistol from Goldberg while O'Neal placed a loaded pistol he was carrying on top of one of the whiskey boxes.[423] Some of the arrested men told officers they had been told that "plans had been made to unload a cargo of liquor three or four times as large as that seized. While Goldberg and O'Neal refused to discuss the case with officers, they grinned when government operatives chided them about being arrested before all of their trucks had reached the address and had been unloaded."[424]

"After nineteen of the men had been placed under arrest, two other workmen walked in, each carrying a crate of axes. They admitted that these axes were to have been used in nailing tops on each of the crates."[425] "One of these men had a box of hatchets under his arm, and the other man had six hatchets loose under his arms... [Sugie] DiGiovanni had the unwrapped hatchets and Joe Mendona had the box of hatchets... Mendona had on his person a .38 revolver fully loaded."[426]

The arrested gang members were transported first to the Masonic Temple Building, where they were placed in two patrol wagons, escorted to the Prohibition Office, and interviewed individually. Goldberg refused to say anything, not even his name or address, but the officers already knew who he was. O'Neal gave his name and said nothing more. Fedele "Sugie" DiGiovanni initially said he had forgotten his first name then gave it as Philip. His "explanation as to the hatchets found on his person was that he had found them on the street."[427] Natale Guinta said his name was Joseph Giunta, and his "explanation as to his presence on the premises was that he had been picked up about ten or eleven o'clock on Oak Street and brought to the premises in a closed car and that he had helped to unload one truck of whiskey."[428] Frank "Yanks" Towle told agents "that on Friday night, the eighteenth, at about ten o'clock he had gone in a closed truck in the direction of West End to the bayou, somewhere in that vicinity, and helped unload a boat of whiskey into the trucks, and that he had come back to 2331 North Rampart Street in a closed car. His memory was that it was a black Chevrolet sedan. They arrived there about one o'clock when they came back from the bayou, and after packing the whiskey into the cases there were no hatchets, and two men were sent for the hatchets..."[429]

After their arrest and questioning, all twenty-one were "taken before United States Commissioner R. H. Carter Jr. and charged with conspiracy to violate the National Prohibition and Tariff Acts."[430] Commissioner Carter released eight of the men on bond, including Frank "Yanks" Towle, who correctly gave his name and address as 1133 Tchoupitoulas street, and Natale Guinta, who incorrectly gave his name and address as Joseph Giunta, 2638 St. Anthony

Street.[431] Fedele "Sugie" DiGiovanni, who incorrectly gave his first name as Philip, was among those including the ringleaders Goldberg and O'Neal, the Todaro brothers and Lentini, the owner of the bakery building, who were denied bond and held in jail.[432]

CHAPTER 25

THE UNITED STATES COURTHOUSE

On February 8, 1933, brothers-in-law Fedele "Sugie" DiGiovanni (being prosecuted under the name Philip DiGiovanni), Natale Guinta (being prosecuted under the name Joseph Giunta), and Frank "Yanks" Towle strode into what is now the historic John Minor Wisdom Fifth Circuit United States Court of Appeals Building at 600 Camp Street. They were present for their jury trial before United States District Judge William I. Grubb of the Northern District of Alabama, who was sitting by special designation in New Orleans[433] to assist local federal Judge Wayne Borah with his burgeoning and overwhelming bootlegging docket. Along with eighteen other members of the Nate Goldberg Bootlegging Gang, the DiGiovanni family brothers-in-law had been indicted on October 20, 1932, by a federal grand jury and charged in three counts: count one, conspiracy to possesses for purposes of selling, delivering, or transporting "intoxicating liquors fit for use for beverage purposes"; count two, possession of liquor for the purpose of sale; and count three, "maintain[ing] a common nuisance...at 2331 North Rampart Street,...where intoxicating liquors, to-wit: whiskey...was sold, kept, and bartered," all in violation of the National Prohibition Act.[434]

At that time, the majestic courthouse edifice, now recognized as a National Historic Landmark, was simply known as the United

165

States Post Office and Court House. The baroque marble three-story building was ornately festooned with Ionic columns, arched doorways, consoled windows, carvings of lions and eagles, the great seal of the United States, and the names of some of its greatest chief justices. It is topped with "a rooftop sculpture, popularly known as 'The Ladies,'" depicting the feminine images of History, Agriculture, Industry and the Arts, created by "[o]ne of the most influential sculptors of the late nineteenth century, Daniel Chester French (1850–1931)... [The edifice] was commissioned by the US Treasury Department in July 1909. It was designed by the New York architectural firm of Hale and Rogers, the principal architect being James Gamble Rogers... [T]he building was completed and occupied in 1915."[435]

The prosecutor was Assistant United States Attorney William H. Norman. The defense team consisted of attorneys Edwin H. Grace, Hugh M. Wilkinson, and A. D. O'Neal.[436]

After jury selection, the government presented the testimony of the four federal prohibition agents who had made the arrests and seized the evidence at the bakery, Agents R. C. Bennett, L. E. Holleman, E. J. Anderman, and J. A. Mollinary. The agents' testimony was supplemented by the testimony of Frank B. Moore, a private photographer who authenticated photographs of the seized evidence and bakery premises taken under the agents' direction; government chemist William O. Whaley, who testified that the seized liquids were in fact "whiskey, containing more than one-half of one percent of alcohol by volume..., fit for beverage purposes, ordinary whiskey commonly used for that purpose";[437] and Assistant Prohibition Administrator E.S. Smith, who had questioned all twenty-one of the defendants after their arrest. An additional prohibition agent, Robert Hume, testified that Lentini, owner and occupant of the abandoned bakery, had pled guilty in 1926 to an offense similar to the charges in the Goldberg gang case, "possession and selling of intoxicating liquors and maintaining a nuisance at 1100 South Franklin Street."[438]

Throughout the government's case in chief, the defense team adhered to the ancient lawyer's adage voiced by the poet Carl

Sandburg: "If the facts are against you, argue the law." Since the Nate Goldberg Bootlegging Gang had been caught in the act by federal agents handling truckloads of Canadian whiskey, the facts were decidedly against the defendants. However, the federal agents admittedly had made their arrests, conducted their search of the abandoned bakery, and seized their evidence without a search warrant and with no warrant to arrest any of the defendants.[439] Thus, at every appropriate point in the trial court proceedings, defense lawyers objected to the introduction of all evidence—the whiskey, the trucks, the hatchets, the guns, the sacks, the crates, the nails—on grounds that the officers' search and seizure violated the Fourth Amendment.[440] Cross-examination of the government's witnesses by defense counsel focused on the absence of warrants either to make the search and seizures of the evidence or to arrest any of the defendants; the fact that the defendants' statements about which the officers were testifying had been merely summarized, not written verbatim; that defendants may have said other things during their interviews that were not recorded; and that some of the defendants had no knowledge that what they had been hired to do was illegal.[441]

When the government rested, defense counsel moved for a directed verdict of not guilty "on the grounds that the evidence adduced at the trial did not sustain the allegations of the counts thereof, or any of them."[442] Judge Grubb promptly denied the motion. The only evidence offered by the defense in its case in chief was the government's written admission that the search and seizure of all evidence had been conducted without a warrant. The defense then reiterated its "motions on behalf of all defendants...to suppress all evidence, and exclude all the evidence, obtained by reason of the said search and seizure."[443] Judge Grubb swiftly denied the motion, and the defense rested. Defense counsel then reiterated defendants motion to dismiss. It was again denied.

Counsel then presented their closing arguments. The court record contains no transcript or summary of what the lawyers said. Judge Grubb then delivered lengthy instructions to the jury.[444] He did **not** include an instruction specially requested by the defense "that mere knowledge of the existence of a crime, or even mental approval of the commission of said crime, or intention to have future participation in the commission of a crime, all without an action exercised by that person pursuant to his knowledge, mental approval or future intention, does not constitute any crime on the part of said person."[445] The jury retired for deliberations and returned a short time later with a verdict that all defendants were guilty of count one (conspiracy) and count two (possession), but not guilty as to count three (maintaining a liquor nuisance).[446]

The defendants were sentenced on February 10, 1933. The ring-leaders, Nate Goldberg and Merchant O'Neal, received the stiffest penalties, fifteen months each in the notoriously tough federal penitentiary in Atlanta. Fedele "Sugie" DiGiovanni and Natale Guinta were sentenced to ninety and thirty days respectively in an unspecified federal jail. They were also fined $100 apiece. Yanks Towle and five others received suspended sentences.[447]

That same day, the defendants sentenced to jail time, including Goldberg, O'Neal, Sugie, and Natale, all challenged their convictions by appeal to the United States Court of Appeals for the Fifth Circuit. As at trial, the basis of their appeal was that the agents' warrantless search, seizure, and arrests violated the Fourth and Fifth Amendments to the Constitution. Judge Grubb signed an order that day that suspended execution of the judgment and all sentences pending the appeal, "upon the defendants furnishing an appeal bond in the sum of two hundred and fifty ($250) Dollars with good and sufficient security to be approved by this court."[448] The same order provided that the defendants were to be released on bond, Goldberg and O'Neal in the amount of $5,000; Sugie in the amount of $2,500; and Natale in the amount of $1,000.

CHAPTER 26

EXONERATION

Nine months later, while the appeal was pending, "Prohibition died on December 5, 1933, when Utah's vote for the Twenty-first Amendment provided the required two-thirds majority to repeal the Eighteenth Amendment."[449] Two months later, in *United States v. Chambers*, the United States Supreme Court put a halt to all bootlegging "prosecutions, including proceedings on appeal, continued or begun after the ratification of the Twenty-First Amendment,"[450] which repealed prohibition. The Supreme Court stated that "when the reason of a rule ceases, the rule also ceases… The law here sought to be applied was deprived of force **by the people themselves** as the inescapable effect of their repeal of the Eighteenth Amendment (Prohibition)… [T]he people are free to withdraw the authority they have conferred and, when withdrawn, neither the Congress nor the courts can assume the right to continue to exercise it."[451] On March 21, 1934, the Fifth Circuit Court of Appeals in New Orleans issued an order in favor of the Goldberg defendants, citing the Supreme Court's Chambers ruling. The order "reversed and annulled" the convictions and sentences of all defendants, including Sugie, Natale, and Yanks.[452] On April 6, 1934, Judge Wayne Borah of the Eastern District of Louisiana federal trial court followed up with an order providing that "the defendants herein are hereby discharged from the said judgment and sentences herein imposed upon them."[453] On June 27, 1933, the New Orleans Deputy Prohibition

169

Administrator authorized the release of Uncle Sugie's Ford truck. It had been impounded since its seizure at the North Rampart Street whiskey unloading venue.

For years earlier, Natale had sent money home to his mother in Castelvetrano "for food and things, for Mother's Day," Nia said, but the Giuntas of Western Sicily were well-off *gabelloti* and "they didn't need it," so Natale's mother, Anna Sanstefano Giunta, "put it away in *la banca*."[454] Nia said that one year in the 1930s when one of Grandma Anna's granddaughters immigrated to America, "they paid me in American money,... The old lady said, she told her [immigrating granddaughter], 'when you get to New Orleans, you give that amount to my daughter-in-law, my daughter-in-law not my son, and you tell them to buy that house.' That's how we bought Tchoupitoulas Street because it was money Paw-Paw and I used to send her. 'You tell my daughter-in-law don't let her husband [Natale] even smell it' because he'd send it back, you know what little it was."[455] And what was Tchoupitoulas Street? Principally, a saloon with living quarters in the back of the building. Natale and Lena (Nia) added a little restaurant component later, where working men from the neighborhood could get a plate lunch of red beans and rice or meatballs and spaghetti to go with their beers, whiskey, and po'boy sandwiches. But it was originally and thereafter mainly a barroom. Thus, the end result of the bootlegging prosecution was that the Guintas walked the nine blocks around the corner from the federal courthouse at 600 Camp Street and opened Mr. Joe's Bar at 1169 Tchoupitoulas Street. They legally went into a business that had been illegal only months earlier. At first, they rented the location. On February 11, 1939, using the money his mother had squirreled away, then sent to her daughter-in-law Lena (Nia), Natale purchased it from the Sterling Realty Corporation for the princely sum of $2,900. At the closing, he plopped down $900 in cash and signed "One (1) Promissory Note for the sum of Two Thousand and No/100 ($2,000) Dollars payable to the Bearer...[at] $30 per month...with...interest at the rate of 6 percent per annum...until paid."[456]

Sugie DiGiovanni did the same in another part of town. He opened Sugar's Bar and filled it with slot machines, leased from his good friend, Anthony "Tony" Carolla, son of Silver Dollar Sam Carolla.[457] Uncle Sugie figured that a barroom full of slot machines would make him rich. About a year into the operation, the New Orleans police inexplicably cracked down on gambling in barrooms. A squad of cops raided Sugar's Bar, and all the slot machines were seized and dumped into the Mississippi River, so Sugie gave it up. He joined the United States Navy and later became a merchant sea-man and dedicated mariner of the Seafarers International Union. At his funeral, he was laid out in his coffin for all to see, including his great-nephew—me, incongruously wearing a suit and tie, with his green and white Seafarers International Union bee-bop hat propped on his head.

CHAPTER 27

ELYSIAN FIELDS
NOVEMBER 26, 1934

The far-right corner of Harold Beucler's thin lips curled upward on his elongated face, pointing skyward toward the vast expanse of his enormous forehead. It was the self-satisfied half-smirk, half-smile he often affected when he was feeling on top of the world. On this Monday night, he was unable to stifle the conceit that accompanied what he thought he had finally attained as his rightful station. After all, it was not long ago that he had been a convict, slaving away at hard labor in the cane fields of the state penitentiary at Angola, Louisiana. Beucler had been "given a penitentiary sentence of ten to twelve years by Judge Frank T. Echezabel in 1926, following his conviction by a jury on charges of assaulting and robbing [a] Chicago salesman of $622 at Canal and Tonti streets January 7 of that year."[458] Beucler could not have thought back then that he would ever reach a position of such self-satisfaction a mere eight years later, at only the age of thirty-one. He had a wife, a girlfriend, a doting mother, a thriving business operating on the recently reinstated legitimate side of the law and a boon companion. He imagined that the Elysian Fields conceived by the ancient Greeks as an afterlife "abode of the blessed...a place or state of perfect happiness,"[459] could not be any better than the Elysian Fields Avenue in New Orleans that was home to both his girlfriend and his widowed mother, whose house he was leaving that night after his daily visit as a devoted son. All seemed right with Harold Beucler.

Twenty-two-year-old Lucille (Lucia, Lou) DiGiovanni also lived on Elysian Fields Avenue, address number 2242, just a few houses away from Buecler's mother. She was a slender, dark-haired, dark-skinned, drop-dead Mediterranean beauty, returned to her New Orleans birthplace for five years after her long exile in Western Sicily and short sojourn in Chicagoland. She was agitated as she waited for Beucler, who was leaving his mother's house. They saw each other. They argued. Beucler moved toward her. Lucille raised the .38-calibre revolver she had taken from her brother's closet. "Beucler fled before the girl's fire as she ran after him, firing four shots… Two of the bullets entered his body, one piercing the heart."[460]

Lucille then ran the short distance back to her neighboring Elysian Fields home, where she sat on the front porch and calmly waited for the police. "Arrested at her home shortly afterward, Miss DiGiovanni admitted that she had shot Beucler, and asserted that he had 'double-crossed' her."[461] Arresting officers Sergeant Peter Berges and Patrolman Paul Poretti reported that they arrested Lucille "on the porch of her home a few minutes after the shooting. 'We went up to the house and asked if she was Lucille DiGiovanni,' Sergeant Berges said, 'and she answered that she was. I asked her if she shot Beucler, and she said, 'I shot that rat.' I told her she had killed him, and she said, 'I'm glad I did a good job.' We asked her where the gun was. She said it was inside, and she took us inside to get it. I asked her why she had shot Beucler, and she said, 'He can't double-cross me.' She wouldn't talk anymore after that, but she went with us to the station without any protest.'"[462]

Police and newspaper reporters[463] at the scene took a statement from the victim's friend, William "Chew Tobacco" Moore, who said he witnessed the killing. Chew Tobacco was Beucler's boon companion, a New Orleans Ninth Warder who made his living as Beucler's right-hand man, doing whatever needed to be done at the beer parlor Beucler owned at the corner of North Robertson Street and Almonaster Avenue. Chew Tobacco told police that he was with Beucler in the passenger seat of Beucler's new Ford after they left the beer parlor and Beucler "stopped for a brief visit to his mother, Mrs. Louis Beucler." According to Moore's statement to the newspaper:

> In accordance with his usual nightly custom, [Beucler] was going to meet his wife, return with her to the beer parlor to check up on the day's receipts before closing the establishment. Miss DiGiovanni was waiting outside Mrs. Beucler's home...when they drove up to [the] residence [and] the girl called to Beucler that she wanted to see him. Beucler continued into his mother's house, where he remained for approximately three minutes... He then reappeared and as he stepped out the door called back to his mother that there was a girl outside waiting to see him... DiGiovanni, who was on the sidewalk a short distance from the door, said, "Come here, Harold, I want to talk to you." Beucler approached and the girl began firing... "I could see the flashes of the gun from where I was sitting in the car," [Moore] related. "Beucler ran away from her and she ran after him, still shooting. He sort-of turned around and tried to grab the gun, but then he fell down. She ran down the street toward her house. I went across the street to a drug store and told somebody else there to call the police and an ambulance. Then I went to Beucler and he was dead."[464]

Beucler's "widowed mother" told the newspaper that she "saw the last of the shots fired and saw her son fall" and that "Beucler's wife was waiting at a theater for her husband when he was shot. The mother said, "After [Harold] had left my house,...I heard him shout, 'Mama! Mama!' I ran to see what was wrong and I saw him fall. I also saw the last of the pistol flashes. I ran out and picked up his head, and kissed him, but he was already dead'... Mrs. Beucler said she thought the young woman was running to assist her son, not knowing at the time that it was she who had killed him. [She] added that she did not know Miss DiGiovanni but 'knew of her.' She quoted her son as having told Miss DiGiovanni that he was married happily and that he did not want to see her anymore."[465]

Lucille was taken from her porch to the police station and then to Orleans Parish Prison, where the usual murder proceedings commenced, both legal and dramatized by the press. She was formally booked and charged by the district attorney with Beucler's murder.[466] She gave her occupation as "wrapper,"[467] explaining that "[a]t the time of the shooting she was working in a New Orleans bakery to obtain money for Christmas."[468] New Orleans Coroner C. Grenes Cole conducted an autopsy and announced the results: "[T]wo…bullets had entered [Beucler's] back. One…entered between the fourth and fifth rib, went through the heart, and emerged through the front of the body. The other entered the ninth and tenth ribs and pierced the liver."[469]

On the afternoon of her arrest, under her full-length photo taken at police headquarters and a headline reading "'I have nothing to say,'" an article about the killing was published on the front page of the local evening newspaper. "It was written by K. T. Knoblock, a veteran reporter and nationally known writer of crime stories."[470] The woman reporter wrote the story from the point of view of Lucille's imagined first person, as if Lucille herself was doing the writing and addressing the writer.

"I have nothing to say," the article began. "The girl who came to see me and said she was a reporter asked me many questions, but I told her I had nothing to say. I killed Harold Beucler, long-faced, thirty-one years old, a married man. When the policeman told me he was dead, I said, 'Well the dirty rat, it looks as if I did a good job.' She asked me why too, and her eyes were kind; I would have told her, if I could. But 'I have nothing to say.' I have nothing to say with my hands

175

folded in my lap, huddled in my long blue coat; my hair is a mess, and it is not a nice place they have put me in. My name is Lucille DiGiovanni. I am Italian, of course. I am twenty-two years old. I live at 2242 Elysian Fields avenue, but now they have got me in a cell in police headquarters. There is a drunkard two cells away whose moans are not nice. I shudder a little as I hear them. But 'I have nothing to say.' What is there that I could say? I killed him; they've got that on me. I couldn't get out by saying I didn't kill him. The rest of it doesn't seem to matter. My reason? That's my business. The girl sat looking at me, but I had nothing to say. She must have read about it in the papers because other reporters came to see me. I told them nothing. I had nothing to say. I heard them ask the police, though. It's in the papers, how I killed Harold. How I look: Italian type, olive complexioned, with dark brown eyes and heavy black hair, wearing a blue coat with a fur collar, pink dress, brown stockings, and low black shoes. How I was brought into the office of the chief of detectives, where Captain Harry Gregson questioned me. I had nothing to say. 'Is your name Lucille DiGiovanni?' he asked. 'Yes,' I replied. 'What cause did you have to shoot Beucler?' 'I had a cause.' 'What was it?' I bent my head but did not answer. 'Was Beucler your sweetheart?' I had nothing to say. 'Have you been keeping company with him?' I told him I had nothing to say, anyway not until I had seen my attorney. My brother is trying to get Chandler Luzenberg **Sr.** Chandler Luzenberg **Jr.** is his son, but he is an assistant district attorney. He says it was just a cold-blooded murder, he says I was running with Beucler, and he thinks jealousy was the motive. 'I have nothing to say.' Last night, when Sergeant Peter Verges arrested me in front of Harold's mother's home at 2210 Elysian Fields Avenue, he says I said, 'Yes, I shot the rat. Is he dead?' He told me he was dead, and he says I said, 'I'm glad I did a good job.' But 'I have nothing to say.' He says I said, 'I would have shot him if I had seen him at Canal and Royal Streets.' That is a busy corner. They said I said, 'You can talk Italian or English to me; I shot him and that's all I have to say.' It happened last night in front of his mother's home; she is Mrs. Louis Beucler, a widow. I shot him as he came out of there, near where I live. He drove up with William Moore, his friend who lives at 1531 St. Roch Avenue, and I called to him, but he ran into the house. Then when he came down, I must have shot at him four times with a .38. Two bullets entered his neck, they told me. His mother came running out and lifted him and he called her 'Mama.' He was in the penitentiary from 1926 until they let him out and he ran a beer parlor at Almonaster Avenue and North Robertson Street. His wife was waiting for him to get her from a picture show when I shot him. 'I have nothing to say.'"[471]

If the killing caused consternation or doubt about the righteousness of Lucille's actions in the DiGiovanni family, neither was reflected in their actions toward her. The Assistant District Attorney who was initially in charge of the investigation after her arrest was Charles Luzenberg **Jr.**[472] Acting through one of his sons and perhaps sensing an opportunity to sow discord and difficulty in the camp of his daughter's opponent, Gaetano retained the prosecutor's father, Charles Luzenberg **Sr.**, as her defense lawyer.[473] The tactic succeeded. On the day after her arrest, she told the assistant district attorney "that she had borrowed from her brother the gun with which she shot

Beucler" and "that she had taken the gun because she thought there were 'muggle heads' at the corner and that when she saw Beucler she shot him."[474] "'No, I didn't love him,' the girl denied vehemently in answer to questions. 'I killed him. I had a good reason.'"[475] When **Jr.** pressed, attempting to question Lucille too aggressively, the young lawyer's father interrupted the son. Luzenberg **Sr.** shut down Luzenberg **Jr.'s** questioning, after which Lucille "refused to make a formal statement" and "steadfastly refused to discuss the affair other than to say repeatedly that she killed the man and was 'glad of it.'"[476] Luzenberg **Jr.** was not part of the team of prosecutors who conducted the State's jury trial six months later while **Sr.** conducted the defense.

Lucille's siblings and cousins rallied around her while she was held in jail without bond awaiting her trial. A brother (probably Sugie, perhaps Jake) and a couple of cousins (maybe Philip Ferraro, Yanks Towle, Giacomo Bucaro, or Pasquale Napolitano) stayed with her in the jail in shifts "so that she would not be alone… After spending the (first) night and part of [the next day] in the Third Precinct station, Miss DiGiovanni was transferred to the Parish Prison. She took the news of the filing of charges calmly, asking only that clean clothes be brought to her at the prison."[477] She was brave but doleful in the jail's squalid conditions. "Huddled in a cell…, Miss DiGiovanni was composed, showing nervousness only by twisting her hands and by pushing back her thick black hair from her face. The condition of her cell seemed to make her miserable and she complained about the noise of drunken Negro women who were held in a cell during the night. 'I couldn't sleep,' she said. 'This board bed is terrible, and even the pillow which [sic] they brought me didn't help. I just sat here and walked up and down all night. I wasn't afraid because my brother and cousin stayed all night. I wish, though, they would give me a glass with some water. I can't drink out of that tin cup everyone drinks out of. I finally got my cousin to wash out a carton in which he had brought coffee and he gave me some water in that. They think I'd cut myself with glass, but I wouldn't.'"[478] She maintained her wits well enough to attempt to win some sympathy from an inquiring reporter, using some of the inaccuracy and deception endemic in the talk of Western Sicilians. She told the reporter she "has six married sisters and one brother" and that she had "attended St. Teresa's school until she was fourteen years old," but "her mother thought she was not doing anything in school and so took her out. She recalled reminiscently that she had been 'bad' in school and...had to be 'whipped often.'"[479]

After almost two months in jail, Lucille was indicted for Beucler's murder by the Orleans Parish Grand Jury on December 11, 1934.[480] Two days later, she appeared in the courtroom of Orleans Parish Criminal District Court Judge William J. O'Hara. Lucille "was brought from the women's department of the Parish Prison by prison matrons and deputy sheriffs. She was wearing a blue coat suit and a blue hat. The young woman remained silent while Alton Humphrey, minute clerk, read the murder indictment. Through her attorney, Charles C. Luzenberg Sr., Miss DiGiovanni pleaded not guilty. She was remanded to jail to await trial."[481] Coincidentally, on the same day as Lucille's arraignment, seasoned murder suspect Battista Pecoraro, forty-eight, the same Mafia muscle who had been accused but never convicted of killing Lucille's eldest brother, Domenico, thirteen years earlier, was arrested on a charge of the shotgun killing of New Orleans grocer Benedetto Cappello, who identified Pecorara as his killer in a deathbed statement to detectives.[482]

CHAPTER 28

TULANE AND BROAD
MARCH 25, 1935

On the morning of the first spring Monday of 1935, after four months in the Orleans Parish Prison, Lucille was again brought to Judge O'Hara's courtroom, this time for trial.[483] The charge was the murder of Harold Beucler, ex-convict owner of a New Orleans beer parlor. The sentence she faced if found guilty was death by hanging.

Lucille appeared in court that day "in a new spring ensemble, with white shoes and white hat. The dress and hat were trimmed in blue. The day of her trial was her birthday, she said."[484] Her defense attorney was Charles Luzenberg **Sr.**, who had been retained to represent her on the night of her arrest and had stayed by her side throughout. The prosecutors were Assistant District Attorneys J. Bernard Cocke and M. E. Culligan.

The trial began with voir dire examination and jury selection. Assistant District Attorney Cocke opened for the State.[485] Lucille "sat motionless and apparently unaffected...and did not flinch as he announced that the state would demand her death on the gallows... A number of prospective jurors were excused because they asserted point-blank that they would not inflict the death penalty upon a woman, regardless of the evidence."[486] Nevertheless, by 1:00 p.m., twelve true and blue New Orleanians were selected, all men, none with Italian surnames.[487]

The State's first witness was the Orleans Parish Assistant Coroner. Lucille "appeared unconcerned as the victim's bloodstained clothes were introduced and Dr. Robert H. Potts described the wounds which [*sic*] had caused death,"[488] including two shots in the back and "two deep scalp lacerations...caused by blows struck by Miss DiGiovanni with the gun as [Beucler] reached for it."[489]

The State's second witness was William "Chew Tobacco" Moore, "[t]he only eyewitness to the shooting."[490] "Moore testified that he had gone with Beucler the night of November 26 from the latter's beer parlor...in Beucler's automobile to his mother's house. He said that Miss DiGiovanni was standing in front of the home and that as Beucler got out of his car she said to him, 'Harold, I want to see you.'"[491]

Hearing this testimony that she "had sought the meeting, stopping Beucler as he got out of his automobile,"[492] Lucille "leaped to her feet and shouted, 'you're a liar, you're a liar,'"[493] drawing Judge O'Hara's sharp rebuke and her lawyer's quick command to sit down and be quiet.

"Moore continued, saying that Beucler entered his mother's house by a side door, came out the front door within a minute, and walked toward Miss DiGiovanni. 'I heard a shot,' he said. 'I turned my head and saw Harold running, and she was running after him, firing at him. I saw the flashes. He fell, and she stood over him and fired again into his body. He raised his hand like he was trying to grab the gun, but she stepped back and struck him on the head with the gun.'" He testified that "no attempt had been made to keep the dead man's marriage a secret and that it was generally known in the neighborhood where the defendant lived."[494]

The State's next witness was Harold's sixty-year-old widowed mother. Mrs. Louis Beucler agreed with Chew Tobacco that it was well-known in the neighborhood that Harold was married.[495] She testified that "she was going to the front door to lock it behind her son when she heard the shots and he screamed, 'Oh, Mama! Oh, Mama!'" She added that "'[a]s I reached the front door...my son was on the ground and this girl was shooting him. She fired two more shots. I ran to him and got down on my knees and held his head in my arms, and then I heard Mr. Moore say, 'He's dead.'"[496]

The prosecution then called to the stand the two police officers who had arrested and questioned Lucille on the night of the killing. The arresting patrolman, misidentified by the newspaper as William Peterson [probably Sergeant Paul Poretti], said that "he found the girl on the porch of her residence, and that she readily admitted the shooting" and "inquir[ed] if he were dead. When the patrolman answered in the affirmative, he said she asserted, 'I'm glad. Then that muggle-head will never double-cross anybody again.' He said that she produced the gun immediately upon his request."[497] Police "Captain William Peterson, who questioned [Lucille] at the precinct station, also quoted her as admitting the shooting and saying she was glad Beucler was dead."[498]

The State's final witness was Harold's thirty-two-year-old widow, "the former Miss Lilly Bourgeois, whom [Harold] married] two years" before the shooting.[499] "Her husband had taken her to a neighborhood theater the night of November 26, she said, and was to call for her and take her home after closing his place of business. Instead, she testified, a nephew came to tell her that her husband had been killed."[500]

The prosecution rested late on that Monday afternoon. Lucille reportedly "appeared increasingly nervous as the afternoon wore on. She fidgeted in her chair, and finally took off her hat, displaying a profusion of jet-black hair."[501] Judge O'Hara decided to push the trial to its conclusion rather than recessing for the day and continuing on Tuesday. Night had fallen when the defense commenced. Lawyer Luzenberg **Sr.** began the defense by calling three character witnesses, all of whom were Lucille's neighbors in the 2200 block of Elysian Fields.[502] All three testified that Lucille "was known as a quiet girl, and had never been in trouble to their knowledge."[503] Finally, Lucille herself testified in her own defense. "She told her story of the killing for the first time on the witness stand. Previously, she had refused to talk to police, prosecuting authorities, or newspapers."[504]

Lucille's testimony echoed the theme her defense attorney had struck in his opening statement: "Beucler had threatened her several times after she ceased keeping company with him when she discovered he was married and that he advanced upon her menacingly in front of the home of his mother...on the night of the killing."[505]

Lucille testified that "she met Beucler soon after moving to Elysian Fields Avenue two years ago,"[506] as Harold "passed her home on his way to his mother's home."[507] She stated that "they became 'engaged' six months later without her knowing that he was married"[508] after Harold "took her to motion picture theaters, asked her to marry him, [and] won her consent."[509]

> QUESTION BY DEFENSE COUNSEL (Q). Had you ever been out with a man in your life before you met Beucler?
>
> Answer by Lucille (A). No.
>
> Q: Did you know he was married or that he had served a term in the penitentiary for assault and robbery?
> A: No.
> Q: Why did you not introduce him to members of your family and your friends?
> A: He was not an Italian, and I knew that my family would never approve of him because of that. That is why I did not meet him at my home.[510]

She testified that "she overheard a conversation from which she learned that Beucler was married. Thereafter, she refused to see him, and he threatened her, once aiming a pistol at her..."[511]

> Q: What happened after you found out that he was married?
> A: Well, I asked him if it was true, and he denied it, and when I told him that I could not go on seeing him anymore, he kept insisting and following me around and asking me to

go out with him...[512] When I told him I couldn't go out with him anymore, he said, 'I'll see about that.'... Once, he slapped me, and another time, he drew a gun and aimed it at me.[513] [After that, she] took to carrying her brother's .38-caliber pistol in her coat pocket for protection... [She] did not complain to her brother or her friends because she was afraid there would be trouble... [514] I had to carry a gun with me. I did it because he had threatened me.[515]

Asked by her lawyer what happened on the night of the killing, Lucille testified that she was walking to the corner drugstore when Beucler stepped out of his car in front of his mother's house and "stopped her, ordering her to 'wait for him. I didn't know what to do... I wanted to go home and I wanted to go to the drug store and I was nervous and afraid and so I started home, and then about one house down the street, I stopped and waited for him.'"[516] She testified that when Beucler came out of the house, he approached her "and demanded that she go out with him...[517] 'I told him for the last time that I couldn't go out with him, and he started cursing me... I started walking away, and he followed quickly.'"[518] Lucille said that Harold "raised his arm, as if to strike her. 'I kind of ducked and pulled the pistol out of my pocket and started shooting... I don't know how many shots I fired, and I don't know what I did until after he fell down and then I went home.'"[519] She said that Beucler "was running toward his car when he fell."[520]

After Lucille's testimony, the defense rested. It was shortly after 10:00 p.m. Despite the late hour, Judge O'Hara forged ahead. In closing argument, the prosecutor "asked for a verdict of guilty as charged, a hanging verdict."[521] Judge O'Hara delivered his instructions to the jury, and the twelve men retired to deliberate shortly before midnight. "The jury was out one hour and thirty-five minutes," and then returned its verdict of **not** guilty.[522]

Lucille sat expressionless at the defense table, except that her deep brown eyes widened into big circles. Her lawyer, Luzenberg **Sr.**, reached his arm around her shoulder and patted her on the back. A brother and a cousin rose up from the gallery, walked toward her, and surrounded her as an escort. She rose from the defendant's chair. She was free to go, released from prison, free to return to Elysian Fields.

In the aftermath of the trial, Gaetano decided that this girl Lucille needed her mother, who was still in San Cipirello with the Pedalinos, her son Vito (Walter), his nascent family, and three daughters-in-law. Don Tano redoubled his efforts to bring his Angelina back to New Orleans. Entreaties were mailed. Bribes were increased. Angelina's Italian passport was stamped as approved for travel to New Orleans on August 7, 1935, and she obtained a United States immigration visa and identification card at the American consulate in Naples on August 24, 1935. Her US Department of Labor "Quota Immigration Visa [card] No. 142" shows that she arrived in New York aboard the Steamship Rex on October 17, 1935. Her 1942 US Alien Registration Card indicates that she arrived in New Orleans in late November 1935, about eight months after Lucille's acquittal.[523]

If the killing, her jailing in the parish prison for four months, and the ordeal of the trial affected Lucille's future life in any way, it was not apparent. Lucille's redoubtable father, Gaetano DiGiovanni, reputedly once told his son Sugie that Lucille was "my only child with any balls." Despite the reservations she expressed under oath at her trial about her family's unwillingness to accept her engagement to a non-Italian, on April 25, 1940, in New Orleans, Lou married James J. Brown, a strapping American country boy from Manilla Village,[524] an island community in South Louisiana's Barataria Bay established "at the turn of the nineteenth century...[by] a group of Filipinos [who] built raised structures on stilts above the water" and became "one of the forerunners of the Louisiana shrimp drying industry... The platform community flourished for several decades until Hurricane Betsy completely destroyed it in 1965."[525] Aunt Lou's husband served on tankers in the United States Navy in World War II.[526] They had two children who were favorites among my mother's thirty-three first cousins. Aunt Lou's family lived for a while on Louisiana Avenue near the river in the old Irish Channel, before moving to a heavily Italian area in Kenner, where Aunt Lou lived until she died in 1998, shortly before my Nia's own death.

When I was a kid, Aunt Lou was the life of every get-together. Her language was raucous; her voice was booming and infused with a semi-Italian, New Orleans Brooklynese 'Yat accent, always too loud for every occasion. Her laugh was infectious. Her commentary was hilarious. She was Nia's best friend and closest companion, embarrassing my grandmother in public at every chance. "Lena," Aunt Lou shouted out to Nia one day in the lingerie section of Krause's department store on Canal Street. "Ya want me to buy ya a pair of these big drawers?" One Easter Sunday afternoon, when Nia and Lou took the girls to an afternoon matinee at the movie theater and Aunt Lou had stuffed her purse with a chocolate Easter bunny from one of the kids' baskets to avoid the high price of theater snacks, she shouted out again, "Lena, you want a piece of this ear?" Thank goodness, it was not a piece of the chocolate bunny's tail she had broken off for a treat. When I was twenty-one, at a Sunday dinner at my parents' house in Terrytown, shortly after my marriage engagement had been announced, Aunt Lou took me aside. In her usual much-too-loud voice, loud enough for all nearby to hear, she advised me, "You're too young to get married. You ought-ta go out and sow some wild oats first."

Somehow, the Beucler killing and trial were mostly kept a secret from the next generations of DiGiovanni offspring and cousins. It was said that after Aunt Lou died, her family was cleaning out Aunt Lou's things in the house in Kenner and found an ancient *pistola*, wrapped in an old towel, at the back of a high shelf of Aunt Lou's bedroom closet. It was the lawyers and paralegals of the family's baby boom generation, in their curiosity about the family history years after Aunt Lou's death, a few scant weeks before Nia died, who dug out the story of the Beucler killing from the voluminous records. My discomfort with the knowledge was on display on the fourth of July 2015, when my wife, Sue, and I took a guided tour of the historic PT boat restoration project at the National World War II Museum in New Orleans. The tour occurred after I had sworn in newly minted United States citizens at a special holiday ceremony. We were assigned a tour guide by the grateful museum director. Our guide was a volunteer museum docent. I recognized him as a distinguished local lawyer who practiced regularly in the courts. He was friendly, knowledgeable, and accommodating in every way. He had the same name as Aunt Lou's victim and looked a lot like the victim's image I had seen on the front page of the November 27, 1934, *Times-Picayune*. How was he related to Aunt Lou's victim, if at all? I did not ask. I did not want to know. I fidgeted my way through the tour and vowed to myself never to mention our connection to the respected lawyer.

My mother's expression was bafflement and surprise when I showed her the newspaper clippings and police records one day in 2015. Mom handed them back to me, saying only, "I still love her. She was still my favorite aunt. I wonder if my cousins know." Me too, Mom. Me too.

CHAPTER 29

TCHOUPITOULAS STREET

The turbulence of the 1920s and early 1930s—the killings, confrontations with police, run-ins with Fascists, cross-Atlantic comings and goings—largely ended for the DiGiovanni and Guinta families with their move to and ultimate purchase of the Tchoupitoulas Street property in the old Irish Channel along the New Orleans riverfront. If Gaetano remained fixated on bringing the remainder of his family home to New Orleans from San Cipirello, he mostly internalized it. Son Vito "Walter" DiGiovanni's family, Jake's Nanina and her children, and the Pedalinos back in Sicily certainly were not forgotten. For years, the New Orleans branch of the family sent them money, clothing, whatever they could spare, for the Sicilians to use or sell, looking forward to the day when they could bring them all to New Orleans. If Natale remained turbulent and taciturn, at least he avoided any new disputes with the police and other civil authorities and restricted his outbursts to his domestic domain, his home, his living being made in the bar and small restaurant business and the immediate neighborhood. His levelheaded wife and the true loves of his life, his children, Ann and Joe, seemed to settle him down considerably, if not entirely.

Natale's new business was Mr. Joe's Bar, 1169 Tchoupitoulas Street. It was conveniently located near the home of his redoubtable father-in-law, Gaetano, who lived with his wife of almost half a century, Angelina, only a few doors down and across the street at 1116 Tchoupitoulas Street. The barroom was in an old structure built

188

in the classic style of what we sometimes call today a New Orleans tradesman's building. The small edifice that housed Mr. Joe's in its large front room, with the kitchen and the Guinta living quarters in the rear, no longer stands. It was expropriated by the state of Louisiana and torn down in the 1980s to make way for an approach ramp carrying traffic onto the newer of the two Mississippi River bridges that make up what now is called the Crescent City Connection. During the expropriation process, a South Peters Street architectural firm periodically circulated a one-page flier called "GNO Bridge No. 2 *News Briefs*" in which the architects tried to alert the public to the threat posed by the bridge's construction to architecturally significant buildings in its proposed path. One such flier included an architectural drawing of the exterior of Mr. Joe's and described it as: "Nicholas Tormè House. This modest brick shotgun was built between 1835 and 1850 in the Greek Revival style but was altered to the Italianate style in the 1880s. The structure was formerly a four-bay double house with two windows and two doors in front and four rooms deep... The building is significant as one of two survivors of a row of three rare brick shotguns which [*sic*] were built of 'colombage,' brick between posts, an ancient half-timber-like technique that was going out of style as early as 1835. This building has housed a popular neighborhood bar and restaurant for many years."[527]

Nia sold the property to the state in 1982 for the offered $40,000, not wishing to contest the amount although my brother Tom had obtained a professional appraisal valuing it at $50,000. Even $50,000 did not accurately reflect the property's prospective value, which these days might be in the millions, given its outstanding location in modern times. The 1982 appraisal report had explained: "The [1984] World's Fair site is on the downtown area near the subject property. There have been extensive reconditioning and upgrading of property value. Since the announcement by the Mississippi River Bridge Authority of the proposed location of the new bridge the immediate area surrounding 1169 Tchoupitoulas Street corner of Erato Street, has been depressed, due to public knowledge that these properties will be taken for the new bridge route."[528] Today, a slow stroll upriver on Tchoupitoulas Street from the New Orleans Central

Business District into what is now the stylish Warehouse District, with eyes cast downward in a careful search, will locate the building's few remains, some old red bricks barely held together by weeds and crumbling mortar, the former foundation that anchored the bar to its place. A few like the old building still stand. One formerly known as Deno's Bar and then the Blue Marlin, 1128 Tchoupitoulas, across the street and a few doors down from the old Mr. Joe's, reflects what Natale's joint must have looked like.

The front doors of Mr. Joe's opened into a small seating area, with six or eight round-topped, wooden-legged tables surrounded by rickety chairs. A massive oaken bar sprouting a tall beer tap stretched across and in front of a cinder block back wall, separating the business area from the kitchen and living quarters. Shelves holding open-topped White Owl and Prince Albert cigar boxes and the same liquors that had gotten Natale into trouble with the feds just a few years earlier were built into the wall behind the bar. Advertisements in the form of statuary busts, garish posters, and decorated placards bearing the logos of the local beers—Jax, Eagle, Falstaff, Dixie—hung on the wall's bare spots between the bottles.

Natale named the bar after himself. "Mr. Joe" was the respectful sobriquet applied to Natale by all who lived in the Irish Channel neighborhood and the customers who frequented his place. He was **Mr.** Joe, not Joe or Natale or anything more familiar. His bearing, burly physical presence, and reputation, including for violent use of firearms, had earned him nothing but respect—and some level of fear—from the working-class polyglot that made up the neighborhood's residents and his saloon's clientele, including Irish, Italian and German immigrants and a significant number of African Americans. "Every Fourth of July and New Year's Eve when I was a kid," Uncle Joe once told me, "My daddy would go outside the bar with his pistol. There was one of those big old US mailboxes set up on the sidewalk right by the bar. He shot that gun into the mailbox until the gun was empty and the mailbox was full of holes. 'Why you do that, Daddy?' I asked him one year. 'I want-a people around here to know what I can do,' he said. Natale just wanted them to understand what he was capable of."

Two circa 1935 photographs of the inside of Mr. Joe's show Natale standing tall behind the bar. He is strong, erect, and unsmiling. Nia is faintly smiling at her husband's right hand in each picture, holding her infant daughter Ann in one arm. Grandma Angelina stands stolidly on Natale's left in one photo. In another, the slender and beautiful young Lucille, less than one year after her murder acquittal, stands in the background, arms crossed around her midsection, smiling broadly. The patriarch Gaetano stands in the foreground at the bar's front in one of the pictures. Unlike the others clad in working clothes, Don Tano is scrupulously attired in a dark threepiece suit and tie, starched white shirt, and polished dark dress shoes. He wears a fedora on his head. His round-rimmed eyeglasses and professorial smoker's pipe protruding from his closed mouth give him the appearance of a visiting potentate, an image sharpened by his brandishing of a long, unbroken loaf of French bread in his left hand, like a scepter. On Don Tano's immediate right stand his adoring three Towle grandchildren: Catherine with her left arm draped around her Grandpa's back, little Frank and Donnie mugging at their sister's knees.

These same 1935 photographs include the images of three of Mr. Joe's bar patrons, all African American men of the neighborhood wearing the rough hats and clothing of day laborers. They sit at a nearby table or stand at the bar, one remembered by my Uncle Joe only as "N—Terry." I frowned disapprovingly at his use of the N-word. "You don't remember his last name?" I asked. "Listening to my daddy talk when I was a little kid," he said, "I thought Terry was his last name."

The fact that Mr. Joe's was racially integrated in 1930s New Orleans, a place where both Blacks and the White Germans, Irish, and Italians that made up the neighborhood were welcome to eat and drink, is not as surprising as an outsider unfamiliar with the nature of the New Orleans riverfront and Irish Channel neighborhood at that time might believe. Though his Irish last name and appearance belie it, Uncle Mike Stapleton was himself a half-Sicilian. His mother's maiden name was Cuccia. Her family had immigrated to New Orleans from Contessa Entellina in Palermo Province. Contessa Entellina was the real name of "Genuardo," the town whose socioeconomic order and people were profiled by Dutch scholar Anton Blok in his authoritative anthropological study, *The Mafia of a Sicilian Village, 1860–1960: A Study of Violent Peasant Entrepreneurs.*[529] Uncle Mike grew up in the neighborhood around the corner from Mr. Joe's, became my uncle Joe's best man at his wedding, and married Sara DiGiovanni of the Rockford, Illinois, branch of the family. Uncle Mike remembered the neighborhood well and wrote about it himself:

"Racial segregation was a way of life in the South..., and equally so in New Orleans. In my neighborhood, though, there was a sprinkling of Black families...who sort of 'coexisted' with their White neighbors."[530] He recalled that he and his sisters and cousins were playmates of the children of one of their Black neighbors. "The girl's name was Dehlia May, and her brother's name was Major... [We] would often play with Dehlia May and Major, unknowing or uncaring about this thing called 'segregation.'"[531] He remembered fondly other African American neighbors who made a lasting impression: "Theresa [who] was probably in her late twenties...had a steady job at the old Mercy Hospital, and provided for her mother, a friendly and cheerful lady [who] had health problems which kept her confined to the house... Earl was a slow-moving, friendly man in his thirties who lived nearby with his wife...[and was] hired by the owners of [the corner meat] market to run [its] fresh fruit and vegetable stand... Pompey...probably in his late thirties owned and operated a shoeshine stand outside of McGittigan's Bar on the nearby corner of Erato and Magazine Streets,"...and Lionel Fourche, who competed with Earl by "treks through the neighborhood pushing a long cart mounted on automobile tires...loaded with a wide assortment of fresh fruits and vegetables... [T]hese particular people and events have remained in my memory, not for any reason related to race, but because they were some of the influences—the drama, the sadness, and the humor that shaped my thinking and my attitudes about people and relationships that were so much a part of my growing up."[532]

In one of the photographs from inside Mr. Joe's, the Black working man and Mr. Joe's regular Terry is holding a foamy glass of beer in his right hand. Terry's right elbow casually rests on the bar's top as he stands comfortably next to my uncle Joe, then three years old, seated next to Terry on top of the bar. I proudly displayed this photograph in a cherry frame on a bookshelf in my judicial chambers for more than two decades. One day, my friend and colleague Judge Louis Moore Jr. popped in to chat and studied the photograph carefully. Judge Moore was one of the first few African Americans to hold a seat on the New Orleans federal trial court bench. He was a native of Bogalusa, Louisiana, in the piney woods north of Lake Pontchartrain. In his youth, Bogalusa had been the site of some of the harshest Jim Crow laws, racial segregation, Ku Klux Klan activity, and race-hate violence in the state. "Who are these folks?" he asked about the people standing around Terry behind the bar, one of whom—Natale—seemed to be raising a can of beer in a toast with his Black customer. When I told Judge Moore they were my grandparents, he looked at me in amazement. "If your grandpa would have done something like that in the 1930s where I grew up, they would have lynched him," he said.

Judge Moore's impression that Natale Guinta must have been some kind of open-minded civil rights trailblazer was mistaken. Natale was interested in his business, not good race relations or human equality. He employed a Black woman, Mary Dixon, as a cook in Mr. Joe's kitchen, not because of any early urge to equal employment opportunity but for her excellent preparation of the plate lunches and poor-boy sandwiches for sale to the working people who frequented his place and her willingness to work for low wages. He was satisfied to take the money of his Black customers for the beer, liquor, and cigars he peddled in his saloon. Nevertheless, the attitudes of Gaetano, Natale, and Angelina about their Black neighbors and customers at times reflected the same views that many in the establishment White population of New Orleans held against them. As Italians in White New Orleans, they often heard epithets like "dago" and "wop" and "Who killa da chief" aimed at their ethnicity and thick accents. I never heard the N-word come out of the mouths of either of my parents. Natale was the one who introduced me to that word and its most virulent uses when, as a boy, I sometimes accompanied him on his rounds after his retirement from the bar business. Why must some people, even those who were subjected themselves to ethnic or racial hatred, identify a caste to castigate as lesser than themselves?

Their shared attitude about the inferiority of Black lives sometimes exhibited itself in the harshest terms. One lazy afternoon, a customer spent the day filching cigars from the open boxes behind the bar when he thought no one was looking. Grandma Angelina spotted him from the corner of her one good eye. She strolled into the kitchen and returned with a giant meat cleaver. To compensate for her shortness and make her aim truer, she climbed up two small steps that led from the floor of the barroom area to the raised platform behind the bar and swung the machete at the customer's thieving arm. "My mama cut a Black man's hand almost off while she was comin' up the steps...," Nia reminded Aunt Lou during one of their recorded interviews. "Remember when Mama almost cut the n—'s hand off because he was stealing the cigars all afternoon?"[533] On another late 1930s day, little boy Joe sassed a Black customer in the bar. "Tell that old lady to get me another beer," the man had said, referring to Nia or Angelina. "Tell her yourself, you lazy n—bastardo," the little boy sneered, using a phrase he had heard his father often employ. The customer slapped the little boy, discipline for his insolence, but both Gaetano and Natale saw and heard him do it. As the two Sicilians reached for their pistols, the customer immediately realized what he had done and hurriedly ran out of the bar. He must have known Mr. Joe's reputation for gunplay and his capacity for violence. The man disappeared from the neighborhood and was never seen there again. On another dark early evening, the women were cleaning up the kitchen and preparing to end their part of the working day before bar-only service run by Natale at night. Little Ann Guinta was sitting atop the bar, waiting for Nia to finish up and put her to bed for the night. Somebody heard a suspicious scraping sound coming from a little storage shed behind the building. Natale grabbed his pistol from under the bar and raced through the door at the back of the building. Nia grabbed Ann, and she and Angelina headed out, trailing Natale, to see what the commotion was. A Black man from the neighborhood was trying to break into the shed. Natale raised his pistol and aimed at close range. "No, Natale, no. Don't kill him in front of your daughter!" Nia shouted. Natale lowered his arm and did not shoot. The man ran away. "I guess I saved that man's life that day," Mom told me decades later.

I hope that any bigotry in my DiGiovanni-Guinta line stopped with my mother's generation. I never heard or saw any signs of race bias in anything Mom or Dad ever said or did. But maybe it was Nia who showed the earliest signs of some sort of desire for racial harmony and acceptance, even if it was in a way that sometimes caused me to cringe in embarrassment or trepidation. In 1962, I received my First Communion in the old Saint Anthony Catholic Church in Gretna with dozens of my seven-year-old second-grade classmates. Among the little first communicants was my Saint Anthony School classmate, Marlin Gusman, the future New Orleans city councilman and first Black Sheriff of Orleans Parish. Marlin was a true civil rights pioneer at the age of seven. He and his brothers had desegregated St. Anthony School earlier that year when their mother had insisted to Monsignor Rombouts, the German-born Saint Anthony Parish pastor, that her sons should not have to travel all the way to Algiers to attend the segregated all-Black Catholic school, Holy Ghost, when Saint Anthony School was only a three-block walking distance from their nearby Gretna home. Monsignor Rombouts agreed. During First Communion Mass in 1962, Nia was seated in the aisle-side end spot of a middle-row pew as Marlin and I and the rest of our classmates marched up the aisle to begin the rite. "Oh, look at the little colored boy," Nia spoke out, loudly enough to embarrass my mother and for all the gathered worshippers to hear as the procession of children passed her seat. "Ain't that nice." In May 1995, in Chief Judge Morey L. Sear's second-floor courtroom in the United States District Court at 500 Poydras Street, all judges of the court gathered with other distinguished guests, my family, and friends for my formal investiture into office. Among the official guests was United States Attorney Eddie Jordan, appointed by President Bill Clinton to serve as the first African American chief federal prosecutor in the Eastern District of Louisiana. From my spot at the front of the courtroom, right below the bench, I saw the first-ever Black United States Attorney in New Orleans take his seat in the courtroom's front row, in the seat right next to my then ninety-one-year-old Nia. Nervously, I watched a mischievous smile grace Nia's face as she grabbed Eddie Jordan by the forearm, bent her head close to his, and began to whisper God knows what into the chief federal prosecutor's ear. I saw a broad grin spring onto the United States Attorney's face and heard an audible chuckle, his head rocking backward, as Nia finished whatever she was telling him and returned her attention to me. As I mingled in the courtroom after the ceremony, accepting congratulations and expressing thanks, one of the outstretched hands I grabbed and shook was the United States Attorney Eddie Jordan's. "I see you met my grandmother," I said. The same bright grin popped onto his face. "I did. I did," he said. "She's something else."

CHAPTER 30

WAR YEARS

The 1941–'45 World War II years brought an ironical mix of benefits and misfortune to the DiGiovanni-Guinta family. The branches of Gaetano's brood who remained in Sicily suffered both the pangs of war and its oddities. Sicily was the theater of operations in which allied troops led by Generals Montgomery and Patton first defeated and expelled the occupying forces of the Axis Powers from European soil. Along with son Giacomo's (Jake's) wife and children and the Pedalino family of daughter Francesca (Nookie), Gaetano's youngest son Vito (Walter) was still in San Cipirello with his wife and children. Although Vito had been born in New Orleans, he had returned to San Cipirello with the rest of the clan in 1922. "[I]n Italy, you know, you have to serve in the army,…it's compulsory. He had to go into the [Italian] army," Nia explained. Vito saw no action and remained largely on the Italian home front. "That was all right, that was just a kick… He [later] eloped with his wife, [Vincenza "Giuzza" Cannella of San Cipirello], and then he had to come to America,… but he had lost his American citizenship."[534] Apparently, even *Il Duce* had the Italian male's sentimental weakness for a man's family and progeny. The Fascist Italian Army had a rule that excused men with four children from service. Either coincidentally or prudently, Giuzza conceived and delivered Vito's (Walter's) fourth child, in time for her husband to be excused from further Army service before the Allied invasion. When the victorious Americans became the latest of Sicily's foreign occupiers, Vito found beneficial employment springing from his birth in New Orleans and resulting ability to speak English. "Yeah," Nia said, "I had one brother that was lucky, Vito. He was an interpreter for the American government [in World War II]. So when the troops came, you know, the Americans got to Palermo, that's the first thing they did, was bomb it, [then hire an interpreter]. So we sent [Walter] a leather coat, you know, a jacket, so [after the war], we got that jacket back and then two extra ones. He must have switched them or something with somebody else."[535]

Uncle Walter's World War II luck extended to his little son Paolo and was partly responsible for a childhood ambition that Paul ultimately realized. One day in 1945, as the war wound down, Vito "Walter" DiGiovanni's family and the Pedalinos were visited in San Cipirello by their American cousin, United States Navy Lieutenant and future New Orleans Judge Andrew Bucaro. The American war hero showered his cousins with gifts and good cheer. Paolo was most impressed, however, by what the lieutenant was wearing on his left wrist: a large and shiny Longines watch. It was a vintage four-teen-karat gold windup timepiece, sleek and sparkling, with bold Arabic numerals marking the hours and a smaller dial beneath its dead center to tick off the seconds. It was the glint of the watch in the Sicilian sun as Lieutenant Bucaro gesticulated greetings and told stories about the US Navy's wartime exploits that captured the boy Paolo's eyes and imagination. *Man, oh, man*, Paul thought to himself, *if I ever get to the States, I'm gonna get me one of those watches.* Paul realized that dream more than a dozen years later when he used some poker game winnings to purchase a similar wristwatch from an Army PX store during his own 1957–'59 two-year stint in the US Army. The watch now adorns the left wrist of an American DiGiovanni nephew who lives in Houston, Texas, a gift from the young man's Uncle Paul.

While Vito was lucky and little boy Paolo was inspired, Nia recalled that not all in the Sicily branch of the Giunta-DiGiovanni extended family were similarly fortunate in the World War II years. "During the war, this happened in the *Duce*'s last year,…they bombed [the Giunta property in Castelvetrano]. My mother-in-law and one of the grand-children,…Catherine, they were buried under the building. And they lived, they both lived for a while."[536]

Back in New Orleans, no bombs were falling. Sugie "Fedele" DiGiovanni was away in the Navy. Aunt Lou's husband was also in the Navy, serving on tankers. Frank Towle was in the Army Air Corps. The children of the family and their civilian parents were all doing their parts on the home front. "We sang more patriotic songs then, took part in scrap metal drives, bought stamps, and war bonds for the war effort, and included a silent prayer each morning [in school] during our general assembly for our country and those in the Armed Forces," Uncle Mike Stapleton recalled.[537]

Despite their status as alien citizens of a belligerent Axis Power—Italy, and their formal registration as such with the United States Justice Department, the worldwide war was a source of conventional American prosperity that Gaetano and Natale had never previously realized. "The war ended the Great Depression. In 1939, the US had a sluggish peacetime economy with 9.4 million unemployed. By 1943–'44 it was fully employed, making one ship a day and one aircraft every five minutes for the 15 million men and women who would end the war in the armed services."[538] Some of the components of those ships, aircraft, and other necessaries for the war effort were being manufactured, assembled, stored in warehouses, or loaded from or onto cargo ships docked in the Mississippi River at the Port of New Orleans, all within walking distance of Mr. Joe's. Service Foundry, a component of the giant shipyards of Uncle Joe's future employer, Avondale Industries, along the Mississippi River; Dixie Mill; Economy Ironworks and others were located within blocks of

Mr. Joe's and employing three shifts of ironworkers and fabricators around the clock. While Natale continued to sling beer, whiskey, and cigars—particularly in the late hours of the night and early mornings—Mom recalled that Mr. Joe's had morphed during earlier hours into Guinta's Bar and Restaurant, "a small 'mom and pop' restaurant in what is now referred to as the Warehouse District of New Orleans. We lived behind the restaurant. Our cook [Mary Dixon, along with her husband, Poppa Wise] was of African American/Creole descent. Our family,...often, during the week, ate whatever was on that day's menu. Since we catered to working-class men, (longshoremen, laundry workers, warehouse workers, etc.) the menu consisted of 'hearty meals'; things like red beans and rice (always on Mondays in New Orleans because they are slow-cooking and allowed women of the house to do the laundry) and dishes like stew and rice (another New Orleans staple). And fish on Friday due to the large population of Catholics who abstained from meat in those days. Sundays were reserved for family and Sicilian dishes, prepared by or otherwise supervised by my grandmother,"[539] Angelina Bucaro DiGiovanni. The workers in the wartime neighborhood flooded the little restaurant and bar for their odd-hours lunches and dinners and their after-hours beers and whiskey. Natale was the bartender and enforcer of barroom order. Lena (Nia) was the brains of the operation. She kept the books, made sure the income outpaced the expenses, inventoried what supplies were needed, directed Natale to obtain them, and stashed away some of the profits for the family in *la banca*. The profits realized by Natale during the boom war years, when coupled with a nest egg saved for him by his mother back in Castelvetrano, who shipped the proceeds to her daughter-in-law, Lena (Nia), emboldened him after the war to purchase the nice Uptown house on Marengo Street, the spacious and comfortable home that transformed Natale in the last decade or so of his life into a realizer of the American dream.

The banana unloading business at the New Orleans port and the nearby New Basin Canal continued to be the foundation, the locus of Gaetano's standing, authority, and influence as Leoluca Trombatore's right-hand man in stevedore labor placement in the

Italian immigrant community. Uncle Mike Stapleton's memories of banana stevedoring were vivid "as a youngster [who] lived on the corner of Annunciation and Erato Streets, just about a three-block walk to the Erato Street Wharf on the Mississippi River... A newly arrived vessel was a welcome sight because it meant that men would be hired to unload the cargo, and there was a large labor pool to choose from... The work crew consisted of a large group of men going up one gangway and into the hold of a ship, many with a burlap bag folded over several times and placed on one shoulder to serve as a cushion, then coming out and under another gangway, each man carrying a large stalk of green bananas draped on top of the makeshift shoulder pad... It was hard work, and it would continue into the night... Occasionally, one of the workers would flick in our direction one of the many tarantulas that infested the stalks... During the unloading process, loose bananas would fall over the side and into the river. Patches of green bananas would form and be washed under the pier, trapped among the huge support pilings... [T]he water beneath the pier was always littered with green bananas...[and] the big river catfish [were] so used to feeding on the abundant supply of green bananas in the water" that they took on a little of the green hue of the bananas in their skin and the boys who tried to catch them spent their time "dodging tarantulas and fishing for river cat using green bananas for bait."[540]

During the war years especially, the New Basin Canal became Don Tano's particular banana stevedoring domain. The New Basin Canal was a navigable waterway connecting Lake Pontchartrain with the center of the city for cargo transport by barge. Its original 1831 Louisiana legislative charter "called for a 60-foot-wide channel at least 6 feet deep, lined with levees, paralleled with a toll road and towpath, with a turning basin in the city and a harbor at the lake... [Its] turning basin [was] the inland quay where vessels would dock... built at the crux of Triton Walk (now Howard Avenue) and Julia Street, a space occupied today by the Union Terminal parking lot and Loyola Avenue at the foot of the Plaza Tower. The canal right-of-way would run 300 feet wide and 6 miles long... [The canal was built by] cheap Irish immigrant labor(,) [t]housands of Irish 'ditchers'...recruited and sent to the New Orleans backswamp. Digging by hand, the workers excavated the channel in sections, using the fill to form guide levees and roads... The first half of the canal...was completed in August 1834, and the rest in 1835... Freight—including...fruits [and] vegetables—came up the waterway while imports and merchandise flowed out the canal to Mandeville, Madisonville, Covington, and beyond. [Its central city turning basin] became a bustling inland port... The shell road became a key cross-swamp artery... The...channel functioned until after World War II but was finally filled in by the early 1950s—just in time for construction of the Pontchartrain Expressway and Mississippi River Bridge."[541]

Gaetano frequently took some of his grandchildren along with him on his surveys and business trips to the New Basin Canal in the early 1940s. Uncle Joe Guinta; Mary (Ma-Mamie) and Yanks Towle's children, Frank, Donnie, Caddie, and Mary Lou; and Sugie's Angie and Gaetano were his most frequent acolytes. For Don Tano and his grandchildren, these trips were like the promenade of a visiting prince. Sometimes the children would pile into the front seat next to Grandpa behind the wheel of a big Ford touring car and go bumping along the rough road, stopping here and there to mix with the longshoremen and the barge operators. More often, they would travel out to what appeared to be Grandpa's personal domain in one of the little trolleys that ran along the tracks of the shell and gravel road bordering the waterway. Gaetano would walk among the working men, exchanging handshakes and listening to their expressions of gratitude, complaints, or requests. In stark contrast to the laborers, Gaetano was always dressed in suit and tie, a broad fedora resting on his head to shade him from the New Orleans sun. Sometimes he would stop to speak with a worksite foreman, nodding solemnly and gesticulating with his pipe in hand slowly to make some point. Always, the children would be given the green bananas that were closest to ripening to peel and munch for snacks. It was in this setting and during their related travels with Gaetano to visit his *paesani* in the French Quarter shops and markets that they sometimes heard Gaetano referred to as *consigliori* (counselor), *mediatore* (mediator), and *pacificatore* (peacemaker). The deference with which the working

men and their bosses treated Gaetano, his air of authoritative familiarity as he toured the docks and the cargo warehouses, his familiar
glad-handing with seemingly everyone he met gave the little children
the impression that Grandpa was a big shot. In their reflective old
ages, both Uncle Joe and Sugie's Angie told me on separate occasions
that watching as children while Don Tano toured the New Basin
Canal led them to believe that "Grandpa owned all those boats, or
maybe he owned the whole canal."

Gaetano paid close attention to all his grandchildren who lived
in New Orleans. Although Fene's siblings considered their oldest sister a recluse, and Fene (Giuseppina) and Natale treated each other
with contempt stemming from some ancient argument over ownership of a cow, Gaetano took special care of Fene's daughters, whose
father Phillip Ferraro had by that time died. Don Tano treated little
Joe Guinta and his Towle grandsons, Frank and Don, like regents of
the crown. One summer, he took the boy Frank Towle with him on
one of his periodic long train rides from New Orleans to Chicago to
visit the Rockford, Illinois, branch of the DiGiovanni family. Little
Frank and his grandpa were seated peacefully on the aisle of a passenger car aboard one of the Illinois Central Railroad's old lines, the
Louisiane or Creole or Northern Express,[542] forerunners to its legendary "City of New Orleans." As the train swayed northward along
the tracks leaving New Orleans, another passenger, seated directly
across the aisle from Gaetano, a New Orleans yokel judging from his
dress and the accent of his speech, heard Gaetano's Italian accent. He
judged the pair from their swarthy appearance and mannerisms and
began to harass the old man and his little grandson.

"Hey, dago," the passenger said, "what are a couple of guinea
wops like you two doing on a fancy trip like this?" Gaetano ignored
him, but the man persisted. "You greaseball dagos ought to stay
home in your shacks with the rats and your whores and your greasy
little kids."

"Leave us alone," Gaetano said. "I'm going up to Chicago with
my grandson to visit my family."

"Chicago?" the man cried. "Don't they have enough dagos and guineas up there without adding two more? Who killa da chief, who killa da chief?"

In a flash of quickness and agility that the taunting passenger could not have expected of an old man wearing a threepiece suit and tie and sporting a broad fedora on his head, Gaetano rose from his seat. He grabbed at the hilt of a cane he regularly carried with him on his walks on the streets and wharves of New Orleans and on his long train rides to Chicago and New York. In one swift movement, before the man could twitch or flinch or utter another slur, Don Tano pulled a sharp dagger hidden in the hollow inside at the top of the cane and grasped it in his right palm. With his left hand and arm, he grabbed the passenger by the lapel of his coat, his left arm stretched against the gasping man's chest, lifted the passenger from his seat, and pinned him against the half-open window of the passenger car as it bumped along northward. Gaetano placed the sharp blade of his dagger firmly but deftly against the man's neck.

"Shut-ta up, my friend, or I slit-ta you throat and throw you out-ta this window." Gaetano thrust the man back down into his seat and retook his own, quickly slipping the dagger into his cane's hidden compartment. The man stood up speechlessly in fright and fear and skedaddled away down the aisle into another car. No further harassment occurred.

My Godfather, then little Joe Guinta, became the closest pal and confidante of both his father and his grandfather. He accompanied the two men everywhere. He hung out with them in the bar. They told him everything about what they were doing and why in a manner that struck little Joe as instructional. "They knew I could keep my mouth shut," Uncle Joe told me seriously years later, only ten months before he died. Little Joe joined them on their fishing trips and rabbit hunts with Mr. Luke Trombatore and his son Mr. Sam. They taught the boy how to shoot and hunt. He accompanied them on their walks through the Tchoupitoulas Street neighborhood, on some of Gaetano's long train trips to Chicago and New York to visit his DiGiovanni siblings, nephews, and nieces and at the bar in Mr. Joe's as they presided over the business. He strode along at

205

their sides into the Italian-owned groceries and shops located in the French Quarter and through the Vieux Carré's open-air markets as Natale and Gaetano obtained the meats, breads, beans, rice, dried pastas, cheeses, spices, vegetables, cans of olive oil, beer, cigars, and other goods for use in the bar and little restaurant. Often, Joe noticed that, especially when he was accompanying his grandfather, no money passed in exchange for the goods the merchants and grocers willingly and pridefully proffered. "*Bacio la mano* [I kiss your hand], *Zu* [Uncle] Tano," some of the older merchants would sometimes say in greeting Grandpa Gaetano.

It was during these years of their earliest childhood that Uncle Joe and Mom began to develop their close and special relationship, a tight bond that lasted a lifetime. As children, Natale appointed his son Joe to act as his little sister Ann's personal chaperone and body-guard. Whenever little Ann went out into the neighbor-hood, Natale would instruct his son: "Non-ja [don't you] let nothin' happen to you little sister, boy, or I break-a you legs." It was Uncle Joe's responsibility to watch over her as she played in the neighborhood and to accompany her to the talent shows, raf-fles, and movie matinees that were the entertainment fare at the old Coliseum Theater "on the corner of Thalia and Coliseum Streets…, generally referred to as the 'Coliseum Show' or as the 'Cow Shed' by the younger patrons."[543] "We became thick as thieves," Mom told me at Uncle Joe's funeral in 2010. "He was the kind of brother I could tell anything. I could have told him that I was an ax murderer, and he would have said, 'Where do you want me to hide the ax?'"

The war years were also Gaetano's eighth decade and last years of life, a time when an uncharacteristic nostalgia seized him from time to time. At those times, he was sometimes observed at a table in Mr. Joe's, seated and gazing thoughtfully across its front room at his wife Angelina as she wiped down the bar or cleaned the drinking glasses. In those momentary lapses into reflection on the past, he could see the fourteen-year-old Ciminna nymph he had kidnapped and married. He wondered if she appreciated the gift of eyesight, albeit through only one good eye, that he had bestowed upon her by coming to America. He wondered if her constant prayers to the Lord Almighty, through the intercession of the Holy Virgin and Saint Vituum, would be a sufficient *pizzu* (wetting of the beak) to do Gaetano any good in the afterlife. As Gaetano passed his seventy-fifth year, he seemed sometimes lost in thought. Was he contemplating a life of tragedy and triumph; of love and hate; of poverty and prosperity; of peace, respect, and violence; of gain and loss—in short, a full and eventful life? Or was he plumbing his gift of prescience in an effort to foresee what might still come for his family and plan for it? His past interactions with the Sicilian retainers of Bourbon princes, *carabinieri* captains, East Texas lumber camp agents, New Orleans detectives and district attorneys, the Fascist Iron Prefect, the *pezzanovanti* of the banana business, had mostly gone his way. His wife had been the steadfast partner of his Western Sicily premonitions, even in times of extended separation, abandonment, and the tragedies of blindness, nine miscarriages or stillbirths, and a murdered eldest son. The DiGiovanni family had multiplied. He sat on a virtual throne atop a pedestal constructed of his grandchildren's adoration. Gaetano was grateful for his special gifts of judgment, counsel, courage, authoritativeness, and prescience. He was thankful that he had been nobody's *fesso* (fool), that he had always acted "out of a refined moral sensitivity" and that whatever "'esteem and consideration [as] an honest person [he had] been able to gain in public opinion [had been achieved] through his [own] actions.'"[544] Much of what he had foreseen for himself on horseback in the passes of the Madonie mountains, in the narrow passages of Via Garibaldi in San Cipirello and Tchoupitoulas Street in New Orleans had become reality. His tangible holdings in property and treasure were small, but "better a friend on the street than an account in a bank," as he often advised.

Don Tano's final days found him uncharacteristically bed-ridden. His family gathered around him on Tchoupitoulas Street. In the Western Sicilian tradition in which Gaetano remained steeped, despite his long years in America, "each father leav[es his] domain to his eldest son as naturally as a king leaves his kingdom to his heir. A father always takes part in confidential negotiations with the eldest son at his side. The latter never speaks. He looks, listens, and remembers everything, in case the older man were suddenly killed."[545] That was the scene at Gaetano's deathbed. The eldest, Domenico, had been killed a quarter century earlier, which left Jake (Giacomo) and Fedele (Sugie) jointly to take his place as the eldest sons. "Sugie had to come in," Uncle Joe recalled of his grandfather's death. "Sugie was in the Navy at the time, wasn't he? He had to come in from San Francisco… It was right at the end of the war."[546] The sons huddled around their father, bending low over the prone Gaetano as he whispered his final instructions and negotiations with death. The remainder of his nuclear family, minus those who remained in Sicily, stood respectfully at a distance. Mom once told me that at one point in this private final conversation, Uncle Sugie's wife, the classy Philippina, innocently wandered too closely to the deathbed. Gaetano must have thought she was attempting to eavesdrop. Though perhaps mistaken, in one of his last demonstrations of authority and strength, Don Tano raised his head slightly, coughed a wad of phlegm and saliva into his mouth, and spit in his daughter-in-law's general direction, cursing her as a "*puttana*" (woman of loose morals) as she retreated into a corner. Among Gaetano's dying instructions were a reflection of his lifelong gift of prescience: his premonition that one day his entire family would be settled in America. His dying instructions were the same directions he had given his children—and himself—since his own last flight from Sicily in 1928: the families of Vito "Walter" DiGiovanni and Francesca "Nookie" DiGiovanni Pedalino, Jake's wife, Nanina, and her children, Dominick and Angie, must be brought back to America, whatever the cost, whatever the time required to accomplish it. No one who might have heard them reported Gaetano's final words.

Don Tano Baiocco, *Zu* (Uncle) Tano, Gaetano DiGiovanni *fu* (son of) Domenico, the great man of the DiGiovanni-Guinta *cosca*, died on November 6, 1945, almost three months after VJ Day in the Pacific. Of course, with his special gift of prescience, he had foreseen the coming of this day. He was almost seventy-seven years old. Ten-year-old Paolo DiGiovanni was still living with his parents Vito and Giuzza in San Cipirello at the time. News of his grandfather's death arrived there by black-bordered telegram. Paolo was with his best friend, one of the little Todaro boys in the home of Don Pepino Todaro across the street when the telegram was read to him. The causes of death listed on the City of New Orleans Health Department death certificate, prepared by Dr. F. L. Loria, were "acute terminal bronchopneumonia, multiple acute cerebral vascular emboli, hypertensive cardio-renal disease."[547] Gaetano's obituary invited not only friends and relatives but also "employees of New Basin Canal and Shell Road" company to the wake and funeral.[548] The obituary proudly identified his son Sugie as "Seaman First Class Fedele" DiGiovanni.[549] A well-attended wake was held at the old Lamana-Panno-Fallo funeral home on North Rampart Street. I can only imagine who might have been among the distinguished mourners. Perhaps Carlos Marcello, who would be identified in the coming decades as Louisiana's "Mafia Kingfish,"[550] was there with his wife, Jackie Todaro Marcello, daughter of Frank Todaro, a capo to Silver Dollar Sam Carolla,[551] whose son Tony, Sugie DiGiovanni's best friend, must also have been a mourner. The New Orleans Todaros were kin to the Todaro family that lived across the street from son Vito "Walter" DiGiovanni's family, which mourned in San Cipirello, and whose Todaro relatives were identified in the Palermo state archives, unearthed by author Gioacchino Nania, as Mafia leaders in San Cipirello during Gaetano's tenure as *gabelloto* of the Tower of Flowers estate during the 1920s.[552] Leoluca Trombatore, "Mr. Luke...Boss,"[553] must have been there. Angelina saw to it that a Requiem Mass was conducted at St. Teresa of Avila Church at the corner of Camp and Erato Streets.

Gaetano was interred in the DiGiovanni vault on Avenue B surrounded by his fellow Italians at Lakelawn Metairie Cemetery. His coffin rested alongside those of his murdered son Domenico and the unknown, unnamed Trombatore man shipped in from New York in 1931. The simple inscription of his name, dates of birth and death, was not the only way in which Gaetano was remembered. In 1953, eight years after Gaetano died, his grandson, eighteen-year-old Paolo DiGiovanni, was finding his transition to American life after his recent immigration to New Orleans more difficult than anticipated. Paolo's uncle Dominick, Gaetano's nephew who lived in Brooklyn, arrived in New Orleans to visit the family. This Uncle Dominick was the son of Gaetano's brother Fedele (Dominick). Uncle Dominick took Paolo aside and began to question him in a manner Paul took to be an interview for employment in some sort of family business venture. "Nah," Uncle Dominick told young Paolo at the conclusion of their talk. "You're too much Cannella, not enough DiGiovanni." On another day soon afterward, Paul was wandering through the French Quarter, idling shortly before he found his first job, window shopping and popping in and out of the old quarter's little shops. One such place was a small store that sold magazines, newspapers, books, and sundries. Its shelves were stocked with Italian language periodicals of all kinds. Paul lingered over one Italian magazine, absorbing its articles and translating them into English in his mind. The store's proprietor, Mr. Cosentino, eyed Paul closely and came out from behind the counter at the front of the store. He was a short man, older in age, perhaps as old as seventy-five or eighty, stout and white-mustachioed. He was wearing a brimless cloth hat and a dingy white apron over his work clothes. The apron rose up to cover his chest, where a wide pocket contained an order pad, two pencils, and a pair of scissors.

"Who are you, young fellow? You want to buy something?" Mr. Cosentino asked in Italian.

Paul was wary. Had he done something wrong, loitering here in America, something he was not aware was an offense of some kind? "I am Paolo DiGiovanni Baiocco."

The older man eyed him astonishedly. He saw something familiar in Paul's visage and bearing. "Are you related to *Zu* Tano DiGiovanni?"

"*Si, signiore*, he was my grandfather," Paul responded.

The old man took one half-step backward, the better to eye Paul from head to toes. Paul saw the slightest sheen of moisture form in the old man's eyes and a wistful look of mixed sadness and nostalgia cross his face.

"A great man, your grandfather. A great man," Mr. Cosentino said. "Take your time. Please, look around. You can have whatever you want. It is my gift."

CHAPTER 31

PORTELLA DELLA GINESTRA MAY DAY 1947

Paolo DiGiovanni, twelve years old, awoke excitedly in the San Cipirello, Sicily, home of his parents, Vito "Walter" and Vincenza "Giuzza" Cannella DiGiovanni. It was Labor Day, May 1, 1947, the date of the planned May Day celebration, a day of festival, fireworks, picnicking, fun, and adventure, all in honor of the working man. Paolo knew that his uncle Carmelo Pedalino, a leading Communist and labor organizer, felt strongly about the rights of the working man and the significance of the May Day celebration. Young Paolo also knew that his Cannella uncles were themselves working men who labored in the Western Sicilian fields and favored the ideals and goals of the agricultural cooperatives that were attempting to grow in importance and standing. This knowledge and the prospect of a good time sparked young Paolo's idea to sneak away from the rest of his family and join the scores of other children and local townspeople at the bucolic scene of the 1947 May Day celebration, the Portella della Ginestra.

As a matter of class, socioeconomic and political struggle in Sicily, the name Portella della Ginestra is a tragic signpost. As a geographical matter, the Portella della Ginestra is a narrow mountain pass running east-west between two branches of the Madonie mountain range. It is guarded on its northern side by the imposing Monte

Pizzuta, whose eastern shadow casts darkness on the odd town of Piana degli Albanesi. On the southern flank of the pass stands the less impressive Monte Cumeta, the peak of a range running westward to the periphery of San Cipirello. At the end of the steep, curving paths from these two nearby towns and their northwestern neighbor, San Giuseppe Jato, the Portella della Ginestra spills into an open plane at the end of a valley. Today, a stylish bed-and-breakfast, located near the village of Piana degli Albanesi and across a lush valley from the notorious mountain town of Corleone, bears its name. The *Agriturismo Portella della Ginestra* is owned and operated by a "consortium of municipalities in the area, *Cooperativo Placido Rizzotto*, named after a labor leader who was shot dead by the Mafia in 1948... [It includes] an organic farming commune," instituted as one of the "'socially beneficial projects'" that "'all the municipalities in the area [which] were part of a long, violent *mafioso* history...wanted to leave behind.'"[554] The property's converted "seventeenth-century farmhouse once belonged to Bernardo Brusca, the capo of one of Sicily's most brutal crime families."[555] His son, Giovanni Brusca, "known in *Cosa Nostra* circles as '*lo scannacristiani*', 'the man who cuts Christians' throats,'" was the murderer who pressed the detonator of the bomb that killed "leading antimafia investigating magistrate Giovanni Falcone and his wife...and three members of their escort" near the small town of Capaci on May 23, 1992.[556]

The 1947 May Day holiday was observed only weeks after Sicily's April 1947 regional elections, in which "the leftist parties, united in a People's Bloc, made huge gains; they took nearly 30 percent of the vote and became the single biggest [elected political] grouping."[557] Specifically, the "highly successful" election results for the "Communist-Socialist coalition" comprising the People's Bloc landed twenty-nine deputies in Sicily's Regional Assembly while the establishment Christian Democrats totaled only twenty and the ultra-conservative Monarchists won only nine.[558] The election tallies resulted in a greater-than-usual atmosphere of gaiety and celebration for the crowds of working-class people and their leaders as they paraded the mountain paths from the three neighboring towns and made their way to the open festival field through the Portella della

Ginestra. "It was here that peasants came together to celebrate May Day in 1947. Families assembled in their best clothes for a picnic, a song, and a dance; their donkeys and painted carts were decorated with banners and ribbons."[559] Some of the flags were a plain red field displaying a white hammer and sickle. Others were the tri-color red, white, and green Italian national flag or bore the ornate Sicilian nationalist crests of their little towns.

The boy and future New Orleanian Paolo DiGiovanni was among the hundreds of children in the festive, celebratory crowd of thousands. He had left behind his parents, siblings, and cousins at their own smaller picnic in town to join the crowds headed for the larger Portella della Ginestra celebration. Paolo was proudly clothed in a hand-me-down khaki shirt and blue cap with golden emblem from an American Boy Scout uniform. He had recently received the shirt and hat with other used clothes in a package from his aunts, uncles, and cousins in New Orleans, who habitually sent them clothing, blankets, linens, and other items during and after World War II. At first, the May Day celebration was just as he had anticipated. The children in attendance were thoroughly engrossed. Music and games were being played. Kites and colorful banners were fluttering in the mountain pass breeze. Picnic food was being served and consumed. The adults looked on in leisurely comfort and anticipation.

The crowds from San Giuseppe Jato and San Cipirello, led by San Cipirello Mayor Pasquale Sciortino "and the leaders of the respective Chambers of Labour [sic] [had] arrived on the spot at 9:00 a.m., when the group [from] Piana degli Albanesi had not yet arrived. In the meantime, the gypsies spread in groups through the meadows both to rest and to consume the food they had brought. The horses and mules were freed from the *bastis* [sic] and left free to graze or lie on the ground."[560] The planned keynote speaker had been "prestigious Communist leader Girolamo Li Causi... But the day before, Li Causi had indicated that, engaged in another demonstration, he would not [appear]. Giacomo Schiro, a shoemaker, secretary of the Socialist section of San Giuseppe Jato," was substituted as a featured orator.[561] The speakers' podium was "a large limestone rock," the iconic "*Sasso di Barbato*" (Rock of Barbato), where "since 1864,...

Nicola Barbato, socialist doctor, one of the founders of the Sicilian *Fasci* (land reform organization), every year spoke to his people."[562]

Carmelo Pedalino was a Communist leader and a well-known orator who must have been elated by the prospect of a May Day observed in the afterglow of victories by the left-wing People's Bloc of Socialists and Communists in the most recent Sicilian elections. Nevertheless, his children and Paul DiGiovanni himself have said that Uncle Carmelo was **not** present at the historic May Day observance of 1947. One of these descendants said that Carmelo was with his wife and children at a family picnic in a park. However, one digitally published article, citing an investigative report of the police commissioner of Palermo, hints otherwise. "When a first stagger of the Piana [degli Albanesi] group arrived, everyone gathered around" the Rock of Barbato, and the first to climb atop the speakers' rock, while "waiting for the official speaker to arrive, [was] Sign[iore] Pedalino of *Federterra*, [who] started talking,"[563] the blog says.

"At 10:15 a.m., the secretary of the People's Bloc from Piana degli Albanesi [the shoemaker, Giacomo Schiro] stood up amid the red flags to open proceedings. He was interrupted by loud bangs. At first, many people thought they were fireworks, part of the celebration. Then the bullets fired [from machine guns planted in the nearby mountain slopes] by the [bandit gang leader Salvatore] Giuliano's men began to find their mark."[564] Children stood frozen in miscomprehension and confusion. Men dived for cover behind boulders or tried to shield their children and womenfolk from the withering gunfire. A hysterical woman "repeated in an anguished wail, 'Where are my children?'"[565] Paolo DiGiovanni leaped to the ground, his twelve-year-old face planted in the alluvial dirt of the Portella della Ginestra plane. Bodies of the dead and wounded began to fall to the ground nearby. "Ten minutes of machine-gun fire from the surrounding slopes left eleven dead, among them Serafino Lascari, aged fifteen; Giovanni Grifo, aged twelve; and Giuseppe DiMaggio and Vincenzo La Fata, both seven years old. Thirty-three people were wounded, including a little girl of thirteen who had her jaw shot off."[566] "Eight hundred spent rounds of ammunition [were subsequently] found at the scene."[567] When the firing stopped, the boy

Paolo DiGiovanni rose to his knees, then stood and scanned his surroundings in shock. He kept his head and did not cry or shout. He saw one man struggling to plug his own severe bleeding from a garish gunshot wound with a picnic napkin. Paolo could see others of the dead and wounded lying around him. None of them were people he knew. Before he gathered himself to escape the disaster and return to his family in town, Paolo scanned his own clothing for wounds. He was unhurt. But the American Boy Scout shirt he had worn to the festival that day was flecked with small red stains, blood spatter from those around him who had been hit by machine-gun fire.

"The impact of the massacre on the local communities was profound and lasting… [All of Sicily expressed] public outrage at the horrors of Portella della Ginestra…"[568] Although Salvatore Giuliano himself remained at large for three more years, several members of his gang were captured and tried for the crimes committed at the Portella della Ginestra. One of those men was Giuliano's cousin and chief gang lieutenant, Gaspare Pisciotta, who was later discovered to have been "an agent of the *carabinieri*" and traitor to his gang's leader. On July 5, 1950, Giuliano himself was shot and killed at the age of twenty-seven in Castelvetrano, birthplace of Natale Guinta. Various disputed versions of his assassination attributed the killing either to *carabinieri* officers in hot pursuit of the fugitive, to the traitor Pisciotta himself or to *Mafiosi* pursuing vendetta against Giuliano because, "[i]n the summer of 1948, he [had] killed five *mafiosi* including the boss of Partinico."[569]

At his trial, Pisciotta claimed that Giuliano's gang had been ordered to commit the massacre at the Portella della Ginestra by Sicilian Christian Democrat Member of Parliament ("MP") Bernardo Mattarella, a politician with reputed close ties to Mafia chiefs; a Monarchist MP named Ettore Messana; and a member of the old Sicilian landed nobility, Prince Giovanni Alliata de Monreale.[570] All were subsequently declared innocent by the Palermo Court of Appeals after their own trial.[571] Pisciotta was convicted and "given a life sentence for his part in the events at Portella della Ginestra… On the morning of 9 February 1954, Pisciotta was poisoned" with strychnine stirred into a cup of coffee while in his cell "in the Ucciardone prison in Palermo—the mafia's university of crime since the middle of the nineteenth century."[572]

Today, a memorial plaque, erected by the modern political leftists whose philosophical predecessors were the intended victims of the attack, can be viewed by tourists and by older people like cousin Paolo who were its actual victims. A snapshot of the plaque taken by Paolo on one of his many subsequent visits to the place where he was born and was present on that fateful May Day can be viewed in Paul's collection of family photographs and travel souvenirs. The plaque reads: "On May 1, 1947, here on the rock of Barbato, celebrating the working-class festival…people of Piana degli Albanesi, San Giuseppe Jato and San Cipirello…fell under the ferocious barbarity of the bullets of the Mafia and the landed barons…"[573] The plaque's inscription makes no mention of Salvatore Giuliani or his band of murderers, thieves, and kidnappers. Like so much else Sicilian, the plaque, at least in part, lies by omission.

CHAPTER 32

FINAL MIGRATION

Nia was asked during her taped interviews about the place where she had lived in San Cipirello. "So what happened to all the properties in Sicily? Is it in the family still?"[574] Nia's answer was like the uttering of

a solemn promise made to her dying father, Gaetano "Don Tano Baiocco" DiGiovanni. "We sold everything we had to get the Pedalinos [and the families of Jake and Vito DiGiovanni] back to the United States," and Carmelo Pedalino did the same. "He sold everything so my sister, Francesca (Aunt Nookie) could come to America. He went and sold everything, our jewelry, everything, to bring his wife [and family] here."[575] Aunt Lou added, "We did without, you know, to give to them [the family members who remained in Sicily]."[576] Nia explained that it was all to fulfill the late-in-life instructions of her father, Don Tano Baiocco. "We did without so we could have them here because Grandpa used to say [to us] and all his children, 'And you all, you all live here, and you're here because of your sisters and me... Now, you all see about the rest of them. You got a sister with eight [soon to be eleven] children,...[still in Sicily].'"[577] Before his death, the old man had often insisted that Vito's family, Jake's wife and two children who remained in Sicily and his youngest daughter Francesca and her brood would be much better off in New Orleans than in Western Sicily, just as the remainder of his family had been.

Carmelo Pedalino posed peculiar obstacles to Gaetano's decree that all of his family must be brought to the United States. The ideas of land redistribution and uplifting the Italian peasantry of the original late-nineteenth-century *Fasci Siciliani* movement, formed by "the oppressed peasants of western and central Sicily," with the goal of "uniting peasants against the landowners and *gabelloti*," must have appealed to him, but "[t]he *Fasci* had nothing in common with [Mussolini's] militaristic, antidemocratic Fascist movement."[578] Carmelo Pedalino was never a Black-Shirt Fascist. Instead, Mussolini's Fascist regime drafted him into the Italian Army, and he rose to the rank of lieutenant. A framed photograph saved in the Pedalino family records shows him standing alone in the snow of an unknown wartime location dressed in the infantryman's cap and long overcoat of an Italian Army officer. Nia said that as a drafted Italian soldier, "he fought for Franco [in Spain], then he fought for Mussolini['s]" army in Albania and Greece.[579] As a man of principle who truly believed in the rights and advancement of the poor and the working man, he was disgusted by the Fascist Party's many failures, including especially its failure to lift Sicily's peasants from poverty and landlessness. When the Germans stormed into Italy, Carmelo left the Italian army and became a nationalist partisan. The Germans captured and interred him when he was caught sabotaging German communication lines. He was released after a few months when a priest who was a Pedalino family friend intervened on his behalf. Carmelo later joined the Communist Party and became a union organizer. After the death of his father-in-law, Gaetano, his political activities and public profile intensified. He became a recognized voice of the Italian Communist Party, whose ascendency in Sicily was more and more being viewed as a threat by the established powers of the Christian Democrats, the large landowners and the Catholic Church. He was a frequent speaker for Communist causes and union organizing in the town squares of the several small villages around San Cipirello and his birthplace, San Giuseppe Jato.

Around Christmas time 1944 or '45, word spread in one of the little villages that Carmelo Pedalino would be giving a speech. The Communist firebrand's oratorical skills, intelligence, and persuasiveness were well-known. Word that Carmelo would be speaking was sure to draw a large crowd, and one quickly gathered that night to absorb what Carmelo had to say. He began his speech with his usual call for justice and land redistribution for the working man. He railed against the oppression of the powers that held them down. One of those powers was the Catholic Church, whose representatives he asserted were unworthy of the goodness of the people for whom they claimed to minister. He identified as an example a local priest, whom Carmelo accused of lustful and decadent fooling around with an unnamed married woman of the town. This was a heretical and hypocritical charge in the minds of the faithful among the townspeople, coming from a man whose reputation for piety was not exactly pristine.

Many in the crowd loudly determined that this speech had gone too far. The crowd, which had been receptive seconds earlier, turned to an angry mob. They shouted curses and threats and flung invectives and rocks picked up from the ground at the slanderous Communist rabble-rouser. Carmelo hurriedly fled under the protection of a small entourage of fellow travelers, his life and limb clearly in danger. Many in the mob armed themselves with guns and clubs and searched for him from house to house. The mob swarmed angrily to a place in town where they mistakenly thought the fugitive was hiding. Carmelo had already absconded into the mountains, leaving his family behind. Nevertheless, the mob surrounded the house and pounded loudly on its shut front door and windows, demanding the fugitive's surrender. From out of nowhere, Don Nardo Battaglia, a known *uomo de rispettato* (man of respect) appeared on the balcony of a building across the street. He raised his right hand, his open palm pointed at the crowd. He shouted in a commanding voice. "No more, people. Go back to your homes. Carmelo Pedalino is the son-in-law of *Zu* Tano Baiocco DiGiovanni. He cannot be harmed." The crowd dispersed.

In 1946, shortly after Carmelo's accusations against the local priest, American author, political activist, and wife of the publisher of *Time* magazine, Clare Booth Luce, converted to Roman Catholicism.[580] She became "ostentatiously Catholic."[581] "[D]uring the 1952 presidential election,…she campaigned on behalf of Republican candidate Dwight Eisenhower, giving more than 100 speeches on his behalf…, [including] anti-Communist speeches on the hustings, radio, and television."[582] In 1953, President Eisenhower appointed her United States Ambassador to Italy, where "'[h]er admirers…—and she had millions—fondly referred to her as *la Signora*, 'the lady,'" but "[t]he country's large Communist minority…regarded her as a foreign meddler in Italian affairs."[583] Ambassador Luce made her first official trip to Sicily in December 1953.[584] At that time, Carmelo Pedalino had remained in Sicily, with some of his family already in New Orleans, and his standing in the regional component of the Communist and then the Socialist Party in Sicily had risen to a point of public prominence. A photograph of Ambassador Luce's arrival at the Palermo airport on that trip shows her being welcomed by the leading men of the Sicilian regional government. One of those men is an assistant to the governor of Sicily, a top Communist/Socialist official, Carmelo Pedalino. A tall *carabinieri* captain stands directly behind him, camera in hand, photographing the occasion for posterity and official police surveillance files.[585]

Some of the Pedalino family, including matriarch Francesca (Nookie) and six of her children, first immigrated to New Orleans in November 1950, shortly after Uncle Jake's wife, Nanina, and their two children, Angie and Dominick, and three years after the Portella della Ginestra massacre. Nia once said, "You remember, we had to furnish a house here so they could stay in it."[586] Carmelo and the rest of his children remained behind in Palermo, intending to emigrate shortly thereafter. They were stopped by the US State

Department from quickly doing so, however, because Carmelo was then a Communist. Carmelo's devotion to his large family was as deep and as true as his adherence to his social and political philosophy. Nia said that shortly after Nookie and most of her children arrived in New Orleans, "one of [Carmelo's] sisters called me [and said], 'My brother's crying for his wife and his children, and we don't know what to do. We might put him in the *manacomio*,' that's the nuthouse, because he was grieving for his wife and his children…"[587] When the last of the Pedalino family came to America in 1955, after two had arrived in 1953, Carmelo's entry was delayed by a few weeks. The US State Department resisted because of Carmelo's Communist past even though he had by then formally switched his political party affiliation from Communist to Socialist.

Vito "Walter" DiGiovanni also returned to New Orleans sometime around 1950, leaving his family temporarily behind in San Cipirello because his departure was enabled by special circumstances. The influential father of Tony Carolla, best friend of Walter's brother, Uncle Sugie back in New Orleans, was Sylvestro "Silver Dollar Sam" Carolla. After years of trying, the US Justice Department succeeded in deporting Silver Dollar Sam "on May 30, 1947, [when he] was escorted by immigration officials to Galveston and flown to Sicily on a military transport."[588] Carolla surreptitiously returned and was "allegedly seen back in New Orleans as early as July 4, 1950."[589] Vito (Uncle Walter), originally an American citizen by virtue of his birth in New Orleans but whom Nia claimed had forfeited his citizenship as a World War II conscript in the Italian army,[590] tagged along with Sam. They traveled from Palermo to Canada, then into Detroit and home to New Orleans. Vito's (Walter's) wife Giuzza and their children, including eighteen-year-old Paolo DiGiovanni, and two of the Pedalino children arrived in New Orleans in 1953, shortly before "when Ann got married" to Joe Wilkinson, as Nia said. After arriving in New Orleans, Walter (Vito) trooped down to the old US Customs House on Canal Street and attempted to regain his compromised United States citizenship by telling the government officials the absolute truth. They subjected Walter to a formal, highly bureaucratized reapplication process. The English-speaking, American-born Walter filled out all the forms and pursued the process assiduously. It took years, but his dogged determination was successful in the end. Uncle Walter officially regained the American citizenship that Mussolini's conscription had robbed from him.

The Pedalinos's settlement in America was not without challenges. Carmelo had a difficult adjustment to life in New Orleans. He could not work in his Italian profession as an engineer. "You see," Nia said, "this whole [Pedalino] family was either teachers or doctors or something,...[Carmelo] had degrees when he was living there [in Sicily], but because he didn't have English, they wouldn't hire him in any of these [American] institutions. He had to go to Tulane and take these classes" to hone his English and become recertified to work as an engineer in the United States. For a while, Jake and Sugie relied on Don Tano's old connections and got Carmelo work "to unload the banana boats," Nia said.[591] Government men in suits would sometimes show up at the family home to ask Carmelo questions. In America, Carmelo also endured the derision and resentment of the DiGiovanni men and their ally, Lucille, because of his rabble-rousing past, the financial burdens they had undertaken in following Gaetano's direction to bring the Pedalinos and other DiGiovanni family members to America and their disagreement with his political views. The rough-and-tumble blue-collar DiGiovannis sarcastically called the well-educated Carmelo "*Il Professore*" (the professor), especially when he went to work temporarily on the banana boats. They ridiculed him when he became a frequenter of the First Baptist Church of New Orleans on St. Charles Avenue, where the congregation attempted to help Carmelo with his English lessons, job placement, and reconciliation with God. According to Nia, it was Uncle Jake DiGiovanni, or perhaps Uncle Sugie, who first said of Carmelo, "'The bastard. First, he was a Fascist. Then he was a Communist. Now he's a Baptist.'"[592] Even after Uncle Carmelo died and was buried in Metairie's Garden of Memories in 1974, his legacy endured with the humbler people of Western Sicily who remembered him for his land reform and labor organizing efforts on behalf of the peasants. The peacemaking Lena (Nia) attempted to keep Nookie close to her heart and home, especially so that Nookie and their mother, Angelina, could see each other with the Pedalino children. Her efforts were not enough. A rift developed between some of the Pedalinos and the DiGiovannis because of their derisive treatment of Carmelo, political and other differences, and the perception among some that sides must be chosen. Long after Carmelo's death, some of the Pedalino women regretted that they had not attended their Aunt Lena's (Nia's) funeral, saying "she was always so good to our momma." It had been forbidden by some of their brothers.

CHAPTER 33

WIDOWHOOD PART 1

No loneliness beset Angelina Bucaro DiGiovanni in her widowhood. She mourned Gaetano's passing in the old style. She wore black exclusively for long years, even dying her underwear black. She lit a second votive candle, contained in a small red vase, and placed it on her bedroom dresser next to an identical candle that was already burning for her murdered son Dominick. Both candles blazed for the rest of her life, two eternal flames flickering to the praise of the Almighty and constant prayer for the salvation of the immortal souls of her husband and eldest son.

At first, Gaetano's death had been a shock. Angelina could not remember Gaetano ever before having been sick or weak. She—not he—was the one who had always been afflicted: with smallpox and blindness in Sicily; with miscarriages and stillbirths in Tunis, Texas, and New Orleans; everywhere with a constitution that left her prone to this minor ailment and that. It seemed to her that Gaetano was impervious to illness and affliction, either physical or emotional; that he was a man of steel. She had never before connected her husband with death unless it concerned someone else's death. In short order, the shock turned to anger—anger that Gaetano had abandoned her again; abandoned her to the Fascists as he fled from San Cipirello; abandoned her to Tchoupitoulas Street as he rode the train to Chicago; abandoned her for the Erato Street wharf and the New Basin Canal as he tended to his domain of bananas and stevedores.

225

Like the shock, however, her anger did not persist. At Gaetano's wake, she recognized that her anger was misplaced. It was near the end of the Requiem Mass at St. Teresa of Avila Church that the shock and anger turned to sadness, and the next phase of her grieving, intermittent sobbing, began.

It was the ever-vigilant Lena, my Nia (Antonia), Angelina's most attentive and felicitous child, who recognized the sadness and took steps to address it. Nia's little daughter, Ann, was not quite ten years old when Gaetano died. When the family returned to Tchoupitoulas Street from Lakelawn Metairie cemetery on the day Gaetano was put to rest, Nia took little Ann aside. "Come on inside," Nia said. "We're gonna pack a little bag for you, so you can go down the street and stay with Grandma for a while so she won't be alone until we fix up a room for her with us." It was not a long trip or a long-distance separation. The Guintas lived behind Mr. Joe's in the same 1100 block of Tchoupitoulas Street and only a few doors down. The females of the new nuclear family, Angelina, Lena, and Ann, frequently traversed the short distance between 1116 and 1169 Tchoupitoulas Street. They were in each other's residences as frequently as they were in their own. For a stretch of weeks, however, Ann was with Grandma at 1116, whenever it was time for evening prayers and sleep. That was the beginning of a seven-year period, from age ten until age seventeen, when Mom began to prepare for her own marriage, that Ann Guinta and Angelina Bucaro DiGiovanni slept together in the same big bed, comforting each other, telling each other stories until they both fell asleep. Angelina told little Ann about her own odd courtship and coming of age. Ann told her Grandma about the wonders of what she was learning in school and about her teen-aged ambition to get married and have a dozen or so children of her own.

It was this period of closeness, among other things, that convinced Mom in her own mind that she was Grandma Angelina's favorite.

"Why would you think that, Mom?" I asked her one day in 2010. I was a little incredulous that Old Ma-Maw would single out Mom among her thirty-four grandchildren as her favorite.

"Why do you think they gave you the old horseshoe and key from the house in Sicily?" she asked. "Because you're my oldest, and all the cousins know I was Grandma's favorite."

I looked at her askance. Was this not Sicilian self-pride, "the unbounded passion of h[er] own ego in h[er] bloodstream—the *mafioso* in a nutshell,"[593] showing itself in my own mother? She saw the look of skepticism on my face.

"I'll give you another example," she said. "When they were living on Marengo Street and I was married and gone, and you kids were still little, we would go over and visit a lot. Grandma and Nia kept a lot of toys there for you kids to play with. When we would get ready to go back to our house in Terrytown, Grandma would bustle around the house picking up all those toys, and she would hide them in the back of her closet so your cousins couldn't find them when they came over to visit. I'd tell her, 'Grandma, you don't have to do that. Let Joe's kids play with them too.' Grandma would say, 'Sure I gotta hide 'em. Those other kids will break these toys if I don't hide 'em.'"

At times, it was little Ann whose fear and sadness over the loss of her Grandpa needed more in the way of care and concern than Angelina needed from her younger incarnation. At those times, it was Angelina who loaned her own strength to little Ann with oft-repeated words of concern for her granddaughter more than concern for herself. Ann would remember Grandma DiGiovanni's words in later times of trouble in her own adulthood: "*Coragio, figghia mia, nun ti scantare*" (Courage, my daughter, don't you be afraid).[594]

It was Gaetano's immortal soul that concerned Angelina most of all. Could it be saved from the eternal damnation men seemed so foolishly intent on courting during their mortal lives? Were not the works that Gaetano had wrought in the interests of his family during his lifetime righteous and just in the eyes of the Lord? Certainly, the merciful and forgiving God in whom Angelina believed would judge Gaetano's life in that vein. But why take chances? Even in the face of Gaetano's earthbound spiritual disinterest and the living of his life in accordance with the Western Sicilian code of *cavalleria rusticana* (rustic chivalry) rather than the Ten Commandments, Angelina had always been a devout, observant, and faithful Catholic. She was a fervent believer in the saving power of God's own Son and the potent interventions available through the Virgin Mother and the communion of saints. She employed every tool available for the salvation of Gaetano's soul through the gifts bestowed upon the faithful by the Almighty through his Holy Church: holy cards and vials of holy water blessed by the local priests; daily rosary recitations; little statuary icons of the Blessed Saints and the Virgin herself; bedroom wall hangings depicting the Sacred Heart, Mary's Ascension into heaven and her crowned depiction as Our Lady of Prompt Succor; and the constantly flickering votive candles. She was convinced that Gaetano's immortal soul could be saved, if only she personally worked hard enough at it. Angelina embraced the essence of Psalms 146–9. "The Lord protects the stranger [foreigner], sustains the orphan and the widow..."[595]

In the early 1950s, Natale Guinta leased Mr. Joe's at a healthy rate of monthly rental income to new operators, brothers Bob and Adam Ciuffi of St. Bernard Parish, who renamed the place Vic's.[596] He and Lena moved the family from the cramped old living quarters behind the barroom to the spacious, clean, quiet, and stylish New Orleans uptown house that they bought at 1113 Marengo Street. In their new home, they could live among the Americans in total middle-class comfort. At Nia's absolute insistence, overcoming the hesitation of both Angelina and Natale, Grandma DiGiovanni moved to Marengo Street with them. They had never before lived in such comfort.

Angelina was given her own bedroom, a private area in the very back of the linear house. She transferred all her religious artifacts and displays to her new little room, which she kept in a constantly darkened state. The window curtains were shut tight at all times to enhance the brightness of the ever-flickering votive candles and maintain the little room's chapel-like atmosphere. When her teenage granddaughter, Ann, first brought her boyfriend and future husband, Joe Wilkinson, around the Guinta home, the young American intuitively recognized the importance of winning over Angelina to his cause in the courtship of her reputed favorite. Young Joe repaired to his art class at Redemptorist High School in the old Irish Channel in his senior year, 1952–'53. There, he refurbished a three-foot-long and two-foot-wide wooden carving of Christ dying on the crucifix. He painted the cross and the crown of thorns in realistic wood hues and the body of the dying Christ figure in realistic flesh tones. He used a garish shade of bloodred at Jesus's palms, feet, forehead, and side; the stigmata, where the Roman soldiers had inflicted their torturous wounds at the direction of Caiaphas and Pontius Pilate. A more frightening and realistic depiction of the horrors of the Crucifixion was never seen. Young Joe presented it to Grandma DiGiovanni as a gift. She loved it. She hung it on her bedroom wall, directly across the pillow on her bed so that she could see and pray to it before falling asleep. Despite his thorough Americanness, Joe Wilkinson was immediately accepted as a suitable future grandson-in-law.

On Marengo Street in her very old age, Grandma DiGiovanni's rigid routine became set on three daily functions: prayer; housework in the form of constant, obsessive cleaning, cooking, and the hand-making of cheese and pasta; and vocally virulent arguments in Sicilian dialect Italian with her son-in-law Natale. Her young great-grandchildren—myself and my older siblings and male Guinta cousins, who were constantly underfoot in her house on frequent visits to Marengo Street, could observe and hear her engaging in all three. Angelina conducted her prayer sessions in the seclusion of her back bedroom, but she left its door open at all times to maintain her connection with the goings-on of the house. She knelt at the foot of her bed, even in her old age, or sat on the bed's edge and prayed more often than the five-times-a-day regimen of the Muslims who had founded her Western Sicily birthplace of Ciminna after the ninth-century Arab conquest. Her daily arguments with Natale were volcanic outbursts that echoed throughout the house like an eruption of the Sicilian Mount Etna. Their arguments sometimes drove the little great-grandchildren through the screen door of the kitchen into the side yard and Nia into the room to separate them and restore order. Angelina and Natale yelled at each other, arguing over God knows what, in that language more suited than any other to histrionics and the casting of ritualistic curses—Sicilian dialect Italian. They waved their arms at each other and pointed their fingers, gesticulating wildly. Occasionally, Natale would pound a tabletop or slam a door, and Angelina would wave her thick round lasagna rolling pin in the air in his direction. I never saw them come to actual blows. The language they employed alone seemed a sufficient substitute for actual violence.

But cleaning and cooking were Grandma Angelina's most frequent avocations. Her cooking was fantastic. Little discs of hand-

made goat cheese were constantly stored in a small open platter in the simple 1950s era refrigerator. She baked Italian cookies of all kinds for her great-grandchildren. She made her own pasta, first dusting the top of the kitchen table with a little flour to prevent sticking, then flattening out the dough that she had prepared separately on a nearby countertop, pressing forward and backward on her round wooden pin until the dough had been rolled out to an acceptable level of thinness. She would train her one good eye, saved for this purpose by Dr. Dugan of New Orleans in the first years of the twentieth century, on the raw leveled-out pasta, then cut it into strips with a sharp knife for whatever purpose she had settled upon: broad flat noodles for lasagna, long strips of thin rope for spaghetti, folded-over pockets of pasta for stuffed cannelloni. A pot of scarlet sauce bubbled constantly on the stovetop, a heaving mass of onions, garlic, celery, basil, thyme, oregano, salt, pepper, olive oil, and crushed tomatoes picked from the garden Natale maintained in the side yard.

The very second her cooking, pasta-making, or baking was complete was the self-same moment when she cleaned up whatever mess she had made. Angelina Bucaro DiGiovanni cleaned incessantly, as she had done throughout her wifely lifetime, sometimes more than twice a day. She swept and mopped the floors, wiped down tabletops and countertops, scrubbed the tub, sink, and toilet of the home's single bathroom, dusted everything from furniture to drapes and woodwork molding. She washed the family clothing and linens in the Maytag in the kitchen, then hung the wet clothes out to dry in the blazing New Orleans sun on lines Natale had draped between two poles in the yard. She washed and dried the pots, pans, dishes, eating utensils, and glassware from every meal and cooking effort by hand. It was her habit, much to Natale's vocal irritation, to begin to clear away the dirty dinner plates and utensils before the eating was completely finished, so she could get a head-start on the cleaning. On the night before she died, all her great-grandchildren were lined up outside her room to enter one by one and kiss her goodbye. When the little children left the house, she rose from her deathbed and swept the place clean. Mom later told us her last words before she died the next morning: "This house could use a good cleaning."

Angela Bucaro DiGiovanni, matriarch of *la famiglia*, died on February 9, 1965, at the age of seventy-seven. Her obituary reported not only the names of her nine children, living and dead, but that she was "also survived by thirty-three grandchildren [one more would subsequently be born], forty-five great-grandchildren [more were on the way], and two great-great-grandchildren [many more would make their marks in the decades to come]."[597] Her wake was the first I ever attended, conducted of course at the Lamana-Panno-Fallo funeral home on North Rampart Street. I was not quite ten years old but old enough to attend an occasion of this kind of magnitude in the family's history. It was the first time I ever saw the preserved body of someone I loved laid out in an open coffin, surrounded by fragrant flower bouquets. The turnout of mourners was enormous. A stir occurred when Carlos and Jackie Todaro Marcello entered the parlor to pay their respects in person, each taking care to shake the hands of Old Ma-Maw's nephew, Judge Andrew Bucaro, and her son, Uncle Sugie. I was stricken by the mixed emotions on full display at the wake: the silent weeping of the surviving women; the solemn expressions of grieving men, holding their heads in their open palms as they contemplated mortality; the occasional outbursts of laughter and chuckles as the mourners recounted moments of hilarity in the broad history of Angelina's family in their memorial storytelling; the shrieks and pitter-patter of the feet of little children as they were allowed to run and play in the funeral home, just as Old Ma-Maw would have wanted. After a Requiem Mass at St. Stephen's Catholic Church near the Marengo Street residence, Angelina was interred with her husband and eldest son in the DiGiovanni family vault in Lakelawn Metairie Cemetery. A small statue of an angel, a young and winged Angelina, safeguards the spot at the base of the vault on Avenue B.

CHAPTER 34

MARENGO STREET

The home where Angelina Bucaro DiGiovanni of Ciminna died and lived out her last years was the final realization of Natale and Lena "Nia" Guinta's shaky and perilous climb to achieve the American dream. In September 1953, they purchased the classically New Orleans house[598] in the solid, tree-lined, decidedly middle-class Bouligny faubourg.[599] Its location was idyllic, even more desirable and expensive today than it was in the 1950s. In one direction, it was walking distance, four-and-one-half blocks, to the stylish and beautiful St. Charles Avenue, where the expansive mansions of some of the old money families of New Orleans stand. Then and now, open-windowed streetcars with clanging bells traverse its broad neutral ground from the New Orleans Central Business District, through the Garden District to the oak-lined University section, and on through Old Carrollton, formerly the separate municipality known as Jefferson City before its annexation in 1870 into New Orleans itself. In the other direction, it was eleven blocks from the Mississippi River and walking distance, only two-and-a-half blocks, to the little commercial strip of shops, groceries, eateries, and drugstores on Magazine Street. The new house was the site of the wedding reception of Joe Wilkinson and Ann Guinta on June 26, 1954, and of family gatherings of all kinds for years thereafter.

The house itself was wood-framed, painted white, with the dark green trim of storm shutters on its windows that people in New

Orleans call "French Quarter green." It was raised off the ground on red brick pillars. The house sat on the right or Mississippi River side of its lot as a passerby might view it while standing at its front on

Marengo Street. On the left or Lake Pontchartrain side of the lot was a fenced-in side yard. The yard was a small green oasis where Natale nursed his fig and Japanese plum trees, green bean vines growing on the side fence, mint and basil bushes sprouting in its gardens and wooden-staked tomato bushes rising alongside the fence that separated the yard from Mrs. Dimm's house next door. A driveway rose from Marengo Street into the side yard. It was two thin strips of concrete on which Natale's 1953 Chevy, "the Blue Flash," would occasionally be parked, but only when it was not being consigned to the street's front curb so Natale could minister to his side yard agricultural pursuits. At the end of the driveway in the back left corner of the lot was Natale's "shed." Its sidewalls, roof, and hinged doorway were constructed of corrugated tin, which had rusted some in the New Orleans rain and sun. It had been built by the house's previous owners as a storage place for their automobile, but Natale did not use it as a car's garage. Instead, he employed its roof to grow snaking vines of cucuzza plants. Natale periodically harvested its long conical green squashes for preparation in tomato gravy by old Ma-Maw. Inside the shed, he built little pens along one wall, which he covered in chicken wire. The pens held little chicks and bunny rabbits that he bought to amuse his grandchildren, especially at Easter time. We gave these little animals names and treated them like pets, and Natale helped us name them. Two of my little chicks were named Choonga and Mary.

The inside of the Marengo Street house was constructed in the classic New Orleans shotgun style, with the rooms running linearly so that every room, except the bathroom, had to be entered and exited to walk from the front to back. The front entry door off the porch opened into a small, separate rectangular foyer, with a door at its back that opened onto a long and narrow side yard porch. A sharp right turn from the foyer opened to the living room, containing a sofa, two comfortable chairs, and a black-and-white television set. The living room flowed into a double parlor, which could be closed off from the living room by shutting hidden pocket doors. This room was originally designed for use as a formal dining room, and perhaps it was employed for that purpose at some point. I remember it exclusively as the bedroom where Natale slept alone in his old age. Into the house through the parlor/bedroom was a short hallway with a door on its right that opened into the house's only bathroom. Beyond the bathroom was the large kitchen, which held not only all of the usual kitchen appliances and sinks but also a pantry and kitchen table and chairs where family meals were both prepared and eaten. The kitchen had two doors to the outside, one on the riverside that opened onto a small porch that was the entryway to the house's connected side apartment rented by the widow Mrs. Kingsmill; the other opened onto the long side porch that overlooked Natale's garden and shed in the side yard. Through the kitchen was the largest bedroom where Nia slept and at the very back of the house was Grandma Angelina's dark and chapel-like bedroom. Until the 1970s, when small window units were installed, the house was not air-conditioned against the sweltering New Orleans summers. Instead of air-conditioning, each room was outfitted with floor-to-ceiling windows, designed to catch the occasional Canadian cool front or breeze from the Mississippi River only eleven blocks away. Giant electrical box fans were mounted to the upper parts of the windows. The fans spun and whirred when no north winds from cool fronts or river breezes were available.

It was on Marengo Street that Natale Guinta, at last, conducted himself and his life in a manner that looked like American conventionality. He took on the persona of a retired country squire. He clothed himself almost always in dark-colored heavy cotton trousers and unpolished working man's laced shoes; white cotton socks; and a white, short-sleeved T-shirt. On the rare cold day in often-tropical

New Orleans, Natale would don a light corduroy or leather jacket, needing nothing heavier to ward off any chill. He had some favorite pastimes. One was attending to his small plots of fruits, vegetables, herbs, and flowering hydrangeas that he grew in his fine home's narrow side yard. Another was simply driving short distances in "the Blue Flash" to purchase the provisions his small yard could not produce on its own. Perhaps Natale's favorite retirement avocations were hunting and fishing. He kept a ferret named "Pete" as a pet because in his Sicilian boyhood ferrets had been used to hunt rabbits. He tied a small cypress flatboat to a tree on the batture of the Mississippi River near the old Woodland Plantation at Port Sulphur, Louisiana, and used the boat for hunting ducks and other critters in the South Louisiana marsh. When his son, my uncle Joe, returned home from his Air Force training program in California in the 1950s, he visited the plantation and found the old rope still tied to the tree and partially covered by the wet river sand. He dug his right hand into the sand and felt the bow of his father's old cypress boat, still intact but buried by years of alluvial silt pushed downstream by the mighty Mississippi. One day, Natale's grandsons will have to organize an expedition downriver and see if they can dig up this family relic and preserve the cypress boat as a testament to the old-age humanity of Natale Guinta.

For the first time in his life, it was in his older age on Marengo Street that Natale Guinta began to exhibit a grandfatherly, even kind and gentle, side of his nature. No one who might have known Natale as a *gabelloto's* oldest son in the olive groves of Castelvetrano, or an infantryman in the Italian army's horrific World War I Alpine theater of war, or on the dark 1920s streets around the French Quarter's "circle of death," or in the whiskey unloading houses of Nathan Goldberg's bootlegging gang, or as Mr. Joe in the Tchoupitoulas Street barroom might have believed some of the things that he did during these days. Make no mistake, he did not transform entirely into Mr. Fred Rogers.[600] The tempestuous daily arguments with Angelina still erupted. Uncle Mike Stapleton, who was Joe Guinta's best friend and life-long companion from the 1930s through the end of Natale's life, once said, "For all those years I knew your grandpa and was around him, even at Joe and Pat's or Ann and Joe's weddings, I can't ever remember seeing that man smile."

Smiles or no smiles, after the Pedalinos made their final immigration to New Orleans in 1953, the younger Pedalino and DiGiovanni men would sometimes visit their Grandma Angelina on Marengo Street. "My brother Dominick used to complain to me about your grandpa," Paul DiGiovanni once told me. "'Uncle Natale is a mean guy. When I go to his house, he tells me 'Domenico, go home.' I'd say, 'Dominick, what-cha talkin' about? Uncle Natale's nice to me. He's funny too.'" For reasons known only to himself, Natale singled out teen-aged immigrant Paolo DiGiovanni for treatment like a favored nephew. Shortly after Paolo's arrival from Sicily, Natale directed his son Joe Guinta to take Paolo out one night to see a local boxing match. The match featured a Natale favorite, an up-and-coming Italian featherweight from New Orleans, paired against a local Irish Channel rival. Before Joe and Paul departed Marengo Street to attend the match, Natale took Paolo aside and instructed him to be on the lookout for some of the finer points of the young Italian contender's boxing style. Uncle Natale illustrated a few moves, lightly thrusting a left jab here, a right hook there, bobbing his bald head a little to the right and then to the left. He then handed Joe a wad of cash to cover the night's expenses. On another summer afternoon, Paul visited Marengo Street and his Uncle Natale took him into the side yard to help with some harvesting of the yard's produce. The older man reached up to pluck one of the larger, drooping, darkening brown figs from beneath the broad green leaves hanging from a low branch. Natale caressed the fig gently between the fingers of his right hand. "Look, Paolo," he said. "*Tette da vecchia signora*" (old lady tits).

Paul DiGiovanni was not the only young man in Natale's orbit who benefitted from his occasional acts of largesse. My dad had thoroughly won Natale over, first through Nia's assurances that Joe Wilkinson was "nothing to worry about, a good boy from the neighborhood," then by young Joe's voracious appetite for the Sicilian dishes at the Marengo Street dining table during the Sunday family dinners, his demonstrations of happiness with and respect for Natale's only daughter and ultimately, after Dad and Mom married, by working hard and producing a large brood of seven grandchildren to Natale's complete satisfaction. One day in 1960, Dad's teenage younger brother, my uncle Jimmy, was the victim of a neighborhood vandal who poured sugar into the gas tank of Jim Wilkinson's Ford jalopy. The engine was ruined. Uncle Jimmy knew his way around an auto engine and was capable of fixing it himself, but the only place for him to work was in the crowded street in front of his mother's apartment in the old St. Thomas Public Housing Project. When Natale heard about it, he insisted that Jimmy tow his car to Marengo Street and park it in his "shed" so that Jimmy could do his engine repairs in the shade of the garage, out of the New Orleans sun and rain. When Jimmy finished his first day of work on the four-day project, he said thanks to Mr. Guinta and started to walk away. "Where you goin'?" Natale asked. "I'm going to catch the bus to go home," Jim replied. Natale reached into his trousers pocket, withdrew the keys to his own car, and tossed them to Uncle Jimmy. "Here you go, boy. You use-a my car." Jim said, "Oh, Mr. Guinta, I can't take your car and leave you here stranded for three days. You might need it for something." Natale insisted. "Uh, uh, boy. You use-a my car as long as you need it."

"He said it in a way that was almost like a command instead of an offer," Uncle Jim recalled sixty years later. An offer Uncle Jimmy could not refuse.

My own memories as a small boy in Natale's company, from my earliest childhood when we lived on General Pershing Street, two blocks around the corner from Natale and Nia's house until he died when I was not yet twelve, are vivid and good. He was my grandpa, the only one I ever knew. My Dad's own father, George Matthews Wilkinson, had died when Dad was eleven, so I never got to meet him. I never feared Natale, even when I saw him beat his hunting beagle mercilessly one day after the dog had the temerity to snap at my younger sister, Terri, or when I listened to him arguing fiercely in Italian with old Ma-Maw Angelina. These outbursts never lasted long, and Nia always intervened to restore peace. To me, these things were just part of the background cacophony of my young life as the Italian boy I thought I was.

Natale fascinated me and my closest-in-age cousin, Joe Guinta Jr. He was methodical, regimented, imposing, fully confident in his own skin. He played solitaire at the kitchen table with a worn-out old deck of playing cards for hours on end. Natale ate one soft-boiled egg every midmorning. He would precisely crack off the eggshell's upper crown with one deft blow of a butter knife, then slurp out the goo of the upper egg before spooning out the remainder into his mouth with the delicacy of a debutante. He hauled giant wheels of parmesan cheese from storage spots in his shed or the kitchen pantry, sliced-off big chunks, and ground them into fluffy powder in a hand-cranked cheese grater he screwed into the top of Nia's table. He would slice open a ripe watermelon, and taste it before distributing smaller pieces to his grandchildren. "Sweet to da-sugah," he would pronounce with satisfaction. Just as he had done with Uncle Joe, Natale took me—his eldest grandson—everywhere he went when I was a small boy. He would bundle me into the front seat of the Blue Flash and then take the wheel. His driving was cautious. He always proceeded at speeds well under the posted limit, leaving the shifting mechanism on the steering wheel constantly in second gear. Occasionally, another driver would honk his car horn from behind the Blue Flash, trying to encourage Natale to move along at a little faster clip. Natale would shout out something in Italian through his car's open window, never moving his eyes from ahead on the road and never increasing his car's speed a single mile per hour. I rode next to him as his passenger to Ortolano's grocery store on the corner of Constantinople and Magazine Streets, only a few blocks from his house. He purchased gallon cans of imported Castelvetrano olive oil, six-packs of Delaware Punch soft drink in returnable glass bottles, long tubes of mortadella and salami, and loaves of French bread for sandwiches. I rode with him out to Elysian ("E-lee-sha-nuh") Fields Avenue and into the French Quarter, where he would stop at outdoor fruit stands and buy eggplants or cauliflower, lettuce or watermelons; only those things he was not growing himself in his own side yard.

We spent a lot of time with Natale playing on the high front porch of his Marengo Street home or in the little front yard patch of grass, protected under his watchful eye. He would sit in a rocking chair and calmly survey his Marengo Street domain. On that porch, I sometimes watched as he carefully carved a red-ripe tomato picked from his side yard stalks, separate the little seeds from the pulp, and then spread the seeds on a small plate that he would place on the porch to dry in the hot sun. He stored the dried seeds in small jars, so he could use them to plant new tomato bushes when the season was right. It was on that porch that I watched one day as he sat in his rocking chair and lifted my younger sister Terri onto his lap. He called Terri "Cherry" and bounced the little girl ever so softly up and down on his knee, as she giggled with delight. Terri reached her little hand up to Natale's face and stroked his cheek, which was covered with the thick short stubble of white whiskers that he had neglected to shave with his straight razor and cup of foaming soap that morning. Little Terri was not deterred by the roughness of his whiskers as she stroked his face softly and repeatedly.

"Pa-Paw," the little girl said, "you need a shave."

"Cherry, Cherry," I heard Natale say. I swear to you, Uncle Mike Stapleton, I saw Natale smile that day.

It was also during this time that Nia cemented her place as Natale's trusted partner, wise counselor, and—yes—beloved companion in the peculiar pairing that had been Natale and Lena Guinta since their arranged marriage in 1931. Natale's Lena (my Nia) could influence and calm him in a way that no one else could, not even Natale's devoted son and daughter. He always stopped his yelling and gesticulating in his mother-in-law's direction during their vitriolic arguments when Nia intervened. Lena made Natale feel secure in their American life—so secure that Natale gave up his last connection to Sicily when he ceded his hereditary property interest in the Giunta holdings to his brother Pasquale Giunta back in Castelvetrano. In doing so, Natale had sought and then acted in accordance with Nia's advice. With some wistfulness over the loss of what might have been inherited by her own son, Nia recounted the reasons for letting go of Natale's inheritance property interests in Castelvetrano. "It's really my fault." She had told her husband, "'Look, your brother's got seven children, Pasquale... Over there, people all are broke, you know, if you don't have land, you don't have nothin', and you have to work for other people.' He said, 'Aww, should we, you think I should?' I said, 'Sure, I don't need ten grand back…' [We were] lucky… So, uh, he said, 'Well. That's fine.' We went to New Orleans, and we had it all. We transferred everything to his brother, gave him an act of sale, and all that should have gone, you know…" to Natale's son, my uncle Joe. "They had a little sort of a camp near the seashore… Your daddy [Uncle Joe] was just a baby,…so we would think later on maybe somebody would want to go to that, live with that certain piece of property that was left, you know, because under Italian law, the first son, the first grandson, you know, is entitled. You know, and even old man Mussolini had said that…"[601]

On April 15, 1954, Lena and Natale appeared before New Orleans lawyer and notary, Peter Gentile, and executed a power of attorney in favor of Rizzo Baldassarre of Castelvetrano giving Baldassarre authority to execute the property deed transfer of Natale's interest in the family property in Castelvetrano to Natale's kin.[602] The document stated in Louisiana civilian law terms that the *causa* (cause, consideration) for Natale's donation was his *l'amore ed l'affetto e sua famiglia* (love and affection towards his family).[603] After Natale signed, lawyer Gentile submitted the document to the Italian consulate in New Orleans, which passed it along to the authorities in Castelvetrano. The transferred property in Castelvetrano was later the subject of a disagreement between Pasquale Giunta, Natale's brother to whom the property had been donated, and his brother-in-law, the Victorino man who was Natale's sister Marguerite's husband. Victorino was a "rich guy, the policeman… He put up a brick wall on my husband's property in Castelvetrano [that had been donated to Pasquale]… The old brother-in-law was a cop. He thought he could do things on the property."[604] The brother-in-law kept moving the fence that separated his property from Pasquale's neighboring tract, slowly but surely encroaching on what Natale had given to Pasquale. At some point, Pasquale Giunta got tired of the creeping encroachment. "Old Pasquale got his ax and knocked the fence down."[605]

A few events on Marengo Street served as reminders of Natale's core self and the things he had been capable of as a stronger, younger, offspring of a Western Sicilian "violent peasant entrepreneur."[606] Not long after Natale's son Joe Guinta enlisted in the United States Air Force in the 1950s, young Joe's obvious intelligence and authoritative air of responsibility and command propelled a rise up the military ranks. One morning, Nia answered a knock on the front door of the Guinta Marengo Street residence. Two men wearing dark suits and thin black ties and carrying briefcases stood at her door. They introduced themselves by name and title and flipped open badges and the photo IDs each carried in small leather wallets. Nia walked back into the kitchen where Natale was seated at the table drinking a cup of coffee and eating a crust of bread smeared with some of Angelina's goat cheese.

"The FBI's at the door, honey," Nia calmly said. "They want to talk to you."

Natale Guinta blanched. His face turned white as his breakfast goat cheese. He gathered himself in silence, pulled himself up from his chair, and shuffled into the front living room with Nia trailing behind him. Nia introduced the FBI agents to her husband and invited them in. Natale plopped heavily and silently into a chair while the two agents took seats on the sofa. Nia remained standing behind the now seated Natale. Nia noticed that the color had not yet returned to Natale's ashen face as the agents opened their briefcases and began to talk.

"Mr. Guinta," one of them said, "your son Lieutenant Joseph Guinta has been selected for an important Air Force intelligence assignment with the Strategic Air Command. His work will require that he first obtain a high-level security clearance that will give him access to sensitive national security data and information. We are conducting a background investigation and preparing our report and recommendation as to whether he should receive that military security clearance. Mr. Guinta, our records indicate that you are not an American citizen and were required a while back to register with the Justice Department under the old, World War II-era Alien Enemies Act. We need to ask you a few questions to bring our records up to date."

Natale nodded wordlessly, relaxing only slightly. The agents warned him that to answer any of their questions falsely was a violation of federal criminal law.[607] Nia stood by in an interested and silently protective mode. The agents began to ask a series of canned

questions. Had Natale ever been active in the Fascist Party in Italy? Was he ever or was he now a member of the Communist Party? Did he agree with Communist views? Did he belong to any social or political clubs that held Communist or anti-American views? Did he still owe allegiance to the Italian government or any other foreign power? Was he an anarchist or subversive of any kind? Did he have any associations with people he knew to be Communists, anarchists, or anti-American in any way? Had he not become an American citizen because of any allegiance or feeling of loyalty to any foreign power? After only about twenty minutes, when Natale had given them one-word no answers to all their questions, the interview ended. The FBI agents rose from their seats, shook Natale's hand, thanked him and Lena (Nia) for their cooperation, and exited through the front door they had shortly before entered. Nia patted Natale reassuringly on the shoulder. The color returned to Natale's cheeks. His anxiety waned and became pride: Pride that his own son could reach such rank among American .50-caliber *pezzonovanti*. Within a few weeks, Lieutenant Guinta received his security clearance. For years afterward, a formal photo portrait of Uncle Joe in his Air Force flight suit graced a dresser top in the parlor that became Natale's bedroom on Marengo Street.

Natale loved his "shed." One day in the late 1950s, a man from the New Orleans Board of Health knocked on the Marengo Street front door. The man explained to Nia that her cranky neighbor, who lived in the house fronting Constantinople Street with a backyard bordering the back of the Guinta lot, including the back left corner occupied by the shed, had complained. The Board of Health man was not there to take or to threaten any official action. "'Talk to your husband'"[608] was all he said to Nia before departing.

Back indoors sitting at the kitchen table, Natale was in an uncharacteristically mellow mood. "'What's the matter, honey?'" he asked Nia. "I'm a honey," Nia said, recollecting the event. "I said, 'we havin' trouble. The Board of Health man was here.'" Natale—still relaxed—responded, "'What's up?'" Nia delivered the bad news. "'He wants us to knock down that shed in the back. He said the people behind us complained. They don't want that shed there because they not gettin' enough air.'"[609]

Natale's relaxed demeanor turned to cold stone reminiscent of his younger self. Rising from the kitchen chair, he told Nia, "'You go back and wait till I get home. I'm gonna get Sugie and Jake. Son-a-ma-bitch, I ain't gonna take-a down my shed,'" and off he went to summon his DiGiovanni brothers-in-law to join him in force to pay a visit to the cranky neighbor.

Nia could envision Natale's plan, a plan rooted in the principles of *cavalleria rusticana* (rustic chivalry), the code learned by Natale as a late nineteenth-century *gabelloto*'s son in Castelvetrano. She tried to forestall him. "'Why don't you go by yourself?'" she told him. "'I already talked to our nice neighbor next door. She said, 'Tell Mr. Guinta don't worry about them people. They crazy. They have to go to city hall. They have to sue you. Your property's been there for years and years, and they can't do a thing.'"[610]

Like most authentic Sicilians of his vintage, Natale was not much for litigation and resort to the civil authorities as a means of dispute resolution. He proceeded immediately with his own plan. No record of the conversation between the cranky backyard neighbor and the three Sicilian men exists. However, no lawsuit was ever filed, no citation from the Board of Health was ever issued, and the shed remained standing in the back-left corner of the Marengo Street property for decades to come as a monument to the resolve of Natale Guinta. When I wrote this passage in 2020, I took a ride across the Mississippi River and into the Uptown neighborhood to see if Natale's shed still stood. It was gone, demolished no doubt by the old home's most recent owners. Apparently, the new residents preferred the open space of a professionally landscaped side yard to a place where an urbanized peasant could keep chicks and bunny rabbits and grow cucuzza squash on a tin roof.

The effect of Grandma Angelina's death in 1965 on Natale, the son-in-law antagonist of Angelina's old age, was metaphysical. If Natale thought that Angelina's death had finally resulted in the vanquishing of his longest-tenured remaining foe, his behavior did not reflect it. Instead, a mystical superstition verging on something like anguish seemed to seize him. Perhaps he missed the verbal clashes with a qualified adversary like Angelina Bucaro DiGiovanni, daughter of a Sicilian *carabinieri* captain. Perhaps it was a lifetime of respect for the *carabinieri* captain's daughter or Natale's *patrono*, Angelina's late husband, Don Tano Baiocco DiGiovanni. Whatever it was, "he wouldn't go in her room after she died. Funny!" Nia said of her husband.[611] Natale lived for two years after Angelina died. Throughout that time, it was like some hole had been bored in Natale's previously impervious psyche. Not only did he avoid venturing into the back room of the house where old Ma-Maw had lived out her days, but he also forcefully rejected any suggestion that it should be altered in any way. The room remained a darkened shrine, preserved just as Angelina had left it, votive candles burning and saintly statuary in place, garishly painted crucifix hanging on the wall, until after Natale died.

Natale Guinta died in Hotel Dieu hospital on January 18, 1967, surrounded by Nia, Mom, and Uncle Joe. He was seventy-eight years old. On the last few nights of his final sickness before he went into the hospital, his grandchildren visited him on Marengo Street, held his hand, or kissed him on the cheek. The official causes of death, assigned by attending physician Frank L. Loria, were "acute cardiac failure due to hypertensive cardiovascular disease," contributed to by "acute hemorrhage from gastric ulcer."[612] His "usual occupation" and employment status were listed as "Restaurant—Retired."[613] His obituary was a simple report of only a few of the basic facts of his life. His wake at Lamana-Panno-Fallo funeral home and the Requiem Mass at Saint Stephen's church near his Marengo Street home[614] were similarly plain and simple. The services were attended almost exclusively by family and the friends of his wife and children. None of the business or Italian community luminaries who had attended the years earlier wakes and funeral Masses of Gaetano and Angelina DiGiovanni were present. Mr. Luke Trombatore had already died four years earlier.[615] No one outside of the family who might have been identified exclusively by his or her close friendship or personal relationship with Natale was present because no such person existed. This is not to say that sorrowful emotion did not accompany Natale's death. After he died, Nia, Mom, and Uncle Joe drove to Terrytown and sat at the kitchen table, where Mom's children saw their reddened and teary eyes as they talked quietly and somberly among themselves. During the wake, Uncle Joe Guinta took his mother and his sister under his outstretched arms. Tearfully, he said, "You might have lost a husband, and you might have lost a father, but I lost my best friend."

After the services, Mom repeated what she had learned from Nia after the death of her own grandfather. She sent her little daughters across the river from the Wilkinson home in Terrytown to spend a few nights with their grandmother, "so Nia won't be alone." During the daylight and early evening hours of their stay on Marengo Street, the girls found Nia in basically the same state of mind that always marked her presence. She chattered with them pleasantly, baked them cookies, and made sure they were occupied with card games to play and television shows to watch. She took them on walks to the Magazine Street shops and saw that they took their baths and brushed their teeth. At night, unlike the experience of little Ann Guinta with her widowed Grandma DiGiovanni, the Wilkinson girls did not sleep with Nia in her bed. Instead, Nia tucked them into that bed herself and sat with them on a nearby chair until she thought they had fallen to sleep. She then tiptoed out of the bedroom into the adjacent kitchen, where she sat alone at the table and sipped a cup of coffee. On every night during their short stay on Marengo Street, from their snugly perches beneath the covers of Nia's bed, where they were not yet really asleep, Nia's little granddaughters heard Nia sobbing.

CHAPTER 35

WIDOWHOOD PART 2

In her widowhood, Antonia "Lena" DiGiovanni Guinta, Gaetano's middle child and most obedient daughter, my "Nia," confirmed all the bona fides and mettle of her DiGiovanni genes. She exhibited strength, independence, guile, resourcefulness, and often hilarious good humor into her old age. Immediately after Natale's death in 1967, things were difficult. After a short period of sorrowful mourning, Nia recovered and lived in the Marengo Street house for more than twenty years. After the death of Mrs. Kingsmill, her longtime renter in the house's small, separate, side apartment, Nia moved into the apartment herself and rented out the big side of the house to Jim and May Fleming.

"Ms. Lena" was hired for a series of jobs as a clerk at nearby grocery stores. She worked for a while at a small grocery store on Decatur Street in the French Quarter. She then moved her employment to the Piggly Wiggly way uptown on St. Charles Avenue, a streetcar ride from her Marengo Street home, and later to Frank A. Von der Haar Fine Foods, an upscale specialty grocery store at the corner of Magazine and General Pershing Streets. Von der Haar's was "an institution that…kept three generations of New Orleanians with good taste and money to accommodate it supplied with food that makes for gracious living… [It was] one of the few groceries left which delivers. It supplied customers all over Uptown and in Old Metairie. The delivery truck ventured as far as the Boston Club on Canal Street," catering to "people with the taste and the money" to live in a "style by which the ladies of some houses never had to stand in line at grocery stores. They called Von der Haar's, accepted the deliveries, and instructed the help in the kitchen in the preparation of the meal."[616] Its proprietor during Nia's tenure was "Ms. Lucy" Von der Haar, Mr. Frank's aged widow. Ms. Lucy ran the store "with loving care," often personally picking out its wares—the fresh trout, Creole tomatoes, watermelons, artichokes, "all kinds of lettuce," from fishermen and farmers only she knew about.[617] When Ms. Lucy died in January 1982, the store closed within a month. Nia was one of "three women—Lilly Lazaroe, [Marion] Apkin and part-time worker Lena Guinta—all widows" left on the payroll and saddened by its closure.[618]

Nia could walk to Von der Haar's the short distance from her Marengo Street home. It was entirely unclear whether she needed the income or just liked the work, the place, and its people. In addition to her Social Security checks, before the state of Louisiana expropriated the Tchoupitoulas Street property to build an on-ramp for the new Mississippi River bridge, she was drawing rent not just from the Flemings for the Marengo Street house but also from the new proprietor of the old Mr. Joe's bar, then known as Vic's. From the day Sue and I married in August 1977 until we moved to a bigger place one year after I finished law school, we lived in a four-room upstairs apartment owned by the Von der Haar family on General Pershing Street, four blocks from Nia's house and half a block from the Von der Haar's grocery. Nia had arranged for us to rent it for $150 per month. One evening during that time, Sue was visiting Nia in her little Marengo Street pad. Nia asked Sue to fetch something for her out of the bathroom medicine cabinet. When Sue opened the cabinet door, a pile of Von der Haar's paychecks came tumbling out onto the bathroom floor. Nia had never cashed them. She used the Von der Haar's butcher's department and the other little grocery stores along Magazine Street as her personal pantry. On her way home from work, she would routinely stop at our apartment and hand Sue a small package wrapped in white butcher's paper containing some sort of meat hand-cut by Joe Guarisco, Von der Haar's veteran butcher.

The packages might contain a giant T-bone, two thick-cut pork chops, a beef liver, or roast beef, all trimmed of excess fat and charmingly obtained by Nia from the butcher himself without charge. She announced her delivery of these goodies to Sue the same way: "Here, honey. Here's a nice chop for you and my grandson." From time to time, she wandered into one of the other little Magazine Street stores or fruit and vegetable stands. She would place her right hand against one cheek and exclaim, loudly enough for the fruit man to hear, "Oh Gawd (God), look at these beautiful bananas. And me, a poor widow on a fixed income." "Here, Ms. Lena," the fruit man would say. "Take a few. On the house." On to the next store or fruit stand, she would stroll and repeat the same scam, just for the fun of it, until she had a whole bunch to use in frying up a batch of banana fritters, covered in powdered sugar.

When Natale died, his fourteen-year-old 1953 Chevy, "the Blue Flash," was transferred to my mother's possession. Nia never owned her own car. Back in the 1930s, shortly after Nia first learned to drive, she crashed Natale's Model A into a cotton-hauling truck while trying to navigate the narrow streets of the French Quarter. Thick bales of cotton came tumbling onto the car. After Nia was extracted from the mess, Natale imposed a forceful ban on further driving by his young wife. Since that day, she was happy to travel everywhere by streetcar or bus. From time to time, she would pop in unexpectedly in Terrytown across the river to visit the Wilkinsons or in Old Metairie across parish lines to visit her Guinta grandkids. She negotiated whatever transfers from one bus line to another might be necessary, then walked the short distances from the nearest bus stop, wherever a bus from New Orleans had deposited her. She would stroll into the Guinta or Wilkinson houses, a scarf wrapped around her head, her shoulders wrapped in a shawl, even in the summertime. She carried a giant purse, out of which she would produce a bag of homemade *biscotti regina* or frosted chocolate cookie rounds or even a whole pan of lasagna for her grandchildren.

Her living alone, solitary bus rides, neighborhood strolls to Magazine Street and the K&B drugstore on the corner of St. Charles and Napoleon Avenues were a constant source of worry for her children, Mom, and Uncle Joe. Their worries were somewhat assuaged by the friendly attentiveness of the Flemings and when various grand-children took up temporary residence in or around Nia's Marengo Street house. My sisters Terri and Judy kept track of her while they rented half a double across the street on Marengo for a few years while they were in graduate and law schools. Nia had negotiated the rental for them with the landlord Parsons sisters, who lived in the double's other half, at a friendly rate of $125 per month. Brother Tom crashed regularly on Nia's living room sofa and kept tabs on her in the early 1980s while he attended Tulane Law School. Cousin Greg Guinta did the same while he studied for his paralegal's certificate.

My wife, Sue, and Nia were particular comforts to each other during the four years 1977–'81 when we lived nearby. I was fully occupied with law school, nighttime and weekend part-time jobs, and the first year of my demanding federal court clerkship. Sue would often make the short stroll from our apartment around the corner to visit Nia on Marengo Street or vice versa. One dark night while I was at work, Sue accidentally stabbed our old refrigerator freezer while trying to clean it of excess ice. A meltdown began. She called Nia to ask if she could walk over and temporarily store our frozen goods in Nia's freezer. "Sure, honey," Nia said. "But it's late. I'll meet you halfway and walk with you." Sue protested. "No, don't do that. I'm only five minutes away." Nevertheless, two blocks into Sue's walk, there was Nia, waiting for her at the corner of Camp and Milan Streets. "Oh, Nia," Sue said. "I told you not to walk out here." "Don't worry about me, honey," Nia replied. She pulled her sweater aside with a sly smile and patted a pistol tucked into the waistband of her pants. Sue later said that it was one of her happiest moments when she and Terri walked into Vonder Haar's grocery one day, and Nia said to Miss Lilly, one of her coworkers, "Hey, I want to introduce you to two of my granddaughters, Sue and Terri." It was during this time in 1981, when I was a law clerk for Judge Morey L. Sear presiding over the federal criminal prosecution of reputed local Mafia boss Carlos Marcello during what was called the "BRILAB" trial, that Nia would gently lobby me for his acquittal, as if I could somehow influence that outcome. "That poor man," she would say.

"They're persecuting him. He's just a poor tomato salesman. There's no such thing as the Mafia."

It was also during this time that I began to list in writing what I later called "the expressions of Antonia DiGiovanni Guinta." Sometimes Nia would pronounce them in Sicilian dialect Italian, sometimes in American English. The expressions were little snippets from conversations with Nia stated usually as a kind of *contadina* (peasant) maxim. Always they provided timely commentary on something she had observed in her children's, grandchildren's, or even her own conduct or in the larger passing of world affairs. When she heard that perhaps the eldest grandson was considering taking a job with a fancy Uptown white-shoe law firm, where former Rexes, Kings of Carnival, presided as partners, she might say, "Better a plain patch than a fancy hole" or "You got a rich mind for a poor behind." If she thought her son or daughter was putting off until tomorrow what should be done today, she might say, "*Dumane', sempre dumane'*" (tomorrow, always tomorrow) or "Times are nearin'." If some casual conversationalist stated what she deemed obvious, she would refer to a then-popular over-the-counter tonic used to combat constipation: "No shit, Mr. Phillips." Or if she distrusted some public authority as unworthy of credence, "He don't know shit from Shinola." When events spun into a frenzied mess that disturbed peaceful living, she grumbled or shouted, "*Camorria!*" If she thought someone's lack of financial success was attributable to laziness, "He's broke as the Ten Commandments." As to one's lack of stature, either physical or intellectual, she would say, "He's so short, the Army couldn't use him as a cannon cork." To an obstinate grandchild persisting in bad behavior, "You got a head like German steel." And of course, in all things, common and uncommon, "*Picchi didi a verita quanna a farfantaria cia basta*" (Why tell the truth when a lie will suffice).

A few incidents finally convinced Uncle Joe and Mom that it was time for Nia to move out of Marengo Street and in with the Wilkinsons in Terrytown. First, she began to give away her possessions. I got a letter opener topped with a stylized, Florentine winged lion. It had been given to her by her brother, Uncle Sugie (Fedele DiGiovanni), as a souvenir obtained while on one of his seagoing ventures to Italy. Cousin Jean Guinta, the only Guinta daughter who died too young in 2021, got an antique chair. Others in the family got some of her costume jewelry, old photos, serving platters, or knickknacks taken and saved from the old Tchoupitoulas Street barroom.

One early morning, she telephoned Uncle Joe. "Can you come over here, honey? I need some help." When her son arrived, she met him on the porch and told him what had happened. In the middle of the previous night, she had heard a strange sound from underneath her bed. Perhaps it was a thief, an intruder come to rob her of her hoard of God knows what. Her mattress creaked as she rose from the bed and went to a nearby cabinet, where she retrieved from its hiding place the ancient *pistola* she had once brandished to protect Sue on her neighborhood walk. She thought she heard the sound again from beneath her bed. Nia bent down low to look under the bed and saw a dark shape. She fired the gun and hit her mark, which splattered a viscous red substance. Nia leaned in to take a closer look. It was a watermelon, now assassinated and smashed to smithereens. She had forgotten that she had purchased it a few days earlier from one of the Magazine Street fruit men and stashed it under her bed to ripen. When he finished laughing and was able to feign anger, Uncle Joe cleaned up the mess and took the gun away for safekeeping in his own Metairie house.

The final straws came when Uncle Joe got a call from the Touro Hospital emergency room one night. Nia was there. She had been on a walk from Marengo Street to the little drugstore at the corner of Prytania and Constantinople Streets to pick up her prescription medicines. She fell to the concrete sidewalk and broke both of her collarbones. She recovered, but not before an intruder attempted one dark night to break into her house. Nia was alert enough to set off her Med-Alert alarm, and the would-be burglar was scared off, but that was when her children insisted that it was time to move from Marengo Street and in with the Wilkinsons in Terrytown. Dad had already converted the old backyard storage garage into a one-bedroom apartment, first for use as the temporary abode of his own elderly mother and then as the same for Nia. Her house on Marengo

Street passed from family ownership. In 2003, Sue and I tried to buy it back for ourselves, driven by sentiment and good memories as much as by the house itself or its great Uptown location, but we could not make the contingent sale of our own house in time, and it passed for good out of the family

At first, Nia seemed content with her new living arrangement. She was able to walk the few steps from the apartment into the main house, where she baked cookies, helped with the cooking and cleaning, and visited her grandchildren and great-grandchildren during their frequent drop-ins, especially on Sundays. Her able-bodied son, son-in-law, and grown grandchildren were happy to drive her for visits with the Guintas in Metairie or her sister Lou in Kenner or her DiGiovanni or Pedalino relatives all over the New Orleans area; to the beauty salon for a stylish "blue-gray" rinse; to church for Mass, funerals, and weddings; to the grocery store, her doctors' appointments and the occasional DiGiovanni family reunion picnics. She never again had to ride the bus. It was in Terrytown where she sat for the first of her genealogical interviews by cousin John Guinta, resulting in volume 1 of the Nia tapes, oft-cited in these pages. Into her nineties, she never lost her marbles, though her considerable street smarts and energy naturally faded. Finally, Father Time defeated her, as he always does, using a couple of strokes as his mechanism. The less Nia could do, the unhappier she became. Contrarily to the lovable sunniness of her lifelong disposition, she became at times—as Mom sometimes complained—"mean as a snake." She made nasty comments about Mom's housekeeping, cooking or mothering abilities, Uncle Joe's work habits, and the failure of her grandchildren to visit as often as she thought they should. When she entered the hospital for the final time, she could not be succored, perhaps because her best friend and closest sibling, Aunt Lou, had died only two months earlier. Nia died on February 19, 1998, in Meadowcrest Hospital (now Ochsner) in Gretna. Mom was surprised when the attending physician listed the cause of death as "pneumonia due to or as a consequence of Alzheimer's disease."[619] It seemed to Mom that Nia had never relinquished her marbles. Proof of that was in one of the last things Nia said to Mom before she died when she foreshadowed our discovery that Nia could not be interred where she always said she would be the last to go, into the DiGiovanni vault on Avenue B in Lakelawn Metairie Cemetery with her assassinated brother Dominick, her sainted parents Gaetano and Angelina, her eldest daughter Anna who had died shortly after her birth and her husband, Natale. Nia's expression, "*Picchi didi a verita quanna a far-fantaria cia basta*" (Why tell the truth when a lie will suffice), became in the end, "You gonna be some surprised when I die." Nia knew what she had never told, but which she must have learned from Don Tano himself—*omerta* (the Sicilian code of secrecy) till the very end: there was a Trombatore already secretly buried there, taking up the space that rightfully should have been hers.

CHAPTER 36

SIX ANGIES

I telephoned Mom on July 28, 2011, just to see how she was doing. "I'm kind-a down today," she said bleakly. "Angie died."

"Oh no," I said, "which one?"

"Dominick's Angie," she said.

It happened again a few months later. "Who's that?" I asked Mom one day, pointing a finger at a gorgeous young dark-haired woman pictured in a black and white snapshot, taken sometime in the 1950s. We were poring over the new family keepsake, a book "made on a Mac" for the 2011 DiGiovanni Family Reunion by my cousin, Angelo Quaglino. "Her," I said, pointing again to the striking Mediterranean beauty.

"Oh," Mom said. "That's Angie."

I laughed out loud. "Which one?"

"Walter's Angie," she replied.

How many Angies did we have in this family? When I was a kid, at a family gathering of any kind, a wedding, a funeral, a picnic, a birthday party, if I needed to call a mostly unfamiliar woman about Mom's age by name for any reason, it was always a safe bet to call her Angie. There were at least six Angies that I knew about myself—not counting Old Ma-Maw, Angelina Bucaro DiGiovanni herself, the original Angie, as far as I knew. "That's Angie," Mom or Nia would often say. What made this identification particularly hilarious was that they were not kidding.

There was Jake's Angie and Sugie's Angie; Walter's Angie, of course, and Nookie's Angie. Then there were the seldom seen, but frequently talked about Angies: Dominick's Angie ("poor Domenico"), usually referred to as "Mickey," off somewhere in Canada or Texas, and Fene's Angie ("poor girl, with all her troubles"), infrequently seen—just like her mother, Aunt Fene, "the recluse" had been.

"You see," Mom had explained to my cousin John Guinta during Nia's taped interview in 1988, "in the Sicilian tradition, your father is named after his paternal grandfather, and the first daughter is named after the father's mother, the paternal grandparents, and the second two children are named after the maternal father and mother. Then after four, you can name them whatever you want."

"That's why we got about fifty Angies in our family," Nia chimed in hyperbolically.[620]

There would have been at least two more Angies in the family, making eight in all, one for eight of the nine adult children of Gaetano and Angelina DiGiovanni, with only the rebellious Lucia (Lucille, Aunt Lou) bucking the naming tradition. Ma-Mamie's (Mary's) Angie died in childbirth and was interred in the Lakelawn family mausoleum, with no name inscribed on the tombstone to mark her brief existence.[621] Mom would have been another Angie, as the second daughter of Natale and Nia, except that her older sister, Anna, named after Natale's mother, Anna Sanstefano Giunta, had died only days after her birth of a congenital heart defect. Like Ma-Mamie's Angie, Anna Guinta was interred without a name inscription in the Lakelawn family vault. After Anna's infant death, Natale decided to abandon the old Sicilian naming tradition and gave his daughter the overtly American name Ann. For Natale, it was not a difficult decision. He never got along with his mother-in-law Angelina anyway. It was only in older age that I could tell the six surviving Angies apart or even tried to differentiate among them and then only by their distinct and sometimes sad stories.

For me, Dominick's Angie, whom the dozens of cousins called "Mickey," was the invisible Angie, the mysterious Angie, the Angie that no one ever really knew, the Angie who most succeeded in escaping (or being forgotten about by) the family. Shortly after Dominick's

Angie died in 2011, my saddened mother told me that this Angie had been an infant when her father was murdered. Gaetano scooped up little Angie and her mother, Domenico's widow, Rosie Milazzo DiGiovanni, and moved them to the perceived safety of White Castle, Louisiana, where Rosie had Milazzo relatives. "When I was a kid, my grandpa would take me on the train with him to White Castle every now and then to visit them," Mom said. When Angie's mother remarried, they moved to Canada and later to Texas. Angie eventually married. Her married name was Gross, and they lived in Houston. On that day in late July 2011, Mom said her distant "cousin Marilyn called me this morning to tell me Mickey died in Houston last week at the age of ninety. Marilyn told me, 'You're the only one of the first cousins I could think of who might care, Ann.' That's probably true," Mom said, as she dug out her wedding photo album. "That's her," Mom said, pointing out this Angie at Mom and Dad's wedding in 1954.

In that same conversation, I told Mom I could remember four of the other Angies, but not Aunt Fene's Angie. Mom said that Angie Ferraro Costella, Fene's Angie, was almost as mysterious as Dominick's Angie, though not quite so, since this Angie had been a local, living in St. Bernard Parish. Mom called her story tragic.

"Fene was a recluse," Mom said that afternoon "Even Nia didn't get to see Fene much because Natale was banned from Fene's house and vice versa" after Natale and Fene got into some kind of dispute over ownership of a Saint Bernard Parish cow. Nia used to say to me that her sister Fene (Giuseppina, Josephine) "had a tough life." Fene was born in San Cipirello, the oldest child of Gaetano and Angelina. Mom said that because of Angelina's blindness, seemingly constant state of pregnancy, and many miscarriages, the burden often fell on Fene when she was young "to take care of all of those kids." Mom said Fene had three daughters, Angie, Catherine ("Kate"), and Margaret, and one son, her youngest, Philip Jr. Fene struggled after her husband, Phillip Ferraro **Sr.** died at a young age. A cousin once asked me—in light of the rest of the family history and the grandfather's too-young death—if I had uncovered any research indicating that Phillip **Sr.** had been poisoned. The cousin had seen that nephritis, a kidney failure ailment more commonly linked to older age conditions like diabetes, was listed as the cause of death on Phillip Sr.'s death certificate. I said I had no such information. I did not say that maybe the diagnosis was related to something that afflicted the older Ferraro's son, Phillip **Jr.** Mom told me that her cousin, Philip **Jr.**, had been a heroin user who served time in the Louisiana State Penitentiary at Angola for drug offenses. "They would ship him off to [stay with the DiGiovanni family branch in] Rockford, [Illinois], whenever he got into trouble," Mom said. "My aunt Mary up in Rockford, once asked him, 'How you doin', Phillip?' Phillip told her, 'I don't know, Aunt Mary, sometimes I feel like God's pulling me one way and the devil is pulling me the other way.' Aunt Mary said, 'Oh yeah, Phillip. Who's winning?'"

Mom told me that in the 1970s, when Mom was a student nurse making rounds at the old Charity Hospital in New Orleans as part of her education, Fene's Angie had a tragic ending. She "went insane," Mom said. "She boarded herself up in her house in Chalmette, and the police had to be called one night because she was causing a disturbance. They took her to the St. Bernard Parish Jail, where she hung herself. The deputies rushed her to Charity Hospital, but it was too late. The hospital was where I heard about it."

Another Angie, Jake's Angie, Angie DiGiovanni McLees, was the Californian. She and her brother Dominick, both born in Sicily, were the only children of the tumultuous marriage of Giacomo "Jake" DiGiovanni and Antonina "Nanina" Cannella DiGiovanni. As to her childhood in Sicily, Jake's Angie sometimes complained in her later life that having to wear wooden shoes as a child in Depression-era Sicily "ruined my feet" and caused them to ache ever after into her womanhood. With her brother and mother, she arrived in New Orleans to rejoin her father shortly after World War II. Angie went straight into the Catholic schools, where she excelled. She was proud that, despite her birth in Sicily, she was an American citizen by virtue of the fact that her father, Uncle Jake, had been born in the United States. She later bragged to her children that in school she had written an essay on the evils of Italian Fascism and earned an A-plus grade. After graduating from Redemptorist High School in the Irish

Channel in 1952, one year before her cousin, my mom Ann Guinta, Angie went on to LSU in Baton Rouge. At a college "mixer," the dark and exotic good looks that she shared with all women blessed with the combination of DiGiovanni and Cannella genes attracted a young chemical engineering student from Little Rock, Arkansas, named Carl McLees. They fell in love. Unlike the DiGiovannis, McLees was an American WASP, a conservative, no-drinking, no-smoking, non-Catholic. Angie was then and ever after a beautiful, sweet, and religious woman whose Catholicism, like her grandmother Angelina Bucaro DiGiovanni's, was important, a core component of her personal identity. So Carl and Angie were married in a Catholic church, but Carl seldom went to church thereafter, an issue that sometimes became a point of contention in their marriage.

Upon his graduation, Carl got his first job with Gulf Oil Company briefly in New Orleans, before he was transferred to Baytown, Texas, for a year, then on to a new position at C. F. Braun Engineering in Alhambra, California, near Los Angeles. It was in the Los Angeles area that the McLees family settled for the long haul and grew to include five children. At first, Angie worked as a stay-at-home mom and housewife. Like her mother and paternal grandmother Angelina Bucaro DiGiovanni, she was constantly cleaning everything in the house, working her fingers to the bone to make sure that the household was just so. She prepared little Italian treats for her children, like "crema," a sweetened, corn starch-based vanilla pudding that her boys lapped up with oversized spoons. From time to time, Grandma Nanina would come to California to visit, twice a year in the 1960s. Nanina's visits were a culture shock to the conservative father of the family, Carl McLees. Unlike the older women with whom the oil industry chemical engineer was most familiar, Nanina smoked cigarettes, drank hard liquor, taught her grandsons how to play poker, spoke in loud shouts, and used foul language. She sometimes subjected her daughter and grandsons to noisy outbursts of criticism. "*Lampione* [lamppost]!" Nanina would shout at one of her grandsons if she thought he was not showing enough energy at whatever schoolwork or other tasks he had been assigned. Nanina's

McLees grandsons seemed amused, but the older McLees was taken aback.

When her children were mostly grown, Angie's innate intelligence, drive, and ambition prompted her to earn her realtor's license and go into the real estate business. She always believed in self-improvement. She could speak Castilian Spanish. Although she was generally easygoing and sweet, if she thought some retailer or other person was trying to take advantage of her, she never took it lying down. Into the transgressor's face or straight to the manager or other higher-up she would go to register her complaints. In her real estate operations, Jake's Angie turned out to be a natural dealmaker and shrewd investor who sometimes bought property for herself behind her conservative husband's back and to his disapproval. She always seemed to make a profit on her deals. To her husband's further consternation, Angie's good judgment, willing but not overbearing advice-giving, and active engagement with clients and others in the real estate business were like magnets for people with problems and troubles. She seemed to have inherited some of the genetic traits of her paternal grandfather, Don Tano Baiocco, Gaetano DiGiovanni, in that people in Los Angeles "found themselves obeying h[er] and asking for h[er] advice and consent for their projects without knowing why."[622] Like *Zu* Tano himself, Angie counseled these people and tried to fix whatever difficulties they were having.

Jake's Angie's sons were impressed by the emotional closeness and affection their mother had for her DiGiovanni and Cannella relatives, despite the distant physical separation of their dwelling places. Angie was proud of her Italian heritage and a staunch defender of the reputation and goodness of her Sicilian family and the Italian people in general. When *The Godfather* movie first aired on television, son David McLees watched it together with his mother one night. A little while into the movie, Angie stood up and yelled at the television screen, "This is all a lie. Italian people are not like this!" David thought in retrospect that she perhaps protested too much. I think that perhaps she had been treated just like her contemporary, my own mom, who declared with sadness in her later years that "my people lied to me my whole life."

The McLees couple's disagreements and differing natures ultimately led to divorce. In Nanina's old age in 1986–'87, she moved in with her daughter where she died. She is buried in Monrovia, California, fittingly separated and far apart from the husband, Giacomo "Jake" DiGiovanni, she could not abide and vice versa in New Orleans. Jake's Angie died herself, much too young at the age of sixty-two. She was a victim of complications of diabetes, the disease carried in the family genes and passed from one DiGiovanni generation to the next, at a time when the controlling medications and treatments for type 2 diabetics that exist today were unknown to her and her doctors. Jake's Angie is buried in Rose Hills Memorial Cemetery in Whittier, California, not far from her mother.

Angie DiGiovanni LeBlanc, Sugie's Angie, was a New Orleans girl through and through and the mirror image of her mother, Philippina Riccobono DiGiovanni. Like her mother, she was a beautiful young woman, voluptuous, dark-haired, alluring in her smiles, sweet as the filling of a cannoli. Her voice was firm and clear, always cast in a tone of authoritative but subdued articulateness. "That was class," Nia had once said of this Angie's mother, Aunt Philippina. Despite her blue-collar New Orleans life and marriage, Sugie's Angie exuded the same kind of class in her bearing, her manner of speaking, the way she revered her parents, and even in the substantial features of her older age. With her husband, she reared a hearty family and looked closely after her parents in their old age. She adored her father, Fedele "Sugie" DiGiovanni, and preserved his pictures and escapades long after Uncle Sugie passed.

It was this Angie who told me the stories of some of her father's exploits as an international seafarer, in barrooms, around the New Orleans docks with his father, and in the company of Sugie's best friend, Anthony "Tony" Carollo, son of Silver Dollar Sam Carollo. Alien smuggling was a post-World War II interest of the powerful Gambino crime family of New York, which sometimes associated with the Carollos in New Orleans.[623] The smuggling of Italians in particular into the country was allegedly one of the specialties of Paolo Gambino, "younger brother of infamous mob patriarch Carlo

Gambino."[624] New Orleans was one of the ports of entry for that operation.

One late night in the late 1940s or early 1950s, young Angie was roused from her sleep by the sounds of a group of men talking outside the home of Fedele and Philippina DiGiovanni on Thalia Street, not far from the docks of the Mississippi River port. Angie peered sleepily through her bedroom window into the alley between their house and its neighbor and out into the connected open street. The talking was coming from seven or eight men huddled together in the semidarkness. She recognized three of them: her father, Sugie, and his friends Tony Carolla and John Pecoraro. A fourth man they called "Paul," whom Angie did not recognize but whom she remembered as wearing an expensive camel's hair jacket, was pointing in the direction of the street, seemingly giving the others instructions. The three or four other unknown men were ill-clothed, young, a little dirty, dark-haired, and dark-complexioned, Italian by every appearance. These men only listened and said nothing. Within seconds, Angie heard the heavy footsteps of others approaching the street toward the alley. At the sound, the men whom Angie did not recognize, including "Paul," hurriedly took off, running away toward the river in the opposite direction from the oncoming footsteps. She heard a whistle blow and the oncoming footsteps quicken to a trot. It was two uniformed policemen, now seemingly in pursuit of the fleeing men. Angie watched her father and his two friends, Carollo and Pecoraro, suddenly but casually stroll together out of the darkness of the alley and into the pathway, seemingly accidentally, of the oncoming policemen. They bumped into each other and became momentarily entangled, the policemen knocked off their strides just long enough by the path-blocking men so that when the officers resumed their pursuit of the fleeing men, they were too far behind to catch them. When the policemen returned to the scene to look for the three men who had slowed them down, Sugie, Carollo, and Pecoraro had disappeared into the night. When the sun rose on the next morning, Angie left the house and looked in the alley. There on the ground, near a brick piling of the raised house, partially hidden under the house itself, was Paul's discarded camel's hair jacket.

Sugie's Angie married a regular American with a classic South Louisiana name, Louis LeBlanc. Like his father-in-law, Louie was a US Navy veteran. He was a hardworking blue-collar man whose nickname was "Shirts," derived from his employment for forty years by a local linen and dry-cleaning company. He was a popular fun-lover at all the family gatherings. Louie was the utterer of one of the family's longest enduring bon mots. One exceedingly frigid early February Mardi Gras in New Orleans found the family revelers huddled inside of Nia's and Natale's Uptown house, near the parade routes of both Rex, King of Carnival, and Comus, Lord of Misrule, instead of out on the streets or in their sunlit side yard, where they were accustomed to beer-drinking and storytelling to celebrate the annual pre-Lenten bacchanal. Everyone was commenting on the un-New Orleans like nature of subfreezing Mardi Gras temperatures.

"Yeah," Louie agreed between quaffs of frosty Jax beer in a bottle. "They ought-a move Mardi Gras to October when the weather's nicer." Some of us now ape Louie LeBlanc's wisdom when similar holiday circumstances arise. "They ought-a move the Fourth of July to October when the weather's nicer," somebody might say while sweating over hot dogs grilling on a barbeque pit on any ninety-five-degree New Orleans July 4. "They ought-a move Christmas to late April when the weather's nicer," somebody might say when Christmas Day turns out to be too frigid for New Orleanians comfortably to bear.

Nookie's Angie was the second of the eleven children of Carmelo and Francesca "Nookie" DiGiovanni Pedalino. She was one of the two Pedalino sisters who repeated Aunt Lou's oral version of history in the 1920s-'30s San Cipirello when Lucille proclaimed loudly, "Two sisters married two brothers."[625] The difference in this instance was that the two sisters and two brothers who married in New Orleans in the 1950s were also first cousins, DiGiovannis and Pedalinos.

Angie Pedalino arrived in New Orleans from Sicily with some of the Pedalino family on their first attempt at immigration shortly after World War II. At first, she stayed for a short time with her Uncle Jake so that there were two young Angies in Jake's and Nanina's New Orleans household for a little while, Jake's own Angie and Nookie's

Angie. The total population of Angies in Jake's house sometimes grew to three whenever Sugie's Angie would visit.

The course of Angie Pedalino's life changed unalterably and for the better in 1953 when the family of Vito "Walter" and Vincenza "Giuzza" DiGiovanni, including their own daughter Angie and son Paolo, arrived in New Orleans from Sicily. It did not take long for young Paolo to fall hopelessly and forever in love with Angie Pedalino. "I put her on a pedestal. She was the best, the love of my life," Paul said almost seventy years later, emotion rising in his voice. Yet in 1953, he could not speak aloud of his love. Paolo was afraid that Angie would say no if he expressed his feelings and that her father, Carmelo Pedalino, would forbid any such romance. For four long years, from 1953 to 1957, the lovesick Paul suffered in silence. He and Angie would sometimes go out together, enjoying each other's company, but never as a couple on a date and always as part of a group of six or eight other young men and women. In some ways, this worsened Paul's suffering. After four years, Paolo reached a love-lorn nadir bordering on implosion. "I couldn't take it anymore," he said. "I was either gonna have to tell her how I felt or leave town."

One night, he arranged to take Angie on a real date, the young couple out together for the first time alone. Paul hired a taxi, and they traveled downtown in the cab's back seat to see the opera (*La Boheme*, of course). Not long after Puccini's Mimi died and the curtain closed at the opera's conclusion, with Mimi succumbing to a fit of coughing caused by consumption and her stricken lover, Rodolfo, crying out her name and sobbing helplessly,[626] Paolo DiGiovanni and Angie Pedalino got back into a New Orleans taxi. About three blocks before arriving at the Pedalino home on Saint Thomas Street, Paul broke the silence by instructing the driver to pull over.

"We gotta talk," Paul said to Angie. He told her how he felt about her. Angie looked deeply, soul-searchingly into Paul's eyes.

"It's impossible," she said. "Daddy would not approve. You know how he feels about your brother and my sister." She was referring to the other first cousins who had already eloped and were married against her father's wishes.

badly. He was ecstatic. He saw it in Angie's
ice. She felt the same way about him as he felt
_e_ undeniably. Who cares about what Carmelo
ul held Angie by both of her hands and saw her
homas Street doorway. He skipped back into the
me to talk with his own father.

Paul, Uncle Walter (Vito DiGiovanni), was a broad-minded man, pragmatic, but a romantic in his own right. He had found the love of his own life in Vincenza "Giuzza" Cannella more than two decades earlier in San Cipirello. He knew the value, the sight, the unrelenting depth of feeling that was true, life-lasting love, the kind of love that would drive a man forever into the bosom of family, the kind of love and family that transforms a boy into a real man. He saw these things now in his own son. "Go see your brother-in-law" was all he said, referring to his other son, Paul's own brother.

Together, the brothers walked to the Pedalino home. Paul paced on the street while his brother went inside. When he emerged, a small grin illuminated his otherwise dark face. "Everything's okay," he said. Carmelo Pedalino had consented to have two DiGiovanni sons-in-law.

Paul had enlisted in the US Army, and he wanted to wait out the two years until his discharge before he and Angie married. He had already waited four years just to declare his lifelong love: what was another two years? But the practical and intelligent Angie Pedalino said no. If Paul were married while in the Army, he would receive the extra pay allotment then awarded to a married soldier. She promised to put the extra pay aside and save it for them to use when Paul was discharged. Since first cousins could not marry in Louisiana, they eloped that night to Mississippi. "We got married under law," Paul said. "But we had our real wedding in St. Patrick's Church on Camp Street in 1959."

Angie spent the two years of Paul's Army service working at the Wembley tie factory in New Orleans. True to her word, she saved Paul's extra pay and more from her own tie-making earnings so that when Paul was discharged from the Army, he walked into a home full of new furniture purchased by his practical and attentive wife. Angie

was a stay-at-home mother and homemaker while her children
growing up, but when Paul and his brother Guy DiGiovanni opene
their own restaurant in Metairie, "the Little Italians," Angie went to
work in the restaurant's kitchen.

"She was the star of the kitchen," Paul said. "She did all the
cooking." The restaurant consistently received rave reviews for the
quality of its Italian food. Angie's star status was confirmed by writer
and restaurant critic Richard Collin, "the New Orleans Underground
Gourmet." Collin came into the restaurant one evening and ordered
Paul's personal favorite dish, a unique pasta concoction prepared with
a mixture of carefully seasoned pine nuts, raisins, cauliflower, and
anchovies, all cooked in Castelvetrano olive oil. It was Angie's creation. Collin swooned when he tasted it. "Who makes this pasta?" he
demanded to know. When chef Angie was introduced to the writer,
Collin declared it "the best pasta dish in the city" and gave it a name:
"Little Italians' unique pasta creation, Macaroni Angelina (a platonic
dish), is one of the best pasta dishes ever conceived,…genius… The
DiGiovannis cook pasta like angels."[627]

When Angie died in 2008, Paolo DiGiovanni was heartbroken.
For years later, into his own old age, Paul continued to say as often as
possible, "She was the love of my life."

Vito's (Walter's) Angie was Angie DiGiovanni Quaglino
Sheppard. By this time, any nonfamily reader of this book must seriously doubt my credibility as an objective assessor of womanly beauty.
I realize that I have described almost every DiGiovanni woman identified in this effort as physically attractive in one way or another.
Walter's Angie, however, was universally recognized—at least among
my parents, siblings, and me—as Hollywood movie star stunning,
one of the most beautiful women we have ever seen. Walter's Angie
shared the dark-haired, dark-eyed, dark-skinned features of her many
relatives, but her sharp Mediterranean features, figure, bearing, and
smile were somehow more striking, more pronounced, more clas-
sical than the others. She had beauty in the class of Sophia Loren
and Claudia Cardinale. Angie was born in San Cipirello, the only
daughter of the six children of Uncle Walter (Vito) and Aunt Giuzza.
After arriving in New Orleans with the rest of her immigrating fam-

ily in 1953 and coming of age, she married into a prominent local Italian family, the Quaglinos, proprietors of hugely successful New Orleans businesses. Tragically, her husband, John Angelo Quaglino, whose father owned a drayage business that delivered flour throughout the French Quarter, died too young in 1968 at age twenty-seven in a terrible automobile accident at one of the busiest intersections of suburban Metairie, Louisiana.[628] His death left Angie with three little children whom she reared with great care and attention. The girl was named Gina. Each Quaglino son bears one of the names of their late father, and both are now successful professionals and family men in their own rights. Angie remarried a regular American named Alan Sheppard. When Angie first brought Alan to her parents' home, introducing him as a prospective husband, Alan's towering height impressed the diminutive DiGiovannis. "That's a big silo to have to fill," Aunt Giuzza said, shrewdly anticipating all the cooking her Angie would have to do to keep Alan fed over the course of a long marriage. Alan embraced his adopted family's Sicilian heritage, accompanied Angie on her trips back to Sicily, and helped stepson Angelo with the production and completion of the invaluable family heirloom Macbook *La Nostra Famiglia* for distribution at the 2011 DiGiovanni-Cannella family reunion.

It was Walter's Angie whose progeny provided me with a delightful surprise and reminder of the broad sweep of our historic extended family. One summer in the late 1990s, the chief judge of my court hired a recent law school graduate to work as one of the court's four staff attorneys. At that time, the staff attorneys were all young lawyers, working at the court for one-year terms, mainly to perform legal research, review state court records and write memoranda for use by the six magistrate judges in habeas corpus and other cases filed by prisoners in their own handwriting without lawyer assistance. The staff attorneys were assigned to no particular judge but did work for all of us, including me. It was a way for young lawyers to gather experience and familiarity with the procedures of the court in their first jobs as lawyers, before moving on to more permanent positions. That summer, the new hire was a stout, short, dark-haired bespectacled young man with the fine Italian name John V. Quaglino. The name meant nothing to me at that time when I had not yet begun delving deeply into the family history or reconnecting with my distant cousins. Perhaps I had become accustomed to thinking about all Angies as exclusively belonging to one of my great-aunts or uncles, Jake's Angie, Sugie's Angie, etc. so that my mind had blocked out the possibility that the Angies might also have last names. It never occurred to me that this young man might somehow be a descendent of the great Gaetano DiGiovanni. We called him Johnny Q.

One afternoon just before the Christmas holidays, Johnny Q and I were discussing a prisoner's petition in my office, and I asked him about his holiday plans. "I'm going to spend some time with my mother making Christmas fig cookies," he said.

"*Cucidati*?" I asked, remembering the sweet delights my grandmother used to make for holidays of all kinds, Christmas, St. Joseph's Day, Thanksgiving, Easter. "Bring me some when you come back to work."

About three weeks later, just after New Year's Day, I was back in my office, working away feverishly on some matter that required my immediate and undivided attention. My judicial assistant buzzed me on the telephone intercom. "Johnny Q's here," she said. "He wants to see you."

"Tell him to come back later," I barked. "I'm busy."

"He says it's important."

"Okay," I relented reluctantly. "Send him in."

Johnny Q strode into my office determinedly. A crooked-mouthed expression I could not describe as a smile was fixed on his face, and a small plastic ziplock bag full of cookies, the Sicilian holiday treat *cucidati*, was in his right hand.

"Here," he said impatiently. "I brought you your cookies. I want you to taste one right now."

"Now," I said, "that's what was so important that you needed to interrupt me. This can't wait till later?"

"It's important, Judge," he replied, thrusting the bag into my hands. "Please, taste one."

I breathed a heavy sigh, reached into the bag, and brought one of the delicacies to my mouth. The bite was heavenly; sweet and fig-filled, the baked dough soft and tender, the white almond icing flecked with red, white, and green sugar sprinkles.

"Oh, my God." I said in ecstasy. "This is absolutely delicious. It tastes just like my grandma DiGiovanni's *cucidati*."

"They ought to," Johnny Q said. "They're made from her recipe."

"What?"

Johnny Q broke into a giant toothy smile. "My mother is Angie DiGiovanni Quaglino Sheppard. Walter's Angie. My grandfather is Vito DiGiovanni, your uncle Walter, your grandmother Lena's younger brother. We have the same great-grandparents."

That "V" middle initial of his name stood for Vito.

CHAPTER 37

WIDOWHOOD PART 3

Ann Guinta Wilkinson was the daughter of Natale and Antonia (Lena, Nia) DiGiovanni Guinta. She claimed to be the favorite granddaughter of Angelina Bucaro DiGiovanni. She married regular American Joe Wilkinson, originally of Plaquemine, Louisiana, and later the New Orleans Irish Channel. Together, they had seven children, including me. After her husband died in 2008, she sparked my search into the family history and the writing of this book, in part so that she could herself discover through my efforts what that history had been. Her mother's stories and the stories of her brother and first cousins are the source of much that is reported in this book. One of Mom's favorite authors, Barbara Grizzuti Harrison, once wrote, referring to her father, in a book I inherited from Mom, "It does not matter to me whether these stories are in any way or every particular true. What is true is that my father told them, and that is what matters."[629] I feel the same way about the stories told by my mother and her Sicilian kin. Often, their stories served as a start-up point, with Mom as an instigator, prompting me to research, explore, and divine large chapters of her family history that she did not know. For example, she did not know what Baiocco was or meant or who Mr. Luke was or what exactly her aunt Lou had done in 1934 until I revealed it all to her. Some of what I learned, I could not bring myself to tell her or write about until after she died.

In her own widowhood, Ann Guinta Wilkinson, also confirmed the mettle of her 100 percent Sicilian genes. She had always been independent of thought and highly intelligent. Shortly before Dad died, they had already moved their long empty nest by selling their family home of more than forty years in Terrytown. They moved into their freshly renovated apartment situated in the one-story cinder block "annex" to the historic William Tell Hall on Newton Street in old Gretna that my brothers Tom and Steve own three blocks from the West Bank levee of the Mississippi River. "Make sure you make this thing elder-friendly, honey," she instructed Steve during the renovation. Dad drew up the plans and specifications and then sat in a lawn chair to "supervise" the work of the hired contractors. He was no longer physically able to do the interior demolition, wall-framing, sheet-rocking, finish carpentry, and painting himself, which would have been his preference.

After Dad died, Mom assumed a widowhood regimen that was eerily similar to the widowhood routines of Angelina Bucaro DiGiovanni and Antonia (Lena, Nia) DiGiovanni Guinta. She cleaned her roomy apartment incessantly. She read and knitted voraciously. She cooked large batches of tomato sauce, meatballs, pasta, red beans and rice, seafood gumbo, fried shrimp and soft-shelled crabs, stuffed artichokes and manicotti shells, stewed rabbit, and cucuzza for herself and all of us. She joined the St. Joseph Church Ladies Club and participated in the mass baking of Italian cookies for special occasions and the spectacular annual St. Joseph's altar, where she helped the other ladies serve food to the hundreds of midday visitors, including myself. She became a front pew daily Mass-goer and communicant. Whenever a new grandchild or great-grandchild was born, she packed herself off to the new mother's house and spent a few days or a week taking care of the new baby, telling its mom, "You rest your nerves, honey." They all called her Nana. Each new baby was rocked to sleep at all hours of the child's early days and nights while listening to Nana sing, "Go to sleep little buckaroo... It's time for bed. Another day is through."[630] Mom was entirely self-sufficient financially. She had no mortgage or other debts of any kind. Her children were all self-supporting. Her pension from her days as a Tulane Medical Center nurse and cancer researcher, her Social Security checks, and the IRA money Dad left her as a beneficiary were much more than she needed for the frugal style of living she enjoyed. In fact, she never spent any of the IRA money. She would simply convert the annually required distributions to certificates of deposit and save them for her children in *la banca*, just as the paternal grandmother she never met, Anna Sanstefano Giunta of Castelvetrano, had done with the money her son Natale sent her from America. That way, Nia had recalled her mother-in-law saying, "'if something happens to me, then you'll all inherit.'"[631] In these ways, Mom's absolute independence and total self-reliance were firmly established for all who loved her to see.

She had relied on Dad as an equal partner for much in their marriage, including often his stamp of approval on certain things she wanted to do. After Dad died, that need for a stamp of approval sometimes shifted to me, her oldest son, or Terri, the oldest daughter who watched out for and stayed closest to Mom in her old age. Mom's purchase of the only automobile she ever selected for herself and drove until her death provides an example.

One afternoon not long after Dad died, Mom made her way the few short blocks to my house and knocked on the side door. At that time, she was driving the car Dad had left behind, an economical Toyota sedan he had purchased and driven as his last vehicle. Mom bustled into my den when I opened the door. She took a seat and reached into her purse, pulling out a thin sheaf of glossy brochures.

"Hey, honey, I think I want to give Dad's Toyota to Terri. It's better than the car she's driving now. Is that okay with you?"

"Sure, Mom. Whatever you want to do is okay with me."

"Good. You know your dad always picked out our cars. I never had any say in that. I think I want to pick out my own new car for myself this time."

"Okay, Mom. Whatever you think."

"Great, honey. I'm gonna get me a new Mercedes." She smiled mischievously and handed me her little pile of brochures. "It's a Smart car. Mercedes-Benz makes them. I want a red one. What do you think?"

I was a little aghast as I looked at the brochures. The Smart car was miniscule, no bigger than a gnat, really, as automobiles go. Its tiny size and lack of protective bulk had me concerned. Mom was not the world's greatest driver. She drove like her father, Natale Guinta. Her ultracautiousness and diminutive height, which kept her hunkered down low in the driver's seat while behind the wheel, made her a little bit of a menace on the road. She was always a possible target for being honked at or crashed into by the many more aggressive drivers with whom she would be sharing the streets of Gretna. For her own safety, I would have preferred to see her driving an Army tank or at least a Hummer or a reinforced Ford LTD POS ("police officer special"), something with a better chance of protecting her bodily safety in an inadvertent collision. I hesitated. But then I remembered her driving habits: no driving in the rain, no highways, no merging, no crossing of bridges, as few left turns as possible (right turns only were her preferred routes of travel). Mom would not really be going anywhere anyway. Her habitual destinations were few: St. Joseph's Church in Gretna (two blocks from her house), the Casey Jones (later Rouse's) grocery store (twelve blocks from her house); the Olde Gretna Pharmacy (only three blocks from her house); my house (six blocks away); her doctors' offices (the longest but least frequent of her trips, usually no more than two miles from her home and all reachable without the use of highways or bridges and with minimal left turns required). I was comforted that she had selected bright red as the car's color; the better for other drivers to see her on the road and take their own precautions.

"Look, Mom," I said. "You don't need my okay for anything. You've still got all your marbles. Your health is good. You can still see and hear. You're rich as Rockefeller. You do whatever you want."

"Thanks, honey."

A few weeks later, she had her tiny red Smart car, paying cash to make the purchase. It was delivered to the off-street parking lot behind the Newton Street building, where she had her own spot so that she would not have to drive it from the showroom across the Mississippi River bridge to Gretna. She loved her little red Smart car. She drove it only to the nearby locations I had foreseen. She made as few left turns as possible. On the rare occasions when it was necessary for her to reach a destination across the river or by using a highway, for funerals or weddings or to visit the Guintas or other relatives in Metairie, she asked one of her children to chauffeur. She decorated the car with a fuzzy animal's tail of some sort hanging from the rear-view mirror, a zebra-skin motif steering wheel cover, and a plastic red, green and white license plate frame sporting the inscription "I love being Sicilian." She drove so little, the distances she traveled were so short, and the Smart car burned so little fuel that she infrequently needed to refill on gasoline. She would not venture to the gas station herself. Buying her preferred brand of gasoline would have required her to cross the busy West Bank Expressway, and arthritis in her hands made it difficult for her to unscrew the gas tank cap. So every four months or so, Mom would ask one of her grown children or grandchildren who lived nearby to take the car for a fill-up. We anticipated the day when one of us grown Wilkinson children would have to drive the car to the dealership for its six-thousand-mile initial servicing and oil change, but that day never came.

Before she died, Mom handwrote a special codicil to her will, giving the car upon her death to my brother Matt, with instructions that he give it to his daughter Hannah, who was then approaching driver's license age of sixteen. Matt's reaction to the news reminded me of my own when Mom first approached me looking for my okay for her Smart car purchase. "I'm not letting Hannah drive that little tin can," Matt said. As executor of Mom's estate, in keeping with Matt's wishes, and figuring Mom would be okay with it in the afterlife, I sold the car and gave the money to Matt. He used it in accordance with Mom's general instructions to get Hannah a used car, but one that was more substantial.

Mom died peacefully in her own home, seated on her own living room sofa on March 27, 2017. She was eighty-one years old. Terri discovered her first thing that morning when she passed by to check on Mom before heading to work. She telephoned me frantically, and I hurried over. Before the emergency medical technicians and police officers arrived in response to Terri's 911 call, we were both able to compose ourselves. Mom's rosary was on the nightstand of her nearby bed, recently used. Jarring and sorrowful as it was to see my formerly strong and active Mom slumped over in the seated position on her sofa, Terri and I were able to recognize what a beautiful death it must have been, the exact kind of passing Mom would have wanted for herself.

Her children and grandchildren made her visitation and funeral service a genuine celebration of her life. My sisters decorated the Lakelawn Metairie funeral home parlor with family photos, flowers, and an intricate poster board illustrating the many highlights of her life. Her obituary cataloged her many accomplishments: "Ann was the smartest girl in her class at St. Teresa of Avila School and the salutatorian of the 1953 graduating class of Redemptorist High School in the Irish Channel. For the first fifteen years of her marriage, she was a dedicated stay-at-home mom to her seven children… When her children were all settled into Christ the King School, she returned to school herself, and earned her RN degree in nursing from Hotel Dieu School of Nursing in 1971 and her Family Nurse Practitioner certificate from…Tulane University…in 1978. She was one of the first licensed nurse practitioners in Louisiana. She worked her entire distinguished medical career in New Orleans, including… for thirty years as Clinical Research Nurse at the Tulane Medical School, Section of Oncology/Hematology, Tulane Cancer Center. She was the confidante and adviser of some of the most distinguished physicians in the city,…mentor to numerous medical and nursing students, some of whom called her 'Mama'," member of numerous professional societies and presenter of cancer research papers.[632]

Her Requiem Mass was concelebrated by two priests from St. Joseph Church in Gretna, including its then-new pastor and its second-generation Sicilian pastor emeritus, Father Frank Carabello. In the eulogies, my daughter Katie (Katherine Antonia) and I attempted to convey the uniqueness of her character and life experiences. We recounted some of the expressions she had passed down to us from Nia and old Grandma DiGiovanni ("*Coragio, figghia mia, nun ti scantare*" (Courage, my daughter, don't be afraid). I retold the funniest story we could recall about her from her childhood on Tchoupitoulas Street: As little Ann, "Mom had gone to the Coliseum Theater to see the movies one afternoon, chaperoned as always by her older brother. In those days, the movie theaters in New Orleans gave door prizes to the patrons, and that day little Ann Guinta's ticket had been drawn, and her door prize was a giant salami. The little girl had been mortified when her name was called, and her brother had worsened her embarrassment by refusing to help her carry the enormous salami home. As the children walked several blocks from the theater to the family bar and restaurant, they passed some neighbors sitting on a porch. One of the neighborhood men, seeing little Ann struggling to carry the salami, which was almost as long as she was short and almost as thick as she was skinny, shouted out, 'Hey, salami, where you goin' with that little girl!' The taunt had been enough to reduce Mom to a wailing fit of tears, which Nia found hilarious upon delivery of the salami and my uncle Joe's explanation for his sister's waterworks when the children returned home."[633]

In the sometimes sorrowful, sometimes joyful nostalgic introspection that the death of a beloved parent brings to offspring in their adulthood, I cataloged the many gifts Mom had given to me. I recalled that when we were kids and the seven of us would become involved in the arguments, scrapes, whining, and complaining that frequently sprung from close living with six siblings, Mom would sharply break up the squabbles. Flashing some of the prescience planted deeply in her genes by Gaetano DiGiovanni, she would say, "Someday, you're gonna appreciate each other and be glad that you've got all these brothers and sisters." Mom was right. The gift of so many siblings has been a gift that never stops giving. In her last few years of life, she had given me the gift of watching Italian movies like *Il Gattopardo* (*The Leopard*) and *Cinema Paradiso* (*Paradise Cinema*) on television in her living room on the movie nights she sometimes hosted. In the years since her death, I have recognized other gifts of the DiGiovanni-Guinta family genes passed to me through Mom: the occasional ability to lapse into the equanimity of Natale and Lena; Natale's hair-trigger temper (itself tempered by Dad's ability usually to control it); an affinity for mediation, judgment-making, giving counsel, and searching for solutions to other people's problems directly from Don Tano Baiocco, Gaetano DiGiovanni; a heckof-a Christmas lasagna (if I must say so myself) passed down from old Ma-Maw, Angelina Bucaro DiGiovanni. One of Mom's lasting gifts for which I am particularly thankful is a familial connection that only she could bestow and that has brought me together physically and psychically with my DiGiovanni kin and ancestors: my intellectual and filial relationship with her authentically Sicilian cousin, Paolo "Paul" DiGiovanni of San Cipirello, Palermo Province, and Metairie, Louisiana.

CHAPTER 38

MY COUSIN PAOLO

On June 28, 2015, I was slowly shaving and showering to prepare myself for another day in my office in the New Orleans federal courthouse. My government-issued cellphone rang.

"Judge Wilkinson," said an excited voice on the other end of the line. It was Marilyn, my longtime trusty judicial assistant, calling breathlessly with what seemed to her to be an urgent message. "I was listening to the voice mail messages when I got to the office this morning. Someone who said he's your cousin Paul DiGiovanni left his number and asked you to call him right away. He said it's 'a matter of life and death.'"

"All right," I said calmly, recognizing the quintessentially Sicilian use of hyperbole Mom's cousin Paolo DiGiovanni sometimes employed in his manner of communication. I hung up with Marilyn and called Paul's number immediately.

"Jay, Jay, Jay," Paul said sadly but excitedly. "Thank you for calling. Our cousin's husband is dying in Palermo. I must fly to them quickly, offer comfort, support, whatever I can. But my green card! She's expired! If I go, I cannot get back into this country. Can you help me?"

"Green card?" I asked. "You don't have a US passport? I thought you were a US Army veteran and became a citizen a while back. What's this about a green card?"

"Yes and no," Paul said. "I never became a citizen. I still have my Italian passport. I got all the papers in the mail a while back to renew my green card, but I just forgot to do it. I had one of our cousins call the immigration office for me. They said I could reapply, but it's gonna take months to get a new one. I gotta go to Sicily now. I guess I might still go anyway. When I first went back to visit San Cipirello in the 1980s, I forgot my green card at home, and they still let me back in."

"Well, airport security's a lot tighter now," I said. "Don't risk not being able to come back. Green cards aren't really my department, but let me get into my office and make a few phone calls. Maybe there's something we can do to speed things up. We wouldn't want to lose you to Italy."

"Oh, thank you, thank you, thank you. Let me know. I gotta do something to get to Palermo."

"Okay, Paul. Just don't do anything till I get back to you."

First, I called the cousin who had already tried to help. She confirmed what Paul had told me and reviewed what had already been done. Then I called a couple of Assistant United States Attorneys who handled immigration matters for the Justice Department. Both said they would check into the procedures and get back to me. When they did, their conclusions were bleak: "It's not sounding great" for quick resolution, one of them said. An application for a new permanent resident card would have to be filed and processed. These things just took a lot of time in the ordinary course of the federal government bureaucracy. One of them confirmed that if Paul traveled to Sicily with an expired green card, he would be denied reentry into the United States upon his return. To make matters worse, the lawyer noted that an alien resident walking around with an expired green card might be committing a federal misdemeanor. One of the lawyers suggested that I telephone the director of the local immigration office myself to see if there was anything that could be done. "Okay," I said. "Thanks for your efforts. What's the name and telephone number?"

When the lawyer gave me the name of the local Immigration and Naturalization Service (INS) official, it immediately rang a bell in my cluttered mind. Hadn't I received some kind of communication from or about this same person lately? I scrolled through my email inbox. There it was, this same official's name, in an email recently circulated by the court clerk in charge of organizing the naturalization proceedings for new American citizens that periodically were conducted in our court. The email said that the local INS office was looking for one of our court's judges to preside over a special naturalization ceremony to swear in newly minted Americans on the Fourth of July at the National World War II Museum in downtown New Orleans. I had conducted many of these court sessions during my years on the bench and found them to be the most pleasant, enjoyable, and satisfying duties I ever performed as a judge. Unlike most court sessions, naturalization proceedings featured flag-waving, pride-evoking, broad smile-beaming, thoroughly happy, and satisfied participants. I always delivered a little congratulatory speech for the new citizens and their family members in attendance that mentioned my own status as the progeny of Sicilian immigrants named DiGiovanni and Guinta. In this particular instance, however, I plead guilty initially to a lapse in my desire to fulfill my judicial duties to the maximum possible extent. I did not really want to put on a suit and tie in the sweltering heat of a New Orleans Fourth of July, on the second day of what I had planned to be a relaxing poolside four-day weekend, and troop across the Mississippi River to conduct what amounted to a court session. Upon receipt of the email, I hoped that any one of the other judges of our court would volunteer. Now with less than a week to go before the July 4 ceremony, I hoped that no one had volunteered so that I could offer my services. Sure enough, when I telephoned the clerk to ask if the INS request had been filled, she said, "Not yet. A couple of judges told me that if no one else volunteered, I should call them at the last minute, and they might do it, but it didn't really seem like they were enthusiastic."

"Fear not," I said. "I'll gladly do it. Let the INS folks know that I'm their man and ask one of them to call me so I can get the details on time, place, and exactly what they want me to do."

Within thirty minutes, I had been copied on an email exchange between the clerk and the INS confirming that I would preside on the Fourth of July and received a phone call from the INS official, who was happy and grateful. On the telephone, we firmed up the details of time, oath-giving, speech-making, attire, and certificate presentation. "Yes," the official said, it would be perfectly fine for my wife to attend. "Just so you know," she added, "we're expecting that the newspaper and television people are going to be there to cover it. We've got about eighty new citizens to swear in, including the new director of the museum."

"All sounds great," I said. "I'm looking forward to it. By the way, are you the same person who might be in charge of the office that handles expired green cards and applications for new ones?"

"I sure am," she said.

I outlined Paul's situation and predicament. I referred to him as my "uncle Paolo" while explaining that he was not really my uncle but was my mother's first cousin whom I had referred to since child-hood as "Uncle Paolo" out of respect and because he was twenty years older than me. "Can you do anything to help us with this?" I asked after my explanation.

"Of course," she said. "If Uncle Paolo has his application for renewal pending, we can prestamp his Italian passport before he leaves for Sicily as evidence of his permanent residency for one year, and he can use that to get back into the country and for any other lawful purpose until he gets his new green card. Just have Uncle Paolo complete the application online on our official website and then bring the confirmation receipt, your uncle, and his passport into my office for processing and we'll get him set to go."

I thanked her profusely and made an appointment for Paul and me to see her at her office on July 1. When I called Paul with the good news, he was so grateful that it was almost embarrassing. He was also proud that he knew someone in the family whom he thought was among the sufficiently .50-caliber *pezzonovanti* to pull strings to get such a thing done (i.e., to make a deal, in Paul's mind: a Fourth of July speech for a special favor). I could not persuade him that big shot status was not a prerequisite—that anyone could have accomplished the same thing just by trying. We made arrangements that I would pick Paul up at his house in Metairie and transport him downtown to my office, where we would e-file his new green card application, then proceed to the INS office on Poydras Street three blocks from my own office to deliver the pending application confirmation and meet with the INS officials.

When Paul and I made our way through the security station and metal detector to enter the INS office, the people there treated us like visiting potentates. Although I was greeted initially as "Judge Wilkinson," I immediately took a back seat from a customer service perspective to Paul DiGiovanni, whom the INS folks referred to as "Uncle Paolo." Paul basked in the spotlight of the attention and respect that was being paid to him. With his humility, exuberance, gratitude, and storytelling in response to their questions, Paul charmed the pants off the INS folks who processed his papers. He told them the circumstances of the family troubles in Palermo and the urgent necessity of his trip. He won them over with his self-deprecation concerning his failure timely to renew his green card and the fervent attestation that he loved "this country." When Paul told them about his youthful service of two years in the United States Army and his honorable discharge in 1959, they offered to expedite any application for United States citizenship that he might pursue, dangling the carrot that I—his "nephew"—might be the perfect official to swear him in. Paul merely smiled at this suggestion, raised his right hand in the air, palm open, and wordlessly bowed his head, as if to indicate in all humility that he was unworthy of such an honor. When they stamped his Italian passport on its "visti/visas/visa" page with the magical inscription that would permit him to reenter the United States after his trip to the deathbed of his cousin's husband in Palermo, Paul sighed a deep breath of pride and relief. He stood and shook the hands of every INS employee in the room, thanking each one with such obvious sincerity and gratitude that all present were proud to be Americans, even those—like Paul and some of the other customers—who were actually citizens of some foreign power.

Paul took off for Sicily the next day. He returned after two weeks, having fulfilled his cousinly ministrations and bearing gifts for me. One gift was a colorful map of Sicily emblazoned on a fine piece of white linen with stylized artistic renderings of its most famous sites and figures (including Mount Etna, the iconic painted Sicilian donkey cart, Palermo's baroque Church of San Giuseppe dei Teatini and the Greco-Roman ruins at Agrigento). Another gift was a *carabinieri pupo* (puppet) with strings attached for my manipulation of its arms, legs, and mouth. It was a colorful, uniformed, plumed hat-wearing little man of the type used in Palermo's traditional miniature puppet theaters, a figurine that "symbolized the thirst for justice, the anger and frustration of the oppressed, and the desire for redemption. A puppet, after all, could speak volumes, while a man couldn't."[634] Paul's third gift was a genuine brass baiocco coin, stamped with the date 1842 on one side and bearing the crest of Pope Gregory XVI on the other. He explained that he had not been able to locate one in the shops of Palermo during his visit, so he scoured the world's ancient coin sources on the internet and purchased this one for me from a Czech collector. I encased the small coin in glass, which I mounted on a wooden base that I hand-cut to size, stained, varnished, and glued on an inscription reading "DiGiovanni Baiocco." I proudly displayed it for Paul at one of our annual family St. Joseph's Altars. He grinned broadly then looked at me and said, "You're crazy."

During the precious time we spent together or chatted on the telephone, Paul confessed that he was not always the sterling human I proclaimed him to be in manhood. "I was a bad kid in Sicily," Paul said wistfully. "I stole. My poor mother [the sweet and patient Giuzza Cannella DiGiovanni]…" He described how, when packages arrived in San Cipirello in the 1940s and early '50s, mailed from the family back in New Orleans, he sometimes opened them, removed the most valuable items, like nylon stockings and bags of coffee, sold them in Palermo and pocketed the cash for himself. It was one of the least serious of his Sicilian offenses that caused the most trouble when the family was preparing to emigrate. "One time, I got a speeding ticket for going too fast in town on a bicycle. My mama gave me the money to go to the police station and pay it, but I kept the money for myself instead. She didn't find out about it until we were getting ready to come to the States. It was still on my police record. We had to pay to have it expunged before we could leave." His proclivities as a Sicilian youth were well-known in the family, some of whom decided to take preemptive action when he arrived in New Orleans in 1953. "Uncle Sugie told me, 'Paolo, you either get good, or I'm gonna drop you in the river.' Yeah, I had a bad reputation when I came to this country, but I made a 180-degree change. People started to say I was a good boy."

Paul's positive American turnaround was so complete that he was able to win the heart of Angie Pedalino; earn the approval of

Carmelo Pedalino; serve through an honorable discharge in the United States Army; and live a long life as an exemplary husband, father, and grandfather, restauranteur, weekend soccer player and coach, mentor, and friend. After Angie died and into his oldest age, particularly after suffering through and surviving a major heart attack at the age of eighty-four and during the isolation and introspection of the 2020 COVID-19 pandemic quarantine, Paul became a thoughtful philosopher whose greatest loves and concerns were for other people. He sometimes proclaimed himself a "socialist," though in a quiet, nonpolitical way and only because he was "for the people." He decried the anti-immigration sentiments of a seemingly growing number of Americans, wondering what might have become of him and his family had such an attitude prevailed in 1953. He reveled in what he saw as a coming-together and growing closeness within nuclear families during the pandemic quarantine, as he watched the little families of his Metairie neighborhood sitting together in their front yards or riding their bicycles past his house. "Family is the most important thing," he frequently told me.

It was also during this time that Paul sought earnestly to "right my past wrongs," as if these self-proclaimed "wrongs" were anything more than youthful mistakes, mere oversights, and common human shortcomings. Among the "wrongs" that weighed most heavily on his mind was the saga of his failed first teenage love in Sicily, the kind of story suitable for Italian operatic treatment.

When he was the young teenage Paolo in San Cipirello in the early 1950s, he fell hopelessly in love with a similarly young beauty, Teresina. At age seventeen, three weeks before he left Palermo for the United States, Paolo went to his sweetheart's home, dressed in his only suit, starched white shirt, scarf, and tie. He knocked on the door. Teresina's father answered.

"*Signore*," Paulo said respectfully. "I am in love with your daughter, Teresina. With all respect, I ask your permission to court her. I want to marry her, but I am leaving for the United States in three weeks."

Teresina's father eyed the young man carefully. He knew that Paolo was the grandson of the late, great Gaetano Baiocco DiGiovanni. He did not want to treat a young man of such lineage lightly or disrespectfully.

"There's a lot of water between Sicily and America," the older man said. "You are young. Go off with your family to America. Write to my daughter frequently from your new home across the ocean. If you feel the same way after a while, return to us, express yourself, and you will have my blessing."

Paolo nodded deferentially in obedient agreement. He left the house and walked down the street, where Teresina and some of her friends were gathered. Paulo told his sweetheart what her father had said. They agreed to write each other.

Once Paolo arrived in America, many letters were initially exchanged. Back and forth went the letters, two or three times a week, between Paolo in New Orleans and Teresina in Sicily. But over the course of six months or so, as Paul fell in love with his future wife, Angie, the frequency of his letters fell away. Paul found that as his unspoken love for Angie increased; his confidence in the face of women decreased. He could not find the courage either to tell Angie how he felt or to write Teresina a "Dear John" letter. Instead, he placed a transatlantic telephone call to his old friend, Fredo, back in Sicily. Paolo knew that Fredo had also been sweet on the beautiful Teresina, but Fredo's respect and friendship for Paul were such that he did not want to step on Paolo's teenage romantic toes. Paul confided in Fredo what his love for Angie had done to him in America and suggested that his old friend move in on Teresina. Fredo seized the opportunity, married Teresina, and they had a long and successful marriage in Palermo, where they reared a fine family of five children.

A quarter century or so later, Paul and Angie, a long-established American-dwelling married couple themselves by then, traveled to Sicily to reminisce, see the old sights of their childhood, and visit family and friends. They arranged to meet with Fredo and Teresina in Palermo. The meeting did not go well. "The tension was so thick," Paul recollected. "It was very unpleasant."

Time passed. Five years after Paul's Angie died in 2008, just short of their fiftieth wedding anniversary and more than two decades after their ill-fated reunion with Fredo and Teresina during their return trip to Sicily, Paul began to reflect deeply on his life. He wanted to apologize to Teresina for not telling her himself in 1954 that he could not marry her, to explain that it was only love, his great and eternal love for Angie, that had caused him to act that way. He began to write a letter of explanation and apology to Teresina. It was a slow and painful process. Months went by and the letter reached seven pages in length, but Paul could not finish it or find the right words adequately to express himself.

Over time, Paul decided to make another transatlantic telephone call, this time to Teresina. When she answered the telephone in Palermo, Teresina was surprised to hear that it was Paolo DiGiovanni. Teresina quickly assumed that he wanted to talk to Fredo and handed the phone to her husband. That day, Paul spoke to Fredo for a long time on the phone. They caught up on sports and the doings of their now-grown children and chitchatted small talk, but Paul never got to talk to Teresina. More time passed, and Paul's nagging need to apologize and explain himself persisted. He called Teresina again, and this time, she was home alone when she answered his call. When Paul announced himself, Teresina exploded in a vociferous rage that lasted forty minutes. She angrily howled every foul epithet she could muster in Paul's direction, making it clear in that beautiful Sicilian dialect that is more suitable than any other for profane excoriation that Paolo was a no-good, rotten son of a bitch for the pain he had caused and the way he had treated her more than fifty years earlier. For more than half a century, Teresina had harbored a horrific grudge against Paolo DiGiovanni and waited for the day when she could unleash it in a stream of curses aimed at her transgressor. Eventually, Teresina hung up, slamming down the phone's receiver with Paul having been unable to get in a word edgewise either to apologize or to give his side of the story.

Paolo DiGiovanni at home alone in Metairie, Louisiana, was deeply saddened for weeks. Over the course of months, even years, his sadness turned to sorrow for Teresina across the ocean in Palermo; sorrow that she had carried this anger around in her heart for fifty-plus years; sorrow for her inability to forgive; sorrow that she could not seem to let it go and recognize with gratitude and love that it had all ended happily for both her and Paul, in her long-lasting marriage to a solid man like Fredo, with the fine family and life of their own they had made together in Sicily, just like Paul and Angie in America.

Another five years of sorrow and regret passed, and Paul decided to try again. He telephoned Teresina at her home in Palermo. This time, both Fredo and Teresina took turns getting on the telephone to berate Paul. Again, Paul could not get in a word edgewise, either to apologize or explain. "You're crazy!" Fredo shouted at him through the telephone line. "You need to be put in an insane asylum!" Teresina echoed when it was her turn. The phone slammed down again, and Paul was left in disappointed silence.

"Jay, Jay, Jay," he said thoughtfully when he recounted this story to me over lunch one day. "I cannot understand why people think this way."

"Well, Paul," I said, "maybe it's time for you to give up on Teresina and just move on to happier things yourself."

"No," he said patiently. "I cannot give up. I think I'll try to call her again after a little time passes since it looks like I will never be able to finish that letter."

"Would you like me to finish the letter for you?" I volunteered. "I could be like Cyrano de Bergerac,[635] and you could be Christian to Teresina as Cyrano's Roxanne. Or I could act like those old-time scribes who used to sit in the public squares in the little villages of Sicily, writing letters for people who could not do it for themselves. I'll sit at a desk in your house in front of a computer screen while you stand behind me and just talk. I'll translate it into good words and put it down on paper for you, and then you can hand-write it in Italian for Teresina. You could stick it in the mail and be done with it."

"No," he chuckled. "I must right my own wrongs and write my words myself. I only tell you this story so you will understand the mindset of a particular Sicilian woman. There may be others out there like her. I count my blessings that I found my Angie and married her. She was just the opposite of Teresina."

I lack ambition at this late stage of my life, but I still have one aspiration. I want to outlive my friend and "uncle" (*Zu* Paolo), my mother's first cousin Paolo DiGiovanni, a man I love and greatly admire. Even though he is twenty years older than me, the odds of my realization of this ambition are small. Paul's Sicilian longevity genes are strong. He has already survived the Great Depression and World War II in Western Sicily, the Portella della Ginestra massacre, transatlantic crossings, the tragedy of the too-early death of a beloved spouse, the haranguing hostility of a spurned lover, a massive heart attack at age eighty-four that would have killed a lesser physical specimen and the COVID-19 pandemic. I have no equal toughening experiences or longevity advantages. Still, I hope I outlive Paul, only so that I can attend his funeral. There, I will attest to his greatness as a human being, express my gratitude and love for having known him, and join with my fellow mourners in a prayer en masse for the salvation of his eternal soul, a prayer so loud and sincere that the Almighty cannot help but hear and grant it. When the prayer ends, I will look out into the funeral parlor for the sight of an aged but still beautiful Sicilian woman. The snow whiteness of her hair and brilliance of her smile will contrast starkly against the fire engine red veil and garishly bright red dress she will be wearing. I will feel no need to introduce myself. I will know she is Teresina.

CHAPTER 39

MY GODFATHER, UNCLE JOE

Again, I was sitting at my desk in my office one afternoon when my trusty judicial assistant Marilyn buzzed me on the intercom. "Your uncle Joe is on the phone and wants to speak to you."

"What's up, Unk?" I said when I picked up the phone, familiarly greeting my mother's older brother, the reigning patriarch of the Guinta family, my Godfather.

"I hear you're doing a lot of research into the family history," he said, straight to the point, without pleasantries or any of his often-employed kidding around.

"That's right," I replied. "I'm deep into it, but I'm not nearly finished. There's a lot more out there."

"Tell me," he said. "In your research, have you come across anything about Kansas City?"

"Yes."

There was dead air on the phone as Uncle Joe paused for a brief moment on the other end. "I need to see you," he said with urgency. "When can you come to my house?"

"Monday afternoon is good," I said. "I'll bring my box of research files." We set the date, June 8, 2009.

On the appointed day, I stowed my banker's box of research files and reference books in the trunk of my car. At that time, they were only a small fraction of the materials I have since accumulated. I drove the short distance from my downtown office to Uncle Joe's house. It was located in Old Metairie, one of the oldest suburbs of New Orleans situated in neighboring Jefferson Parish. His house was built near the same Metairie Ridge where Mrs. Leonardo Cipolla had hidden while waiting for her uncle Gaetano DiGiovanni to retrieve her from the murderous carnage that resulted in the death of Uncle Joe's own uncle, Domenico DiGiovanni, on Tupelo Street in 1921. It was a new house, constructed only a few years earlier, but on the same piece of ground where he and his wife, my Godmother Aunt Patricia (Nonnie), had lived for years. It was a style of suburban home that could only have been conceived by someone like my uncle who had lost everything in the catastrophic flooding of Hurricane Katrina in 2005. Having been wiped out by one hurricane's flooding, he had vowed not to be destroyed again. The flooded old house was demolished and a new one was built on high stilts, like the fishing camps that dot South Louisiana's estuarian coastline, twenty feet above ground level. Under the raised living quarters was an open-air area for bench swings, seafood boiling, grilling, storage, and outdoor leisure. The small home's living area high above the flood plain was kept simple, big enough only for my uncle and his wife to live out the days of their old age and retirement in comfort and privacy. It was reachable from the ground below in two ways: a long front staircase leading to a wide porch and the doorway to its living room, or an elevator traveling from the driveway up to a side doorway to the kitchen. I walked up the stairway, carrying my box of research materials over one shoulder, and knocked on the door. Uncle Joe opened it immediately and expectantly.

We greeted each other with a hug and smiles, and I plopped my materials down on his kitchen table. "Where's Nonnie?" I asked when I noticed we were alone and I did not see my aunt in the living room or the kitchen. "I sent her off to visit one of her friends," he said. "I told her I'd pick her up and bring her home when we finished." We were alone. He offered me a beverage, and I opted for a soft drink, which he poured over a few cubes of ice into a tall tumbler. I took a sip, and Uncle Joe sat down next to me. He got right down to business.

"So what do you know about Kansas City?" he wanted to know.

I reached for my volume of Critchley's history of American organized crime and began to search for a particular set of dog-eared pages. "I know that three DiGiovanni brothers were the Kansas City Mafia chiefs going back to the early 1920s. I know that they had close ties with the St. Louis mob. I've got a few newspaper articles that say that Leonardo Cipolla, one of the two big shots probably responsible for Uncle Dominick's murder in 1921, may have been killed in St. Louis about a year after Dominick was shot, right before the other big shot, Vito DiGiorgio, was definitely killed in Chicago in 1922."

Uncle Joe frowned a deep frown. "Okay," Uncle Joe said. "I brought you here to clear my father."

I said nothing. I was more interested in observing Uncle Joe and listening closely to whatever he was about to say. Clear his father? I thought to myself. Clear him of what?

"When is the earliest that you think my father was in New Orleans?" Uncle Joe asked.

At the end of that question, I knew exactly what it was for which Uncle Joe sought Natale Guinta's exoneration. I concluded right then in my own mind, but did not and would not say and had never before considered, that he wanted to clear his father of the 1922 vendetta assassinations, reportedly of Leonardo Cipolla in St. Louis and definitely of Vito DiGiorgio in Chicago, at about the one-year anniversary of his uncle Dominick's murder. I also knew other things that I did not mention to Uncle Joe. I knew that Natale's obituary had reported that when he died in 1967, he had been "a resident of this city [New Orleans] for the past forty-five years."[636] I knew that Natale's 1967 death certificate, with Nia as the "informant" to the recording physician, stated that Natale's "[l]ength of stay in New Orleans [was] forty-five years."[637] I knew that Natale had been arrested in New Orleans in the reputed Black Hand episode in 1923, shortly after the DiGiovanni family pulled up its New Orleans stakes and returned to Sicily for seven years. Uncle Joe Guinta, Natale's friend, confidante, and only son, must have known these same things. Doing the simple arithmetic, the obituary and death certificate indicated that Natale had arrived in New Orleans in early 1922, shortly before the reputed Cipolla and confirmed DiGiorgio killings. Why would my uncle conclude that I might be thinking there was any possibility that his father, my grandfather Natale Guinta, was involved?

I looked squarely into Uncle Joe's face, saying nothing. He had shifted his eyes downward so that our eyes could not meet. His expression was pure torture. He loved his father. He wanted me to love him too. If my research showed that Natale had arrived in New Orleans after 1922, that would be the basis on which Uncle Joe could clear his father with me.

Try as he did to maintain his usual air of animated authority, I could see the conflict that was bubbling inside my Godfather. Despite his long Americanization, his rise to the rank of lieutenant colonel in the United States Air Force, his college education in one of the finest private universities of the South, his professional career as an engineer for one of America's biggest shipbuilders, his genetic makeup and upbringing were 100 percent Sicilian. He was the son, best friend, and confidante of Natale Giunta of Castelvetrano, the grandson of Don "Tano Baiocco" Gaetano DiGiovanni of San Cipirello. Uncle Joe was torn. On one hand was the truth-telling urge that all of his upstanding Americanization and my status as his Godson urged him to employ. On the other was the obligation of *omerta* springing from his Sicilian genes and boyhood mentoring. Too late for *omerta*, he must have decided. This Godson of his had already dug too deeply toward the truth and was equipped with exactly the kind of capabilities that might unearth it, regardless of what his uncle told him. Too late also because Uncle Joe had perhaps inherited Gaetano's gift of prescience. Perhaps he foresaw that his own fatal heart attack, which occurred suddenly and unexpectedly to those in his immediate family, was only about ten months in the future.

Uncle Joe struggled with his decision about what to say to me. What to tell this Godson of his about the circumstances that led to his father's membership in the DiGiovanni family? Should he tell the truth as his father had told it to him, or some other version, close enough to seem like the truth but just off enough to satisfy the pull of his own and the genes of his nineteenth-century Sicilian

ancestors? I recalled the written explanations of the experts and historians of nineteenth- and early-twentieth-century Southern Italian
and Sicilian culture: "[Italians] know the truth... But collectively,
they seem sometimes to forget truth's unique importance. They often
ignore it, embellish it, embroider around it, deny it, as the case may
be. They lie to please, to round off a picture, to provoke an emotion,
to prove a point... They must keep secrets."[638] "[T]ruth is a peculiarly precious and dangerous commodity... [Its telling must be tempered by being] prodigiously good at keeping their mouths shut [and
by the ability to] communicate in codes, hints, fragments of phrases,
stony stares, significant silences..."[639] "[T]ruthfulness should be
ordinarily preferred, without abandoning deception altogether...
[I]n the ordinary circumstances of life, use truthfulness in such a
way as to gain the reputation of a guileless man. In a few important cases, use deceit. Deceit is the more fruitful and successful the
more you enjoy the reputation of an honest and truthful man; you
are more easily believed."[640] Right then and there, I could see him
decide on a middle ground. *Picchi didi a verita quanna a farfantaria
cia basta.* (Why tell the truth when a lie will suffice.) He would try
to make 1922 seem like 1931, and Kansas City seem like Chicago or
St. Louis, without expressly saying so; or maybe his own father had
done the same to him.

"My daddy once told me that he had come to New Orleans
to meet and marry Lena, my mother, your grandmother. It was my
grandfather, Gaetano, who contacted Natale while he was a railroad
worker in Tampa. Gaetano promised Natale one of his two daughters, either Lena or Lucille, in marriage, if Natale would come to
New Orleans and do something for him in Kansas City. Natale did
what Gaetano asked him to do, and he picked Lena. They got married in 1931."

"How did Gaetano even know who Natale was?" I asked.

"I don't know," Uncle Joe said. "They were about the same age.
They were both born in little villages in Western Sicily that were only
about seventy miles apart."

"What did Natale do for his future father-in-law in Kansas
City?"

"I don't know."

Silently, I thought about the things Uncle Joe had **not** said. The only year mentioned was the year we all knew Natale and Lena had married. Uncle Joe did not say what year Natale had come to New Orleans. He did not say when Gaetano had contacted him or proffered the bargain for a daughter's hand in marriage. He did not say what year Natale had done what Gaetano asked him to do. He did not really say that Natale had done this thing **in** Kansas City. I was sorely tempted to commence a thorough lawyerly cross-examination, but before I could ask another question, without prompting, Uncle Joe launched into his own long description of the father, Natale Guinta, whom he knew and idolized as a boy in the 1930s and '40s. I could not bring myself to interrupt him.

"Daddy had a ferocious temper, a really short fuse," he said. "He was the enforcer of order in the barroom, especially at night, when the women who worked in the restaurant left and just the bar stayed open. I remember one night, when I got to stay up late in the barroom, one of the women complained that a customer got fresh with her. Natale pulled a pistol from behind the bar and pistol-whipped the man bloody, then dragged him out the door and threw him into the street. Mama heard the ruckus from the back and came in and pulled me away by the neck, but I had already seen what Daddy could do. It sounded like someone hitting a watermelon."

Uncle Joe recalled another day when a man came into the bar, stole some salt shakers off the tables, and ran. Natale grabbed his shotgun, ran onto Tchoupitoulas Street, and fired. Uncle Joe, who was outside, heard the shot and saw the man hit the ground. "You got him, Daddy," the little boy shouted. They ran up to the man together and found that he had not been shot but had run into a street pole in his haste to escape and knocked himself unconscious.

"I shoot over his head," Natale said. "Non-ja (don't you) think I could hit him if I try?"

Uncle Joe also recalled that Natale was equally quick to grab for a knife in the barroom. Once, Natale's niece, Anna Napolitano, who lived far uptown on Constance Street near Audubon Park, came to the bar to complain to Uncle Natale that a man in her neighborhood had treated her disrespectfully. After getting a description of the man and the details of what had happened, Natale pulled a large knife from behind the bar and left in a rage. "I'm-a kill him," was all Natale said. Uncle Joe did not know what had happened after that.

Uncle Joe was certain of Natale's excellent marksmanship. On hunting trips, and sometimes right there on Tchoupitoulas Street, Natale would pick off small birds in flight, seemingly without effort, usually with a shotgun. He told me about the annual New Year's Eve assassination of the mailbox across the street. He added that from time to time, Natale and a neighbor (with whom he was more or less friendly) would stand in the middle of Tchoupitoulas or Erato Streets and fire their shotguns into the air. The pellets from the shells would rain down on the streets like hail falling from the sky, and they would laugh. When he was older, Uncle Joe summoned up the courage to say to Natale, "Why do you do that, Daddy? You could hurt somebody."

"I want-a [want] people to know who they deal with," he said. "I want 'em to know what I can-na [can] do."

At times during his long narration, Uncle Joe's eyes became cloudy in a fog of nostalgia. At times, there was anguish and worry on his face as he contemplated the effect the stories were having on me. I remained silent, listening carefully, mentally recording it all for later commitment to a memo to myself. Uncle Joe paused. The sorrowful, fearful look in his eyes showed me that Uncle Joe knew that his beloved father was capable of murder. He knew that Natale would have done anything Gaetano asked. He did not want to believe this about the man he loved so dearly, whom he respected and thanked for giving him life and love, especially the successful, respectable life and love that Natale had made for the Guinta family in America.

It was then and there that I decided on my own course of action. I loved my uncle. He needed peace and contentment in his old age, not accusations and recrimination. While I was no match for my uncle in any contest of Sicilian wits—I was only half-Sicilian after all—I decided to deceive him. *Picchi didi a verita quanna a farfantaria cia basta* (Why tell the truth when a lie will suffice). I did the best I could (and think I succeeded) in convincing Uncle Joe that

Natale could not have killed either Cipolla or DiGiorgio. Cipolla perhaps and DiGiorgio certainly were assassinated in 1922, perhaps within days of each other. The DiGiovannis fled New Orleans and returned to Sicily shortly thereafter. I lied and told Uncle Joe that I had found no evidence that Natale had made it to New Orleans at that time. Gaetano DiGiovanni did not return to New Orleans from Sicily until 1928. Nia (Lena) returned in 1929. Natale married Nia in 1931. I suggested to Uncle Joe that, based on what his father told him, Natale must have come to New Orleans from Tampa shortly before that. I told him it sounded like whatever Natale did for Gaetano in Kansas City was done long after Cipolla and DiGiorgio were killed.

"You know about that intent to murder indictment on my Daddy that Greg [Guinta, his son, my first cousin] found when he was doing his paralegal certificate studying in the 1980s, huh?" he asked.

"Yeah, I know about it. Nia showed it to me back then after Greg gave her a copy."

"Yeah," Uncle Joe said. "Daddy got in an argument with the fruit and vegetable man, another Italian. He was gonna pistol-whip him because Natale thought the guy cheated him on some things he was trying to buy from him for the restaurant."

"Uh-huh," I said, knowing this was untrue. I knew from the indictment itself, the newspaper articles and the court records that Natale's arrest for stalking the fruit and vegetable man, a suspected Black Hand act of lying in wait with intent to kill, had occurred in 1923, more than ten years **before** "the restaurant" at the old Mr. Joe's had gone into operation in the late 1930s. Why mislead me in this way, if not in an attempt further to "clear" his father of the 1922 vendetta killing? Had he himself been misled by his father, Natale? This was the same explanation Nia had given me when she showed me the indictment herself on Marengo Street after Greg delivered it to her in the 1980s. Had Nia similarly misled her son, Uncle Joe? *Picchi didi a verita quanna a farfantaria cia basta* (Why tell the truth when a lie will suffice?). I said nothing else.

I could see the tension evaporate from Uncle Joe's face and body language. His shoulders relaxed. He breathed a shallow sigh. He seemed satisfied that he had succeeded in his earlier stated objective for our private meeting: "I brought you here to clear my father." Or did he know instead that I was lying and that he had not convinced me at all? I decided to change the topic slightly.

"Tell me something about the character of our grandfather, Gaetano," I said.

"Grandpa was a man of respect," he said. He then smiled broadly, thoroughly relaxed now that the subject was no longer his father's theoretical culpability. "Grandpa had three favorite grand-children: Kaddie [Towle Miller], Mary Lou [Towle Landry], and me. Grandpa used to take me with him to a schoolyard near where we all lived around Tchoupitoulas and Erato and Euterpe Streets. The schoolyard had a padlock, but Grandpa could always open it. We would go into the schoolyard, and Grandpa had a garden there; tomatoes, some other fruit, and vegetable plants. He kept some rabbits there in a pen. We'd pick the tomatoes and fruit. That's where Grandpa taught me how to shoot. It was like he owned the place."

Uncle Joe said his grandfather also took him on little excursions to the New Basin Canal and the stalls and shops of the French Market (including the now-famous Central Grocery) and Esplanade Avenue, where Gaetano would tell little Joe to pick out whatever he wanted, and things would be given to him without any money ever changing hands. Unlike any of the other men Uncle Joe knew, "Grandpa was always dressed in suit and tie. People called him *Zu* [Uncle] Tano or *Consigliori*." He recalled being asked by Natale to take "Mr. Luke" Trombatore rabbit hunting in Mr. Luke's old age. He remembered attending Mr. Luke's wake and funeral with his father after Mr. Luke died in 1963 and being told by Natale, when several of the older men gathered to remember him, to step away so that they could speak in private.

Uncle Joe and I jointly concluded that a man of Gaetano DiGiovanni's character and background could not under any cir-cumstances have accepted the unavenged murder of his eldest son. He had read the newspaper articles passed to him by my mother about his uncle Dominick's murder. Uncle Joe thought it wholly out of character that Gaetano would have gone to Chief of Police Molony and Assistant District Attorney Craven within ten days of his son's murder in May 1921, as *The Times-Picayune* stories report. I hypothesized that Gaetano was smart enough to realize that he had to size them up for himself and make some sort of deal with them since he had in his house at that time the "material witness" the authorities so badly wanted to question, Mrs. Leonardo Cipolla, Gaetano's niece by marriage, undoubtedly a Bucaro. He seemed impressed by my analysis. Uncle Joe did not know (or would not say what he knew) about other key details. When did Natale first come to the United States? He knew he arrived in New York, but when? Why was Natale so shaken on that day in the 1950s when Nia roused him in their house on Marengo Street and announced that there were FBI agents at the door to see him?

Uncle Joe said he had never told my mother what Natale told him about coming to New Orleans at Gaetano's invitation to choose between Nia and Aunt Lou in exchange for the favor in Kansas City. He said he had never told his own children.

"Then why are you telling me?" I asked.

"You'll know what to do with the information," he said.

"What's that?" I asked.

"You can do whatever you want with it."

I decided to tell no one about it at that time. Although I typed it all out in a memo to myself, I buried the memo in my file box at home. It has taken me more than a decade to put it down formally as I have done on these pages. What was it that caused this delay? What was it that Uncle Joe meant when he said I would know what to do with the information? I hope I have complied with his wishes. I hope he knows what I know: that Uncle Joe's depth of love for his father was vast and true and that I recognized his worries and concerns in telling me these things only ten months before Uncle Joe died himself. His concerns were that the story of his parents should not die with him and about the ultimate destiny of a man he loved, the fate of his beloved father's eternal soul—the soul of Natale Guinta whose salvation I have prayed for myself since that day.

EPILOGUE

Many of the sites of the lives of the DiGiovanni-Guinta family of New Orleans, including the family's great catastrophes and triumphs, no longer exist. Nothing bears the address of 843 Tupelo Street, where Uncle Dominick was assassinated. The corner of Religious and St. Mary Streets, where Black Hander Natale Guinta was chased down by police after lying in wait with intent to kill, is now an entryway to a Walmart store. The former 2242 Elysian Fields Avenue, where Aunt Lou waited calmly for the police after killing her married boyfriend a few doors down, is a vacant lot under the elevated Interstate 10 eastbound highway. The gangs of Italian banana unloading stevedores at the docks of the Mississippi River have disappeared. The New Basin Canal, where Gaetano once influenced banana boat unloading jobs, has long been filled and covered. Its shell road has been replaced by the smooth pavement of the Pontchartrain Expressway that transports commuters through the toney Lakeview residential neighborhood. The former canal now is the site of tree-lined jogging paths, a Gaelic cross monument to the Irish immigrants who died building it, and a conical hill-like structure hiding the deserted nuclear fallout shelter built by Civil Defense authorities at the peak of the US-Soviet Union Cold War of the 1950s and '60s. Mr. Joe's bar and the last residence of Gaetano and Angelina DiGiovanni in the 1100 block of Tchoupitoulas Street have vanished, one replaced by a Mississippi River bridge overpass and ramp, the other by a modern condominium building.

Many of the most important things remain. The DiGiovanni interment vault on Avenue B of the old Italian section of Lakelawn Metairie Cemetery still receives placement of flowers on All Saints'

Day. The 1100 block of Marengo Street is still a desirable neighborhood where an American family can grow and prosper. San Cipirello,

Ciminna, and Castelvetrano
still stand in Western Sicily.
These days, in the older age
of my siblings and me, I
can peer into the faces of
my sister Lynn and see the
visage of my great-grand-
mother Angelina Bucaro
DiGiovanni looking back
at me or my sister Judy and
see the smile of Antonia
(Lena, Nia) DiGiovanni
Guinta, or I can size up my
brother Tom and recognize
the spitting image of the
Natale Guinta I knew as a
child. As always, "nothing is more important than *la famiglia* (the
family); the foundation of all things Italian… [I]t is essential for individuals with an Italian background to recognize the contributions of
their ancestors and to pass on a sense of Italian pride to their children
and grandchildren."[641]

Thus, most importantly, the extended American family estab-
lished by Gaetano and Angela DiGiovanni remains. Together,
Gaetano and Angelina reared nine children: Giuseppina (Josephine,
Fene), Domenico (Dominick), Giacomo (Jake), Antonia (Lena,
Nia), Fedele (Sugar, Sugie), Maria (Mary, Ma-Mamie), Lucia
(Lucille, Lou), Vito (Walter), and Francesca (Nookie). Their children
produced thirty-four grandchildren, including Joe Guinta and Ann
Guinta Wilkinson, two Dominicks, two Gaetanos, and six Angies.
La famiglia's hundreds of descendants springing from Gaetano and
Angelina DiGiovanni, their great-grandchildren and infinite num-
bers of children yet to come, are spread across America. Their names
are now more frequently American than Italian. They argue, they
err, they disagree, they sin, they have their troubles and travails, but

mostly, they thrive, prosper, and form the honorable pillars of their American communities. They love each other and their common heritage, thankful for what Gaetano foresaw and Angelina dreamed.

"Gawd (God)," Nia said in her audio-taped 1988 interview. "We have a family."[642]

DiGIOVANNI-GUINTA FAMILY TREE

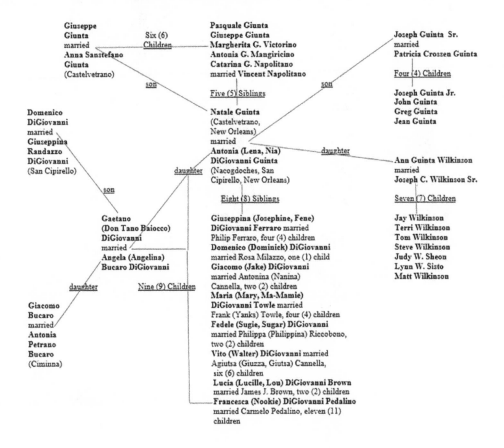

Giuseppe Giunta married Anna Sanstefano Giunta (Castelvetrano) — Six (6) Children

Pasquale Giunta
Giuseppe Giunta
Margherita G. Victorino
Antonia G. Mangiricino
Catarina G. Napolitano
married Vincent Napolitano

Joseph Guinta Sr. married Patricia Crossen Guinta

Four (4) Children

Five (5) Siblings

Joseph Guinta Jr.
John Guinta
Greg Guinta
Jean Guinta

Domenico DiGiovanni married Giuseppina Randazzo DiGiovanni (San Cipirello)

Natale Guinta (Castelvetrano, New Orleans) married Antonia (Lena, Nia) DiGiovanni Guinta (Nacogdoches, San Cipirello, New Orleans)

Ann Guinta Wilkinson married Joseph C. Wilkinson Sr.

Eight (8) Siblings

Seven (7) Children

Gaetano (Don Tano Baiocco) DiGiovanni married Angela (Angelina) Bucaro DiGiovanni

Giuseppina (Josephine, Fene) DiGiovanni Ferraro married Philip Ferraro, four (4) children
Domenico (Dominick) DiGiovanni married Rosa Milazzo, one (1) child
Giacomo (Jake) DiGiovanni married Antonina (Nanina) Cannella, two (2) children
Maria (Mary, Ma-Mamie) DiGiovanni Towle married Frank (Yanks) Towle, four (4) children
Fedele (Sugie, Sugar) DiGiovanni married Philippa (Philippina) Riccobono, two (2) children
Vito (Walter) DiGiovanni married Agiutsa (Giuzza, Giutsa) Cannella, six (6) children
Lucia (Lucille, Lou) DiGiovanni Brown married James J. Brown, two (2) children
Francesca (Nookie) DiGiovanni Pedalino married Carmelo Pedalino, eleven (11) children

Jay Wilkinson
Terri Wilkinson
Tom Wilkinson
Steve Wilkinson
Judy W. Sheon
Lynn W. Sisto
Matt Wilkinson

Nine (9) Children

Giacomo Bucaro married Antonia Petrano Bucaro (Ciminna)

INDEX

A Lie Will Suffice
A DiGiovanni Family History

BIBLIOGRAPHY

A Lie Will Suffice
A DiGiovanni Family History

Books

About Palermo. è un produtto realizzato da: 99idee s.r.l., Via Ausonia, 76, 90100 Palermo (giugno 2001).

Baiamonte, John V., Jr. *Spirit of Vengeance: Nativism and Louisiana Justice, 1921–24.* Louisiana State University Press, 1986.

Barzini, Luigi. *The Italians: A Full-Length Portrait Featuring Their Manners and Morals.* Simon & Schuster 1964, 1st Touchstone ed., 1996.

Black's Law Dictionary. West Revised 4th ed., 1968.

Blok, Anton. *Mafia of a Sicilian Village, 1860–1960: A Study of Violent Peasant Entrepreneurs.* Harper Row 1974.

Bonanno, Bill. *Bound by Honor.* St. Martin's Press, 1999.

Bondanella, Peter and Julia Conaway. *Cassell Dictionary of Italian Literature.* Greenwood Press, 1979.

Chandler, David. *The Criminal Brotherhoods.* London: Constable, 1976.

Coppola, Francis Ford. *The Godfather Notebook.* Regan Arts, 2016.

Couch, Harvey C. *A History of the Fifth Circuit 1891–1981.* Bicentennial Committee of the Judicial Conference of the United States, Federal Judicial Center, 1984.

Critchley, David. *The Origin of Organized Crime in America: The New York City Mafia, 1891–1931.* Routledge, 2009.

Davis, John H. *Mafia Kingfish: Carlos Marcello and the Assassination of John F. Kennedy*. McGraw-Hill, 1989.

De Vito, Carlo. *The Godfather Classic Quotes*. Cedar Mills Press.

Dickie, John. *Cosa Nostra: A History of the Sicilian Mafia*. Palgrave Macmillan, 2004.

Evans, Harold. *The American Century*. Alfred A. Knopf, 1998.

Gelli, Jacopo. *Codice Cavalleresco Italiano (Italian Code of Chivalry)*. 1887.

Glazier, Ira A. and Filbey, P. William. *Italians to America: Lists of Passengers Arriving in U.S. Ports, 1897–1902*. Vol. 12. Scholarly Resources Inc., 2000.

Harrison, Barbara Grizzuti. *Italian Days*. Atlantic Monthly Press, 1989.

Hess, Henner. *Mafia and Mafiosi: The Structure of Power*. Farnborough: Saxon House, 1973.

Holland, Tom. *Rubicon: The Last Years of the Roman Republic*. Anchor Books: Random House, 2005.

Horne, Alistair. *The Price of Glory: Verdun 1916*. St. Martin's New York, 1961.

Kefauver, Estes. *Crime in America*. Doubleday & Co., 1951.

Long, Robert Emmet. *The Achieving of The Great Gatsby: F. Scott Fitzgerald 1920–25*. Associated UP, Cranbury, New Jersey, 1979.

Lyons, Joseph. *CBL, Author and Diplomat*. Chelsea House, 1988.

Marshall, S. L. A. *World War I*. Houghton Mifflin Co., 1987.

Menen, Aubrey. *Art & Money: An Irreverent History*. McGraw Hill, 1980.

Moramarco, Federico and Stephen. *Italian Pride: 101 Reasons to Be Proud You're Italian*. Citadel Press, 2000.

Nania, Gioacchino. *San Giuseppe e la Mafia: Nascita e Sviluppo del Fenomeno Nell'Area Dello Jato (Saint Joseph and the Mafia: Birth and Development of the Phenomenon in the Town of [San Giuseppe] Jato.*" Microsoft Bing trans. https://books.google.com/books?id=m9f1KaQUPCkC&printsec=frontcover#v=onepage&q&f=true (Edizioni della Battaglia 2002).

Niceforo, Alfredo. *Contemporary Barbarian Sicily*. Quoted in Dickie *supra*. 1897.

Ouseley, William. *Mobsters in Our Midst: The Kansas City Crime Family*. Kansas City Star Books, 2011.

Puzo, Mario. *The Godfather*. Penguin Publishing Group and Fawcett Crest Books, 1969.

Puzo, Mario. *The Sicilian*. Bantam Books, 1985.

Quaglino, Angelo. *La Nostra Famiglia*. MacBook, 2011.

Sheon, Lila. *NaNa's Kitchen*. Recipe booklet self-published for family and friends. New Orleans, Louisiana, 2003.

Smith, Tom. *The Crescent City Lynchings: The Murder of Chief Hennessy, the New Orleans "Mafia" Trials, and the Parish Prison Mob*. Lyons Press, 2007.

Stapleton, Michael W. *A House in the Channel*. Unpublished booklet of short stories. Metairie, Louisiana, 2011.

The American College Dictionary. Random House, 1970.

The Catholic Bible: New American Bible, Personal Study Edition. Oxford University Press, 1995.

Wilkinson, Jay, *My Dad's Eulogy*. Self-published for family and friends. Walter W. Eckert Binder & Specialty Co. Inc., New Orleans, Louisiana, 2009.

Magazines and Periodicals

Cacibauda, Joseph L. "The Sicilians of Louisiana." *Italian America*. (Summer 2009).

Feather, Bill. "Mafia Membership Charts, New Orleans 1920–1970s." *Informer* 3, no. 3 (July 2010).

Kendall, John S. "Blood on the Banquette." 22 *Louisiana Historical Quarterly* 831 (July 1939).

Lombardo, Robert M. "The Black Hand." *Journal of Contemporary Criminal Justice* 18, pt. 4 (2002).

Smith, Sandy. "Brazen Empire of Crime, Part 2." *Life* 63, no. 10 (September 8, 1967).

Warner, Richard N. "The First Crime Boss of Los Angeles?" *Informer: The Journal of American Mafia History* 2, no. 3 (July 2010).

Internet Resources, Blogs and Articles

Ambler, Jay C. "Organized Crime Research: Kansas City (PLR International 1998–2008), March 23, 2021. http:/AmericanMafia.com/Cities/Kansas_City.html.

Barry, Gearold. *Demobilization, 1914–1918*, December 4, 2018. https://encyclopedia.1914-1918-online.net/article/demobilization.

Bernstein, Adam. "Post-Mortem." *The Washington Post*, June 5, 2008. www.italianjazz.com/interview.php at §5.

Brister, N. "A Street by Any Other Name, June 15, 2009. http://www.neworleans.com/arts/history.

Campanella, Richard. "185-Year-Old New Basin Canal Continues to Affect Thousands of New Orleanians Every Day." *Cityscapes: A Geographer's View of the New Orleans Area.* First published in *The Times-Picayune*, December 8, 2017. https://rich-campanella.com/wp-   content/uploads/2020/02/Picayune_Cityscapes_2017_12_The-New-Basin-Canal.pdf.

"Chef Natale Giunta." June 15 and July 12, 2010. http://www.natalegiunta.it/news.php.

"Ciminna." September 10, 2010. http://sicilia.indettaglio.it/eng/communi/pa/ciminna.html.

"Contessa Entellina, Images of Blok." *Reportage Sicilia blog*, October 20, 2012. http://reportagesicilia.blogspot.com/2012/10/contessa- entellina-le-i…

Feather, Bill. "Mafia Membership Charts: Unconfirmed Members Charts." November 21, 2017. https://mafiamemberscharts.blogspot.com/2017/11/unconfirmed-members-chart.html.

Hammer, Joshua. "Mafiosos' Retreats, Peacefully Repurposed in Sicily." *The New York Times Reprints*, July 10, 2010. http:/www.nytimes.com/2010/07/04/travel/04explorer.html.

Hunt, Thomas. "Who Was Who: Carolla, Silvestro (1896–1972)." *The American Mafia: The History of Organized Crime in the United States*, June 29, 2015 (hereinafter "Hunt"). http://mob-who.blogspot.com/2011/04/carolla-silvestro-1896-1972.html.

"La Cosa Nostra: Sam Carolla." May 19, 2009. http://www.lacndb. com/php/Info.php?name=Sam%20Carolla.

Lea, John. "The Structure of Traditional Organized Crime," 2008, September 21, 2011. http://www.bunker8.pwp.blueyonder. co.uk/orgcrim/3802.htm.

Louisiana Historical Marker, Town of Jean Lafitte, La. *The Historical Marker Database.* https://www.HMdb.org.

"NOLA History: The Neighborhoods of Uptown New Orleans." October 12, 2011. https://gonola.com/nola/ history- the_neighborhoods_of_uptown_new_orleans.

"San Cipirello." June 14, 2010. http://sicilia.indettaglio.it/eng/ comuni/pa/sancipirello.html.

"Senti le rane che cantano..." ("You Can Hear Frogs Singing..."). Portella della Ginestra. *L'Infanzia della trame* ("The Childhood of Plots"). Quoting "Report of Police Commissioner Cosenza of Palermo, Subject: Serious Crimes Committed in Piana degli Albanesi on the Occasion of the Labour Day on 1 May 1947," May 8, 1947, and Provvisionato, Sandro, *"Misteri d'Italia,"* Laterza (1993). May 31, 2021. Google trans., https:// sites.google.com/site/sentileranechetano.sched/gli-anni/ portella-della-ginestra-l- infam.

"Sicily for Tourists—History of Castelvetrano." September 10, 2009. http://www.regione.sicilia.it/turismo.

"The American Mafia: Kansas City Crime Bosses." June 9, 2009. http://www.onewal.com/maf-b-kc.html.

Wikipedia. "Ciminna." September 20, 2011. http://en.wikipedia. org/wiki/ciminna.

Wikipedia. "Clare Booth Luce." August 28, 2015. https://en.wikipedia.org/wiki/Clare_Boothe_Luce#Ambassador_to_Italy.

Wikipedia. "Don Vincenzo Randazzo." June 15, 2010. http//:en. wikipedia.org/wiki/list/List of Sicilian Mafiosi by City.

Wikipedia. "Federterra." May 31, 2021. https://en.wikipedia.org/ wiki/ National_Federation_of_Agricultural_Workers_Italy.

Wikipedia. "Paolo Gambino." March 22, 2016. http://mafia.wikia. com/wiki/Paolo_Gabino.

Wikipedia. "Savatore Giuliani." September 10, 2009. http://www.
en.wikipedia.org/wiki/Salvatore-Giuliano.

Newspapers

Gambit Weekly, New Orleans, Louisiana, 2013.
New Orleans Item, 1921.
New Orleans States, 1921.
The New York Times, May 10, 1921.
The Times-Picayune, New Orleans, Louisiana, 1921–2017.

Pamphlets

Fifth Circuit Pattern Jury Instructions (Civil). West, 2009.
"John Minor Wisdom United States Court of Appeals Building."
U.S. General Services Administration, Public Buildings Service.
1994.

Court Records and Police Reports

Arrest Report. New Orleans Police Department. Lucille DiGiovanni.
November 26, 1934.
Arrest Report. New Orleans Police Department. Digiovanni [*sic*].
Dominick, July 4, 1920.
State of Louisiana v. Natale Guinta. Case No. 17, 996, Docket "A."
Orleans Parish Criminal District Court, 1923–24.
Succession of Natale Guinta. Case No. 82-19783. Civil District Court,
Parish of Orleans, State of Louisiana, December 21, 1982.
United States v. Nate Goldberg et al. Crim. No. 16, 832. United States
District Court, Eastern District of Louisiana, New Orleans
Division, 1932–34.

Movies, Plays, Songs and Operas

Arnold, Eddy. "My Little Buckaroo." https://www.azlyrics.com/lyr-
ics/eddyarnold/mulittlebuckaroo.html.

Tornatore, Giuseppe. *Cinema Paradiso* (*Paradise Cinema.* Miramax Films, 1988.

Visconti, Luchino. *Il Gattopardo* (*The Leopard*). Titanus, 20th Century Fox, 1963.

Puccini, Giacomo. *La Boheme*, Act IV. 1896.

Rogers, Fred M. "It's a Beautiful Day in the Neighborhood." 1990. https://www.misterrogers.org.

Rostand, Edmond. *Cyrano De Bergerac* (trans. *Gertrude Hall.* Doubleday & McClure Co., 1808.

Coppola, Francis Ford. *The Godfather, Part 1*. Paramount Pictures, 1972.

Audio-Recorded Interviews

Guinta, John, Interviews of Antonia DiGiovanni Guinta and Lucia DiGiovanni Brown, volume 1 (1988), volume 2 (1991), page references to written transcript by Jay Wilkinson (November 2009).

Personal Family Documents

Alien Registration Card, Angela Bucaro DiGiovanni, February 24, 1942.

Alien Registration Card No. 4328082, Gaetano DiGiovanni. US Department of Justice, February 24, 1942.

Alien Registration Form of Natali [*sic*] Giunta, November 7, 1940.

Certificate of Baptism of Antonia DiGiovanni issued October 10, 1989, Sacred Heart Church, 504 North Street, Nacogdoches, Texas, 75961.

Certificato di Nascita, Comune di Castelvetrano (Birth Certificate of the City of Castelvetrano), Natale Giunta, (certified copy issued June 25, 1954).

Certificate of Death, Natale Guinta, City of New Orleans File No. 670000489 (January 19, 1967).

Death Certificate of Antonia Guinta, State of Louisiana Office of Public Health—Vital Records Registry No. 640337 (1998).

Deed, DiGiovanni Family Cemetery Vault, Officials Records of Lakelawn Metairie Funeral Home (1921).

Italian Passport, Angela Bucaro DiGiovanni, November 8, 1923.

Marriage Certificate of Natale Guinta and Antonia DiGiovanni, City of New Orleans, issued January 1, 1931.

Marriage Certificate of Natale Guinta and Antonia DiGiovanni, City of New Orleans Health Department, Bureau of Vital Records, re-issued September 22, 1947, Book of Marriages No. 52, folio 1407.

Procura Speciale, Executed Before Peter Gentile, *Notaro Publico* (April 15, 1954).

Visa, Angela Bucaro DiGiovanni, U.S. Department of Labor, August 24, 1935.

Statutes and Court Decisions

Alien Registration Act of 1940. "The Smith Act," 76th Congress, 3d Session, Ch. 439, 54 Stat. 670, 18 USC § 2385 et seq.

National Prohibition Act, "the Volstead Act," 41 Stat. 305-23, ch. 85 (1919).

US Const., 18th Amendment (prohibition); 21st Amendment (repeal of prohibition).

United States v. Chambers, 291 US 217, 226 (1934).

18 USC. § 1001.

Miscellaneous Sources

DiGiovanni, Paolo "Paul," Metairie, La., Translations of family sayings from English to Sicilian dialect Italian.

FBI report dated July 11, 1967, Bureau File no. 92-6054 (cited by Critchley).

Gregory M. Guinta, "The Great Gatsby in the Aftermath of World War I. Unpublished University of New Orleans student essay, 1986. Citing and quoting Alistair Horne, *The Price of Glory: Verdun 1916* (with internal quotation to Barleusse, "Le Feu'). St. Martin's New York, 1961; Robert Emmet Long, *The Achieving of The Great Gatsby: F. Scott Fitzgerald 1920–25*. Associated UP, Cranbury, New Jersey, 1979.

Letter of Marvin L. Jeffer, Appraiser, to Thomas Wilkinson. September 21, 1982.

Papers of Clare Booth Luce, United States Library of Congress, Lot 11236-1, Nos. 15(g)—17 (G), Photographs of Official Trip to Sicily, December 1953. Library of Congress Prints & Photographs Division, Washington, DC, 2002.

"Wells Fargo Warehouse, Nicholas Tormè House." *GNO Bridge No. 2 News Briefs* (Daniel, Mann, Johnson & Mendenhall, 512 S. Peters Street, New Orleans, La.) (undated est. 1980s).

Wilkinson, Joseph C. Jr. General Civil Jury Instructions of United States Magistrate Judge Joseph C. Wilkinson, Jr. United States District Court, Eastern District of Louisiana (1995–2020).

ENDNOTES

A Lie Will Suffice
A DiGiovanni Family History

1. Sicilian dialect translation by Paolo DiGiovanni, Metairie, Louisiana.
2. "Bandit Feud: 3 Murdered—3 Killed in Feud, Auto, Booze and Bank Gang," *New Orleans States*, May 9, 1921, at 1 (emphasis added).
3. Luigi Barzini, *The Italians: A Full-Length Portrait Featuring Their Manners and Morals* (Simon & Schuster 1964, 1st Touchstone ed. 1996) (hereinafter "Barzini"), 328, 254.
4. *Id.* at 164 (quoting Francesco Guicciardini).
5. John Dickie, *Cosa Nostra: A History of the Sicilian Mafia* (Palgrave Macmillan, 2004) (hereinafter "Dickie"), 24–25.
6. *Black's Law Dictionary* 1429 (West Revised 4th ed., 1968).
7. General Civil Jury Instructions of United States Magistrate Judge Joseph C. Wilkinson, Jr. (quoting in part *Fifth Circuit Pattern Jury Instructions (Civil)* sections 2.11, 2.18, 3.1 (West, 2009); *see generally* John S. Kendall, "Blood on the Banquette," *Louisiana Historical Quarterly*, 22, 831 (July 1939) (hereinafter "Kendall") ("Here, as always in dealing with the Mafia, we are forced to fall back on circumstantial evidence.").
8. Dickie, *supra* n. 5, at 231.
9. Barzini, *supra* n. 3, Foreword at ix–x.
10. http://sicilia.indettaglio.it/eng/comuni/pa/sancipirello.html (June 14, 2010).
11. Peter Bondanella, Julia Conaway Bondanella, *Cassell Dictionary of Italian Literature* (Greenwood Press 1979), 188–89.
12. Barzini, *supra* n. 3, at 198.
13. Audio tape: John Guinta Interviews of Antonia DiGiovanni Guinta and Lucia DiGiovanni Brown, volume 1 (1988), volume 2 (1991), page references to written transcript by Jay Wilkinson (November 2009) (hereinafter "The Nia Tapes Vol. 1 and Vol. 2"); Vol. 2 at 3.
14. *Id.*, vol. 2 at 4.
15. Barzini, *supra* n. 3, at 256.
16. The Nia Tapes, *supra* n. 13, Vol. 2 at 7.

17. Aubrey Menen, *Art & Money: An Irreverent History* (McGraw Hill 1980), 71.

18. Barzini, *supra* n. 3, at 263–64.

19. *Wikipedia*, "Don Vincenzo Randazzo," June 15, 2010, http:en.wikipedia.org/wiki/list/List of Sicilian Mafiosi by City.

20. *See* Gioacchino Nania, *San Giuseppe e la Mafia: Nascita e Sviluppo del Fenomeno Nell'Area Dello Jato* (*Saint Joseph and the Mafia: Birth and Development of the Phenomenon in the Town of* [San Giuseppe] Jato) 66, 94 ("*In San Cipirello,*...parte del gruppo (in San Cipirello, part of the group [was]...Randazzo Filippo...; *id.* at 66; "*Montaperto...Gabelloti: Fratelli Randazzo Calogero e Santo* (Randazzo brothers); *id.* at 94 (Microsoft Bing trans.). https://books.google.com/books?id=m9f1KaQUPCkC&printsec=frontcover#v=onepage&q&f=true (Edizioni della Battaglia 2002) (available only digitally and in Italian) (hereinafter "Nania") (copy on computer file with author).

21. Barzini, *supra* n. 3, at 258.

22. *Id.* at 253–54.

23. John V. Baiamonte, Jr., *Spirit of Vengeance: Nativism and Louisiana Justice, 1921–24*, xv, Author's Note (Louisiana State University Press 1986)(hereinafter "Baiamonte") (citing Anton Blok, *Mafia of a Sicilian Village, 1860-1960: A Study of Violent Peasant Entrepreneurs* (Harper Row 1974) (hereinafter "Blok") and Henner Hess, *Mafia and Mafiosi: The Structure of Power* (Farnborough: Saxon House, 1973).

24. *See* Nania, supra n. 20, at 94 ("Torre dei Fiori (Tower of Flowers)...*Gabelloto: Gaetano fu* ("was" or "son of") *Domenico, affiliato alla maffia*") ("affiliated with the Mafia") (Microsoft Bing trans.).

25. The Nia Tapes, *supra* n. 13, vol. 2 at 8, 26.

26. *Id.* at 9.

27. Dickie, *supra* n. 5, at 49-50.

28. *Id.* at 58.

29. *Id.* at 66.

30. *Id.* at 154.

31. *See id.* at 196 (cattle rustling in 1943), 249, 262 (cattle rustling in 1956); Blok, *supra* n. 23, at 51, 130, 142 (cattle rustling in 1925).

32. Dickie, *supra* n. 5, at 75.

33. http://sicilia.indettaglio.it/eng/communi/pa/ciminna.html (September 10, 2010); *Wikipedia*, September 20, 2011, http://en.wikipedia.org/wiki/ciminna.

34. The Nia Tapes, *supra* n. 13, vol. 2 at 5.

35. *Id.*, vol. 1 at 6–7, 12–13; vol. 2 at 8–10.

36. *Id.*, vol. 2 at 10–11.

37. Dickie, *supra* n. 5, at 75.

38. Barzini, *supra* n. 3, at 21, 253–54, 259.

39. The Nia Tapes, *supra* n. 13, vol. 1 at 13.

40. Blok, *supra* n. 23, at 49.

41. The Nia Tapes, *supra* n. 13, vol. 1 at 13, vol. 2 at 7–8.

42. Dickie, *supra* n. 5, at 15–16 (quoting Alfredo Niceforo, *Contemporary Barbarian Sicily* (1897).

43. The Nia Tapes, *supra* n. 13, vol. 1 at 13; vol. 2 at 8.

44. Barzini, *supra* n. 3, at 257.

45. Tom Holland, *Rubicon: The Last Years of the Roman Republic* (Anchor Books: Random House, 2005), xviii, 181 (quoting Livy, 39.6).

46. http://www.natalegiunta.it/news.php (June 15 and July 12, 2010).

47. *Certificato di Nascita, Comune di* Castelvetrano (Birth Certificate of the City of Castelvetrano), certified copy issued June 25, 1954 (copy on file with author).

48. The Nia Tapes, *supra* n. 13, vol. 1 at 2–3; vol. 2 at 17, 18, 20.

49. "Sicily for Tourists—History of Castelvetrano," http://www.regione.sicilia.it/turismo (September 10, 2009).

50. The Nia Tapes, vol. 1 at 10.

51. *Id.* at 9–10.

52. *Id.* at 11.

53. Dickie, *supra* n. 5, at 132.

54. John Lea, "The Structure of Traditional Organized Crime (2008) at 3, http://www.bunker8.pwp.blueyonder.co.uk/orgcrim/3802.htm (September 21, 2011) (hereinafter "Lea") (quoting Blok).

55. Dickie, *supra* n. 5, at 133.

56. Lea, *supra* n. 54, at 3.

57. Alien Registration Act of 1940, popularly known as the Smith Act, 76th Congress, 3d Session, Ch. 439, 54 Stat. 670, 18 USC § 2385 et seq.

58. Alien Registration Form of Natali [sic] Giunta, Nov. 7, 1940 (Official Records of the United States Department of Justice, Immigration and Naturalization Service) (copy on file with author).

59. *Id.* at 1.

60. *Id.* at 2.

61. Dickie, *supra* n. 5, at 149.

62. S. L. A. Marshall, *World War I* (Houghton Mifflin Co., 1987), 174–75.

63. Gearold Barry, *Demobilization, 1914–1918*, December 4. 2018,.

64. Gregory M. Guinta, "The Great Gatsby in the Aftermath of World War I" (unpublished Tulane University student essay, 1986), 6–8; (copy on file with author) (citing and quoting Alistair Horne, *The Price of Glory: Verdun 1916*, 60–70 (internal quotation to Barleusse, "Le Feu'), 177, (St. Martin's New York 1962); Robert Emmet Long, *The Achieving of The Great Gatsby: F. Scott Fitzgerald 1920–25* (Associated UP, Cranbury, New Jersey 1979), 143.

65. Ira A. Glazier and P. William Filbey, *Italians to America: Lists of Passengers Arriving in U.S. Ports, 1897–1902*, vol. 12 (Scholarly Resources Inc., 2000), introduction, x–xi.

66. *Id.*

67. David Critchley, *The Origin of Organized Crime in America: The New York City Mafia, 1891–1931* (Routledge 2009), 31 (hereinafter "Critchley").

68. *Id.* (quoting Bill Bonanno, *Bound by Honor* [St. Martin's Press, 1999], 6).
69. Barzini, *supra* n. 3, at 259–60.
70. *Id.* at 237.
71. Critchley, *supra* n. 67, at 31.
72. Barzini, *supra* n. 3, at 260.
73. The Nia Tapes, *supra* n. 13, vol. 1 at 5–6.
74. *Id.* at 8; vol. 2 at 9.
75. Dickie, *supra* n. 5, at 91–111.
76. *Id.* at 91.
77. *Id.*
78. *Id.* at 108.
79. In addition to the birth dates and places of his children, evidence that 1898 is the year of the DiGiovanni family's first trek to America is provided in Gaetano's obituary upon his death in 1945, which describes him as "a native of San Cipirello, Italy, and a resident of New Orleans, Louisiana, for the past forty-seven years." *The Times-Picayune*, November 7, 1945, § 1, 2.
80. Baiamonte, *supra* n. 23, at 3.
81. Joseph L. Cacibauda, "The Sicilians of Louisiana," *Italian America* at 6–7 (Summer, 2009).
82. Critchley, *supra* n. 67, at 39.
83. *Id.* at 29.
84. *Id.* at 46.
85. *Id.* at 38 (quoting Francesco Ortoleva, unsuccessful Corleone election candidate, 1889, *id.* at 37–38).
86. *Id.* at 54.
87. The Nia Tapes, *supra* n. 13, vol. 1 at 3.
88. *Id.*; vol. 2 at 26.
89. *Id.* at 3; vol 2 at 28–29; Certificate of Baptism of Antonia DiGiovanni issued October 10, 1989, Sacred Heart Church, 504 North Street, Nacogdoches, Texas, 75961 (recording baptism date on March 26, 1904 and birth date on February 10, 1904) (copies on file with author). Nia speculated that the family of "Dominick DiGiovanni [who] lives in Lake Charles [Louisiana]" and from whom she once received a letter, "came to America with my father...all of those that were in Texas, we got to be related some kind of way... Yeah, there's another Gaetano DiGiovanni that left San Cipirello with our Daddy. He's my Daddy's first cousin... It could be a cousin...it's the same branch, you know." The Nia Tapes, *supra* n. 13, vol. 1 at 3–5, 11.
90. The Nia Tapes, *supra* n. 13, vol. 2 at 4.
91. *Id.*, vol. 1 at 4.
92. *Id.* at 8.
93. *Id.* at 8–9.
94. John H. Davis, *Mafia Kingfish: Carlos Marcello and the Assassination of John F. Kennedy* (McGraw-Hill, 1989), 17 (hereinafter "Davis").

95. *Id.*

96. *Id.* at 17–18.

97. *Id.* at 18.

98. New Orleans native and jazz musician Sam Butera once said in an interview in the *Washington Post* that when he was growing up in New Orleans, "whenever people wanted to insult Italians they would whistle and say, 'Aayy, who killa da chief?'" Adam Bernstein, Post-Mortem—*The Washington Post* www.italianjazz.com/interview.php at §5 (June 5, 2008); *See generally* Tom Smith, *The Crescent City Lynchings: The Murder of Chief Hennessy, the New Orleans "Mafia" Trials, and the Parish Prison Mob* (Lyons Press, 2007) (hereinafter "Smith-Chief").

99. Critchley, supra n. 67, at 60; Obituary of Leoluca Louis Trombatore, *The Times-Picayune*, January 11, 1963, § 1, 2 (hereinafter "Mr. Luke Obit").

100. *Id.* The math in both Critchley's writing and the obituary is slightly off. If Mr. Luke lived in New Orleans for fifty-eight years and died in 1963, he must have arrived in New Orleans in 1905.

101. Critchley, supra n. 67, at 60 (citing FBI report dated July 11, 1967, Bureau File no. 92-6054; David Chandler, *The Criminal Brotherhoods* [London: Constable, 1976], 185).

102. *Id.* at 55–56 [citations to internal quotes omitted].

103. *Id.* at 60.

104. *Id.*

105. Davis, *supra* note 94, at 29–30.

106. Thomas Hunt, "Who Was Who: Carolla, Silvestro (1896–1972)," *The American Mafia: The History of Organized Crime in the United States*, June 29, 2015, http://mob-who.blogspot.com/2011/04/carolla-silvestro-1896-1972.html (hereinafter "Hunt").

107. Critchley, *supra* n. 67, at 60.

108. Estes Kefauver, *Crime in America* 171–87 (Doubleday & Co., 1951) (hereinafter "Kefauver").

109. Hunt, *supra* n. 106, at 1.

110. Mr. Luke Obit, *supra* n. 99.

111. The Nia Tapes, *supra* n. 13, vol. 1 at 13; vol. 2 at 31.

112. *Id.*

113. Kendall, *supra* n. 7, at 826–27.

114. Deed, DiGiovanni Family Cemetery Vault, Officials Records of Lakelawn Metairie Funeral Home (1921) (emphasis added) (copy on file with author).

115. *Id.* (backside) (emphasis added).

116. Critchley, *supra* n. 67, at 40 (citing Dickie at "5" [actually 168–69]).

117. Barzini, *supra* n. 3, at 263.

118. "Murder charges were filed in criminal district court Friday [December 14, 1934] against Battista Pecoraro, forty-eight years old,…and Ciro Lisotto… two of seven men apprehended as suspects in the fatal shooting…of Benedetto Cappello, thirty-eight-year-old grocer…[who] was struck from behind by

a shotgun charge as he drove his automobile…" "Murder Charged Against Pair in Death of Grocer," *The Times-Picayune*, December 15, 1934, at § 1, 4 (hereinafter "Pecoraro Charged"); *See* Bill Feather, "Mafia Membership Charts, New Orleans 1920-1970s," *Informer: The Journal of American Mafia History* 2, no. 3 (July 2010): 47, 49; (hereinafter "Feather-Informer") ("Pecoraro, Baptiste, Alias Batista,…1920–40s, Boss?"). It is unknown what relationship, if any, Batista Pecoraro might have had to Sugie DiGiovanni's later friend, John Pecoraro, *see* text *infra* at page 262, or to "Giovanni Pecoraro, born 1867 in Piana Dei Greci,…acquitted in 1898 of embezzlement while operating as a broker living in San Cipirello,…[and] mowed down in March 1923…in a [New York] 'bootlegger' feud.'" Critchley, *supra* n. 67, at 67–68.

[119.] Baiamonte, *supra* n. 23, at 34.

[120.] New Orleans Police Department Arrest Report, July 4, 1920, "Digiovanni [sic], Dominick, 1237 N. Johnson St.,…Held for Federal Authorities viol. Volstead Act…" (record maintained at New Orleans Public Library, Louisiana Archives, Main Branch, 219 Loyola Avenue, New Orleans, Louisiana; copy on file with author).

[121.] "Two Bank Robbers Killed, Found Dead After Band Had Shot Man in Independence, Louisiana," *The New York Times*, May 10, 1921, p. 19.

[122.] "Gang Linked in Killings," *New Orleans Item*, May 9, 1921, at § 1, 1 (hereinafter "Gang Linked").

[123.] *Id.* at 2.

[124.] *Id.* (emphasis added); *see also* "Double Killing Baffles Orleans Police," *New Orleans Item*, May 9, 1921, at § 1, 2 (hereinafter "Double Killing").

[125.] Gang Linked, *supra* n. 122, at 2.

[126.] *Id.*

[127.] *Id.* at 1.

[128.] Meigs O. Frost, "1 More Feud Arrest Near," *New Orleans Item*, May 10, 1921, at § 1, 1, 4 (hereinafter "1 More Feud").

[129.] *Id.*

[130.] "Vendetta Feared as Police Bare Big Bandit Plot," *The Times-Picayune*, May 10, 1921, § 1, at 1) (hereinafter "Vendetta Feared").

[131.] Double Killing, *supra* n. 124, at 2.

[132.] 1 More Feud, *supra* n. 128, at 1.

[133.] *Id.*

[134.] *Id.*

[135.] *Id.* at 4.

[136.] *Id.*

[137.] *Id.*

[138.] *Id.* at 1.

[139.] *Id.* at 4.

[140.] *Id.*

[141.] *Id.*

142. *Id.*

143. Richard N. Warner, "The First Crime Boss of Los Angeles?" *Informer: The Journal of American Mafia History*, vol. 2, no. 3 at 5, 9 (July 2010) (hereinafter "Warner").

144. Critchley, *supra* n. 67, at 57.

145. Baiamonte, *supra* n. 23, at 11.

146. Warner, *supra* n. 143, at 7.

147. Baiamonte, *supra* n. 23, at 11.

148. Critchley, *supra* n. 67, at 57.

149. Warner, *supra* n. 143 at 8.

150. *Id.*

151. *Id.* at 9–10; Critchley, *supra* n. 67, at 57.

152. Critchley, *supra* n. 67, at 57.

153. Warner, *supra* n. 143, at 11.

154. Baiamonte, *supra* n. 23, at 18.

155. *Id.*

156. *Id.* at 164–65.

157. Meigs O. Frost, "Boy Tightens Net on Gang," *New Orleans Item*, May 11, 1921, at § 1, 4.

158. "Cipolla Caught Pistol at Hand After 3 Days," *The Times-Picayune*, May 12, 1921, at § 1, 4 (hereinafter "Cipolla Caught").

159. *Id.* at 4.

160. Meigs O. Frost, "Quiz More in Gang," *New Orleans Item*, May 12, 1921, at § 1, 8 (hereinafter "Quiz More").

161. Cipolla Caught, *supra* n. 158, at 4.

162. Quiz More, *supra* n. 160, at 8.

163. *Id.* at 1. **B**ucaro's name is misspelled as starting with a "D" in this story. Later stories correct the spelling.

164. Obituary of Judge Andrew G. Bucaro, *The Times-Picayune*, October 30, 2003, at § B, 5; Obituary of Giacomo "Jack" Bucaro, *The Times-Picayune*, March 23, 1939, at § 1, 2 ("son of the late Archangela and Andrea Bucaro").

165. Quiz More *supra* n. 160, at 8.

166. "Thwart Cipolla Plot; Jail Two as His Aides," *The Times-Picayune*, May 13, 1921, at § 1, 2 (hereinafter "Thwart Cipolla Plot").

167. Quiz More, *supra* n. 160, at 8.

168. Cipolla Caught, *supra* n. 158, at 4.

169. *Id.*

170. Quiz More, *supra* n. 160, at 1.

171. *Id.*

172. *Id.*

173. *Id.* at 8.

174. *Id.*

175. Cipolla Caught, *supra* n. 15, at 1.

[176.] Quiz More, *supra* n. 160, at 8.

[177.] Thwart Cipolla Plot, *supra* n. 166, at 2.

[178.] Cipolla Caught, *supra* n. 158, at 1, 4.

[179.] Quiz More *supra* n. 160, at 8

[180.] *Id.*

[181.] *Id.*

[182.] Cipolla Caught, *supra* n. 158, at 4.

[183.] Quiz More, *supra* n. 160, at 8.

[184.] Cipolla Caught, *supra* n. 158, at 4.

[185.] Quiz More, *supra* n. 160, at 8.

[186.] *Id.* at 8.

[187.] *Id.*

[188.] *Id.*

[189.] *Id.* at 1, 8.

[190.] *Id.* at 8.

[191.] *Id.*

[192.] Thwart Cipolla Plot, *supra* n. 166, at 1.

[193.] *Id.*

[194.] Meigs O. Frost, "Gangmen Lose Writ Fight," *New Orleans Item*, May 13, 1921, at § 1, 12.

[195.] *Id.*

[196.] *Id.* at 1, 12. This is a misspelling of the name of the accused gunman, Batiste Pecararo.

[197.] Obituary of Dominick DiGiovanni, *The Times-Picayune*, May 13, 1921, at § 1, 2.

[198.] "Nine Are Indicted on Murder Plot Hold-Up Charges," *The Times-Picayune*, May 14, 1921, at § 1, 1 (hereinafter "Nine Indicted").

[199.] *Id.* at 1–2.

[200.] Meigs O. Frost, "Double Murder Motive Looms Clear," *New Orleans Item*, May 14, 1921, at § 1, 2 (hereinafter "Double Murder Motive").

[201.] *Id.*

[202.] Nine Indicted, *supra* n. 198, at 1–2.

[203.] Double Murder Motive, *supra* n. 200, at 2.

[204.] *Id.* at 1.

[205.] *Id.* at 2.

[206.] Frank Cabibi, Letter to the Editor, "No Need to Meet, Declares Italian," *New Orleans States*, May 22, 1921, at § 1, 3 (hereinafter Cabibi").

[207.] Dickie, *supra* n. 5, at 13, 15.

[208.] Andrew J. Gieda, "New Orleans Police Fear Another Vendetta," *New Orleans States*, May 15, 1921, at § 1, 1.

[209.] *Id.* at 1–2.

[210.] *Id.* at 1.

[211.] *Id.* at 2.

212. *Id.* at 1.
213. "Italian Editor Flays Criminals," *New Orleans States*, May 16, 1921, at § 1, 8.
214. *Id.*
215. *Id.*
216. *Id.*
217. Cabibi, *supra* n. 206, at 3.
218. *Id.*
219. *Id.*
220. "Rini Is Ready to Confess, He Tells Craven," *New Orleans States*, May 20, 1921, at § 1, 1.
221. "Rini is Exonerated of Toledo Slaying," *The Times-Picayune*, May 19, 1921, at § 1, 2 (hereinafter "Rini Is").
222. "Police Told Where Mrs. Cipolla Is Hiding," *New Orleans States*, May 18, 1921, at § 1, 1 (hereinafter "Police Told").
223. "Rini Grilled by Craven in Parish Prison Friday," *New Orleans Item*, May 20, 1921, at § 1, 1 (hereinafter "Rini Grilled").
224. "Murder of Deamore Planned by Gang," *New Orleans States*, May 17, 1921, at § 1, 1.
225. "Murder Charge Against Three May Be Dropped," *The Times-Picayune*, May 20, 1921, at § 1, 14; *see also* Rini Grilled, *supra* n. 223, at 9.
226. "Wife of Cipolla Found and Story of Assassination Suspect Is Shaken," *The Times-Picayune*, May 25, 1921, at § 1, 1, 2 (hereinafter "Wife Found").
227. *Id.* at 2.
228. *Id.*
229. "Mrs. Cipolla is Questioned by Craven," *New Orleans States*, May 27, 1921, at § 1, 1.
230. "Six Italian Gunmen Seek Venue Change," *New Orleans Item*, May 28, 1921, at § 1, 2; *see also* "Italian Woman's Story is Sought," *The Times-Picayune*, May 28, 1921, at § 1, 3.
231. "Police Arrest Man in Connection with the Double Murder," *The Times-Picayune*, May 15, 1921, at § 1, 1 (emphasis added).
232. "Cipolla to Face Killing Charge, Officer Asserts," *The Times-Picayune*, May 16, 1921, at § 1, 1; "2 More Suspects Nabbed in Crime Plot," *New Orleans Item*, May 15, 1921, at § 1, 1 (emphasis added).
233. *Id.*, Cipolla to Face...at 1.
234. "Cipolla and Two Others Charged in Murder," *New Orleans States*, May 16, 1921, at § 1, 1 (hereinafter "Cipolla and Two Others").
235. "Cipolla in Trio to Face Charges of Murders Here," *The Times-Picayune*, May 17, 1921, at § 1, 1, 4; *see also* Wife Found, *supra* n. 226, at 2.
236. Cipolla and Two Others, *supra* n. 234, at 8.
237. Rini Is, *supra* n. 221; Police Told, *supra* n. 222.
238. "Indict Cipolla on Charge of Double Murder," *New Orleans Item*, June 7, 1921, at § 1, 1 (hereinafter "Indict Cipolla").

239. "Cipolla Indicted by Grand Jury," *The Times-Picayune*, June 8, 1921, at § 1, 6.

240. Indict Cipolla, *supra* n. 238, at 1.

241. Baiamonte, *supra* n. 23, at 53–54.

242. *Id.*

243. Kendall, *supra* n. 7, at 854.

244. Baiamonte, *supra* n. 23, at 165.

245. Mario Puzo, *The Godfather* (Penguin Publishing Group and Fawcett Crest Books, 1969), 299 (hereinafter "Puzo-Godfather") (emphasis added). The movie version of this line was altered from Puzo's original novel version as follows: "Tattaglia's a pimp. He never could've out fought Santino. But I didn't know it till this day that—it was Barzini all along." *See* Carlo De Vito, *The Godfather: Classic Quotes* (Cedar Mills Press, 2007) (movie version); Francis Ford Coppola, *The Godfather Notebook* (Regan Arts, 2016) (referencing and reproducing Puzo-Godfather novel version with notes). In my opinion, Puzo's original version of this line is a truer reflection of the late-nineteenth- and early-twentieth-century Western *mafiosi* mindset.

246. Barzini, *supra* n. 3, at 183–84 (quoting Jacopo Gelli, *Codice Cavalleresco Italiano* (*Italian Code of Chivalry*) (1887).

247. Kendall, *supra* n. 7, at 854 (emphasis added).

248. Barzini, *supra* n. 3, at 186–87.

249. Blok, *supra* n. 23, at 174. Blok provides numerous anecdotal examples of "the social acceptance of homicide" in his in-depth anthropological study of Western Sicily in the late nineteenth and early twentieth centuries. *Id.* at 206–207 n. 15.

250. Vendetta Feared, *supra* n. 130, at 1.

251. Dickie, *supra* n. 5, at 15. *But see* The New Testament, Romans 12:17–19, *The Catholic Bible* (Oxford University Press, 1995), 246 ("Do not repay anyone evil for evil... Beloved, do not look for revenge but leave room for the wrath; for it is written, 'Vengeance is mine, I will repay, says the Lord.'").

252. Warner, *supra* n. 143, at 6; *see also* Kefauver, *supra* n. 108, at 22 (quoting testimony of Narcotics Agent Claude A. Follmer: "[T]here are possibly twenty-five or thirty [Mafia] members here in Kansas City. The more important ones are fellows like...Pete and Joseph DiGiovanni...").

253. Jay C. Ambler, "Organized Crime Research: Kansas City (PLR International 1998–2008), March 23, 2021, http:/AmericanMafia.com/Cities/Kansas_City.html.

254. William Ouseley, *Mobsters in Our Midst: The Kansas City Crime Family* (Kansas City Star Books, 2011), 15; *see* Critchley, *supra* n. 67, at 27, 34, 249 n. 109.

255. "The American Mafia: Kansas City Crime Bosses," June 9, 2009, at 2 of 3, http://www.onewal.com/maf-b-kc.html.

256. Kefauver, *supra* n. 108, at 24–25.

257. "Blackhand Seen in Orleanians' Death in Chicago," *The Times-Picayune*, May 14, 1922, § 1, 7 (hereinafter "Blackhand Seen).

258. Warner, *supra* n. 143, at 10 n. 48.

259. Bill Feather, "Mafia Membership Charts: Unconfirmed Members Charts," https://mafiamemberscharts.blogspot.com/2017/11/unconfirmed-members-chart.html (November 21, 2017) (emphasis added).

260. Baiamonte, *supra* n. 23, at 59 (citing *The Times-Picayune*, May 14, 1922, May 10, 1924).

261. "Mystery Shrouds Angles of Crime," *The Times-Picayune*, May 10, 1924, at § 1, 2.

262. The Nia Tapes, vol. 1 at 8; family tree prepared by Michael W. Stapleton (copy on file with author).

263. "Orleanian Held Vendetta Victim," *The Times-Picayune*, May 1, 1922, at § 1, 1.

264. Kendall, *supra* n. 7, at 853.

265. Blackhand Seen, *supra* n. 257, at 7.

266. Warner, *supra* n. 143, at 12.

267. Blackhand Seen, *supra* n. 257, at 7.

268. *Id.*

269. Critchley, *supra* n. 67, at 58.

270. Warner, *supra* n. 143, at 11-13.

271. *Id.* at 12.

272. Kendall, *supra* n. 7, at 852-53.

273. Baiamonte, *supra* n. 23, at 165.

274. Obituary of Andrew G. Bucaro, *The Times-Picayune*, October 30, 2003, at § B, 4.

275. Sandy Smith, "Brazen Empire of Crime, Part 2," *Life* 63, no. 10 (September 8, 1967): 91, 96.

276. The Nia Tapes, *supra* n. 13, vol. 2 at 23–24.

277. *Id.*, vol. 1 at 7, 15–16; vol. 2 at 24.

278. Kendall, *supra* n. 7, at 848–49.

279. The Nia Tapes, *supra* n. 13, vol. 1 at 9; vol. 2 at 24–25.

280. Critchley, *supra* n. 67, at 20–22.

281. Dickie, *supra* n. 5, at 171–72.

282. Critchley, *supra* n. 67, at 20–21 (quoting Robert M. Lombardo, "The Black Hand," *Journal of Contemporary Criminal Justice* at 18 pt. 4 (2002): 401).

283. *Id.* at 26–27.

284. *Id.* at 29, 46

285. Kendall, *supra* n. 7, at 819.

286. The sources concerning the incident of October 9, 1923, involving New Orleans grocer Anthony Tumarello, including the quotations in the following paragraph, and the subsequent criminal proceedings against Natale Guinta are the following: *The Times-Picayune*, October 11, 1923, at § 1, 1, 7, 9; *State of Louisiana v. Natale Guinta*, Case No. 17,996, Docket "A," Orleans Parish Criminal District Court (1923–24) (record maintained at New Orleans Public Library, Louisiana Archives, Main Branch, 219 Loyola Avenue, New Orleans, Louisiana) (hereinafter "*State v. Guinta*") (copies on file with author).

287. *The Times-Picayune*, January 19, 1967, at § 1, 2 ("Natale Guinta,…a native of Italy and a resident of this city for the past forty-five years.") (hereinafter "Natale's Obituary").

288. Certificate of Death, Natale Guinta, City of New Orleans File No. 670000489 (January 19, 1967) (hereinafter "Natale's Death Certificate") (copy on file with author).

289. N. Brister, "A Street by Any Other Name," June 15, 2009, http://www.neworleans.com/arts/history; "Final Recommendations to Rename 37 New Orleans Street, Parks," February 25, 2021, Nola.com.

290. Kendall, *supra* n. 7, at 848–51.

291. *State v. Guinta*, bond.

292. "Blake Pontchartrain, New Orleans Know-It-All," *The Gambit Weekly*, February 5, 2013, at 14.

293. "Three Dismissed by Chief on Corruption Charge to Appeal to Police Commission," *The Times-Picayune*, October 15, 1924, at § 1, 3 (hereinafter "Three Dismissed").

294. Smith-Chief, *supra* n. 98.

295. *State v. Guinta*, Tumarello letter.

296. *State v. Guinta*, nol prosse dismissal.

297. Dickie, *supra* n. 5, at 27, 65.

298. Blok, *supra* n. 23, at 62.

299. *Id.* at 210–211.

300. Nania, *supra* n. 20, at 94 ["*Gabellotto*: DiGiovanni Gaetano *fu* Domenico, *affiliato alla mafia*."].

301. *Id.* at 92.

302. *Id.* at 5.

303. *Id.* at 40.

304. *Id.* at 55.

305. *Id.* at 40.

306. *Id.* at 55.

307. *Id.* at 86.

308. *Id.* at 85.

309. *Id.* at 16, 49.

310. *Id.* at 66, 71. The Todaros lived across the street from the DiGiovannis in 1930s–40s San Cipirello. Randazzo was the maiden's name of Gaetano's mother.

311. Mario Puzo, *The Sicilian* (Bantam Books, 1985) 49.

312. Nania, *supra* n. 20, at 69–70.

313. *Id.* at 69.

314. *Id.*

315. The Nia Tapes, *supra* n. 13, vol. 2 at 9.

316. *Id.*, vol. 1 at 15; vol. 2 at 35.

317. *Id.*, vol. 2 at. 34.

318. *Id.* at 32.

319. *Id.*

320. *Id.* at 33.

321. *Id.*, vol. 2 at 21; Nania, *supra* n. 20, at 92.

322. The Nia Tapes, *supra* n. 13, vol. 2 at 21.

323. *Id.* at 25.

324. Angelo Quaglino, *La Nostra Famiglia* (Macbook, 2011), 11 (limited copies self-published for family and friends only on file with author) (hereinafter "Quaglino Macbook").

325. The Nia Tapes, *supra* n. 13, vol. 2 at 32, 34.

326. *Id.*

327. *Id.* at 21, 33–34.

328. *Id.* at 32–33.

329. *Id.* at 33.

330. *Id.*

331. *Id.*

332. *Id.*

333. *Id.*

334. *Id.*

335. *Id.*

336. *Id.* at 25.

337. *Id.* Although Nia said Carmelo had been a chemist, some of his descendants later corrected her and advised that Carmelo had been an engineer in Sicily.

338. *Id.*

339. *Id.* at 34.

340. "Three of City's Raiding Squad Under Charges," *The Times-Picayune*, October 7, 1924, at § 1, 1, 3.

341. *Id.* at 1, 3.

342. *Id.* at p. 3.

343. *Id.*

344. *Id.*

345. *Id.*

346. Three Dismissed, *supra* n. 291, at 1.

347. *Id.*

348. *Id.*

349. *Id.* at 3.

350. *Id.* at 1, 3.

351. *Id.* at 3.

352. *Id.*

353. *Id.* at 1.

354. "Policemen Freed on Bribe Charge in Ten Minutes," *The Times-Picayune*, December 19, 1924, at § 1, 1.

355. *Id.* at 3.

356. *Id.* at 1.

357. Blok, *supra* n. 23, at 142–43.

358. Dickie, *supra* n. 5, at 148.

359. *Id.*

360. *Id.* at 148-49.

361. *Id.* at 150.

362. *Id.* at 151.

363. *Id.* at 152.

364. *Id.* at 153.

365. Harold Evans, *The American Century* (Alfred A. Knopf, 1998), 167–68 (hereinafter "Evans").

366. Dickie, *supra* n. 5, at 153.

367. The Nia Tapes, *supra* n. 13, vol. 1 at 8, 11; vol. 2 at 35.

368. Dickie, *supra* n. 5, at 153.

369. Nania, *supra* n. 20, at 92–94.

370. Blok, *supra* n. 23, at 183.

371. Nania, *supra* n. 20, at 92.

372. *Id.* at 92–94.

373. Dickie, *supra* n. 5, at 155; Blok *supra* n. 23, at 185.

374. Dickie, *supra* n. 5, at 155.

375. *Id.* at 156.

376. Blok, *supra* n. 23, at 183–84.

377. Dickie, *supra* n. 5, at 157.

378. The Nia Tapes, *supra* n. 13, vol. 1 at 7, 15.

379. Alien Registration Card No. 4328082, Gaetano DiGiovanni, United States Department of Justice (February 24, 1942) (copy on file with author).

380. The Nia Tapes, *supra* n. 13, vol. 1 at 8, 11, 14.

381. *Id.*, vol. 2 at 36.

382. *Id.*, vol. 1 at 14-15; vol. 2 at 35.

383. *Id.* at 36.

384. *Id.*, vol. 1 at 15–16; vol. 2 at 36.

385. Dickie, *supra* n. 5, at 158.

386. *Id.* at 159.

387. The Nia Tapes, *supra* n. 13, vol. 1 at 8, 16.

388. *Id.* at 17.

389. *Id.* at 18.

390. *Id.* at 16.

391. *Id.* at 9, 16.

392. *Id.* at 17.

393. *Id.* at 17–18.

394. *Id.* at 17, 19.

395. *Id.* at 19.

396. Dickie, *supra* n. 5, at. 101.

397. *Id.* at 101-2.

398. The Nia Tapes, *supra* n. 13, vol. 1 at 20.

399. *Id.*

400. *Id.* at 20–21.

401. Marriage Certificate of Natale Guinta and Antonia DiGiovanni, City of New Orleans, issued January 1, 1931 (copy on file with author).

402. Marriage Certificate of Natale Guinta and Antonia DiGiovanni, City of New Orleans Health Department, Bureau of Vital Records, re-issued September 22, 1947, Recorded in Book of Marriages No. 52, folio 1407 (copy on file with author).

403. The Nia Tapes, *supra* n. 13, vol. 2 at 28.

404. Barzini, *supra* n. 3, at 198.

405. Puzo-Godfather, *supra* n. 245, at 289.

406. "Four Dry Agents in Raid Capture 21 Men Packing $65,000 Cargo of Whiskey," *The Times-Picayune*, March 20, 1932, at § 1, 1 (hereinafter "Raid").

407. *Id.*

408. The brand of the seized liquor was identified by the arresting federal prohibition agents, who testified at the gang members' trial. *United States v. Nate Goldberg et al.*, Crim. No. 16,832, United States District Court, Eastern District of Louisiana, New Orleans Division (1932-34) (hereinafter "Goldberg Case Court Record") (copy on file with author), Goldberg Case Court Record, "Bill of Exceptions No. II" at 3 (testimony of Federal Prohibition Investigator Bennett).

409. Raid, *supra* n. 406, at 7.

410. *Id.*

411. *Id.* at 1, 7.

412. *Id.* at 7.

413. Goldberg Case Court Record, "Bill of Exceptions No. II" at 13 (testimony of Federal Prohibition Investigator Anderman).

414. Raid, *supra* n. 406, at 7.

415. *Id.*

416. Goldberg Case Court Record, "Bill of Exceptions No. II" at 1.

417. Raid, *supra* n. 406, at 1.

418. *Id.* at 7.

419. Goldberg Case Court Record, "Bill of Exceptions No. II" at 2-3.

420. Raid, *supra* n. 406, at 1.

421. Goldberg Case Court Record, "Bill of Exceptions No. II" at 18 (testimony of Federal Prohibition Investigator L. E. Holleman).

422. Raid, *supra* n. 406, at 1.

423. Goldberg Case Court Record, "Bill of Exceptions No. II" at 9.

424. Raid, *supra* n. 406, at 7.

425. *Id.*

426. Goldberg Case Court Record, "Bill of Exceptions No. II" at 3.

427. *Id.* at 4–5.

428. *Id.* at 7.

429. *Id.* at 5.

430. *Id.* at 1.

431. *Id.* at 7.

432. *Id.*

433. Judge Grubb was a frequent visiting judge in New Orleans and the courthouse where he conducted the Goldberg gang trial. He was "the district judge who sat most often with the [Fifth Circuit] Court [of Appeals headquartered in New Orleans]...; frequently enough that it is safe to venture the observation that he participated in more Court of Appeals decisions than some judges who were members of the [Fifth Circuit] Court." Harvey C. Couch, *A History of the Fifth Circuit 1891–1981* (Bicentennial Committee of the Judicial Conference of the United States, Federal Judicial Center 1984).

434. Goldberg Case Court Record, Indictment.

435. "John Minor Wisdom United States Court of Appeals Building," Pamphlet of the US General Services Administration, Public Buildings Service at 2 (1994) (copy on file with author).

436. Goldberg Case Court Record, Bill of Exceptions No. II" at 39.

437. *Id.* at 23.

438. *Id.* at 22.

439. *Id.* at 12, 15, 17, 21.

440. *See, e.g., id.* at 10, 12, 13

441. *See, e.g., id.* at 11–12, 15, 17, 21.

442. *Id.* at 26.

443. *Id.*

444. *Id.* at 27–38.

445. *Id.* at attachment to 39.

446. *Id.* at 38.

447. *Id.*, Handwritten attachment to true bill with sentences and jury foreman's signed verdict form (February 8, 1933).

448. *Id.*, Notice of Appeal and Order (February 10, 1933).

449. Evans, *supra* n. 365, at 245.

450. 291 US 217, 226 (1934).

451. *Id.* (emphasis added).

452. Goldberg Case Court Record, *Goldberg et al. v. United States*, Case No. 7037 (5th Cir. Order Filed Mar. 21, 1934).

453. *Id.*, *United States v. Goldberg et al.*, Crim. No. 16,832 (ED La. Order April 6, 1934).

454. The Nia Tapes, *supra* n. 13, vol. 1 at 10.

455. *Id.*

456. Act of Sale of Property, Orleans Parish Conveyance Office Book 500, Folio 503, Mortgage Office Book 1560, Folio No. 479, February 14 and 16, 1939 respectively (copy on file with author).

457. Davis, *supra* n. 94, at 44–47, 59

458. "Ex-Convict Shot by Girl as He Steps from Mother's Home," *The Times-Picayune*, November 27, 1934, at § 1, 2 (hereinafter "Ex-Convict Shot").

459. *The American College Dictionary* (C. L. Barnhart, Jesse Stein, eds., Random House, 1970), 391.

460. Ex-Convict Shot, *supra* n. 458, at 1.

461. *Id.*

462. *Id.* at 2.

463. In one of those circling twists of coincidence or destiny that history often delivers, the front-page story by the Associated Press that ran just right of and next to the story of the murder of Beucler by my aunt Lou on the front page of *The Times-Picayune* that day bore the headline "Reveille's Staff Quits in Protest of Censorship." With a dateline of Baton Rouge, Louisiana, the lead read: "The editor and five staff members of the Reveille, Louisiana State University student newspaper, resigned today because the university forbade them to print anything objectionable to Senator Huey P. Long." *Id.* at 1. Forty-two years later, I was a News Editor of the LSU Daily Reveille.

464. Ex-Convict Shot, *supra* n. 458, at 1.

465. *Id.* at 2.

466. "Formal Charge Placed Against Woman in Killing," *The Times-Picayune*, November 28, 1934, at § 1, 12 (hereinafter "Formal Charge').

467. New Orleans Police Department Arrest Report, November 26, 1934 (records maintained at New Orleans Public Library, Louisiana Archives, Main Branch, 219 Loyola Avenue, New Orleans, Louisiana) (copy on file with author).

468. Formal Charge, *supra* n. 466, at 12.

469. Ex-Convict Shot, *supra* n. 458, at 1–2.

470. K. T. Knoblock, "Story of Last Night's Killing from Silent Girl's Viewpoint," New Orleans Item, November 27, 1934, at 1, 4.

471. *Id.*

472. Ex-Convict Shot, *supra* n. 458, at 1.

473. Formal Charge, *supra* n. 466, at 12.

474. *Id.*

475. *Id.*

476. *Id.*

477. *Id.*

478. *Id.*

479. *Id.*

480. "Miss DiGiovanni and Frank Early Accused by Jury," *The Times-Picayune*, December 12, 1934, at § 1, 8.

481. "Lucille DiGiovanni Pleads Not Guilty," *The Times-Picayune*, December 14, 1934, at § 1, 6.

482. "Seven Men Held in Investigation of Ambush Death," *The Times-Picayune*, December 14, 1934, at § 1, 6; Pecoraro Charged, *supra* n. 117, at 4.

483. Sources for this account of the trial are "Girl is Found Not Guilty in Killing of Saloon Keeper by Jury's Verdict," *The Times-Picayune*, March 26, 1935, at § 1, 1–2 (hereinafter "Girl Is Found"); "Free Girl in Murder Case," New Orleans Item, March 26, 1935, at § 1, 1, 7 (hereinafter "Free Girl").

484. Girl is Found, *supra* n. 483, at 1; The Nia Tapes, vol. 2 at 22.

485. Girl is Found, *supra* n. 483, at 1.

486. *Id.*

487. The jurors were C. J. Evans, J.O. Grout, K. L. Koster, U. L. Rodrigues, Albert Weckerling, Charles Aprill, George Cunts, Arthur E. Egdorf, Richard Faust, Louis C. Fernandez, Leonard C. Ocha and Robert Oliver. *Id.*

488. *Id.*

489. Free Girl, *supra* n. 483, at 7.

490. *Id.*

491. Girl is Found, *supra* n. 483, at 1.

492. Free Girl, *supra* n. 483, at 7.

493. Girl is Found, *supra* n. 483, at 1.

494. *Id.* at 1-2.

495. *Id.* at 2.

496. *Id.*

497. *Id.*

498. *Id.*

499. Ex-Convict Shot *supra* n. 458, at 2.

500. Girl is Found, *supra* n. 483, at 2.

501. *Id.*

502. The character witnesses were druggist Lawrence Esher, Mrs. A. Caffarel and Mrs. Henry Hyde. *Id.*

503. *Id.*

504. Free Girl, *supra* n. 483, at 1.

505. Girl is Found, *supra* n. 483, at 1.

506. *Id.* at 1.

507. Free Girl, *supra* n. 483, at 2.

508. Girl is Found, *supra* n. 483, at 1.

509. Free Girl, *supra* n. 483, at 2.

510. *Id.*

511. Girl is Found, *supra* n. 483, at 1.

512. Free Girl, *supra* n. 483, at 2.

513. Girl is Found, *supra* n. 483, at 1.

514. Free Girl, *supra* n. 483, at 2.

515. Girl is Found, *supra* n. 483, at 1.

516. Free Girl, *supra* n. 483, at 2.

517. *Id.*

518. Girl is Found, *supra* n. 483, at 1.

519. Free Girl, *supra* n. 483, at 2.

520. Girl is Found, *supra* n. 483, at 1.

521. Free Girl, *supra* n. 483, at 2.

522. Girl is Found, *supra* n. 483, at 1.

523. Italian Passport, November 8, 1923; US Department of Labor Immigration Visa, August 24, 1935; US Alien Registration Card, February 24, 1942 ("Length of residence in United States 6 yrs., 4 mos.") of Angela Bucaro DiGiovanni (copies on file with author).

524. The Nia Tapes, *supra* n. 13, vol. 2 at 22.

525. Louisiana Historical Marker, Town of Jean Lafitte, La., *The Historical Marker Database*, https://www.HMdb.org.

526. The Nia Tapes, *supra* n. 13, vol. 2 at 23.

527. "Wells Fargo Warehouse, Nicholas Tormè House," GNO Bridge No. 2 *News Briefs* (Daniel, Mann, Johnson & Mendenhall, 512 S. Peters Street, New Orleans, Louisiana) (undated est. 1980s) at 1 (copy on file with author).

528. Letter of Marvin L. Jeffer, Appraiser, to Thomas Wilkinson (September 21, 1982) (original on file with author, "Succession of Guinta" file).

529. Blok attempted to shroud in secrecy the real identity of the village whose characteristics and people he so assiduously studied and wrote about by giving it the fictitious name Genuardo in his book. *See* Blok, *supa* n. 23, at 5 n. 1 ("For obvious reasons I have changed the names of certain persons and places."). Other researchers have determined by studying Blok's many photos of the village that it was in fact Contessa Entellina. Ernesto Oliva, "Contessa Entellina, Images of Blok," *Reportage Sicilia blog*, October 20, 2012,.

530. Michael W. Stapleton, *A House in the Channel* (unpublished booklet of short stories) (Metairie, Louisina, 2011) (on file with author) (hereinafter "Stapleton").

531. *Id.*

532. *Id.* at 3–6.

533. The Nia Tapes, *supra* n. 13, vol. 2 at 27.

534. *Id.*, vol. 1 at 12.

535. *Id.*, vol. 2 at 34.

536. *Id.*, vol 1 at 10; vol. 2 at 20.

537. Stapleton, *supra* n. 530, at 13.

538. Evans, *supra* n. 365, at 314.

539. Lila Sheon, *NaNa's Kitchen* 3 (recipe booklet self-published for family and friends only by Gaetano and Angelina DiGiovanni's great-great-granddaughter and Ann Wilkinson Guinta's granddaughter) (2003) ("Foreword by Ann Wilkinson") (copy on file with author).

540. Stapleton, *supra* n. 530, at 26.

541. Richard Campanella, "185-Year-Old New Basin Canal Continues to Affect Thousands of New Orleanians Every Day," *Cityscapes: A Geographer's View of the New Orleans Area*, first published in *The Times-Picayune*, December 8,

2017, https://richcampanella.com/wp-content/uploads/2020/02/Picayune_Cityscapes_2017_12_The-New-Basin-Canal.pdf.

542. https://www.chicagorailfan.com/rpasscs.html

543. Stapleton, *supra* n. 530, at 16–18.

544. Barzini, *supra* n. 3, at 184 (quoting Jacopo Gelli, *Codice Cavalleresco Italiano (Italian Code of Chivalry)* (1887).

545. *Id.*, *supra* n. 3, at 260.

546. The Nia Tapes, *supra* n. 13, vol. 2 at 29.

547. Death Certificate of Gaetano DiGiovanni (reproduced in Quaglino Macbook, *supra* n. 324, at 23).

548. Obituary of Gaetano DiGiovanni, *The Times-Picayune*, November 7, 1945, at § 1, 2.

549. *Id.*

550. Davis, *supra* n. 94, title.

551. *Id.* at 28-30; Feather-Informer, *supra* n. 118, at 47; *see* 49 ("Todaro, Frank, 1889-1944, Birthplace [Immig.] San Ciparello [*sic*], Sic. [1911]…1920–40s. Underboss").

552. *See* Nania *supra* n. 20, at 85.

553. Feather-Informer, *supra* n. 118, at 49.

554. Joshua Hammer, "Mafiosos' Retreats, Peacefully Repurposed in Sicily," *The New York Times Reprints*, July 10, 2010, 2 of 4, http:/www.nytimes.com/2010/07/04/travel/04explorer.html.

555. *Id.* at 1 of 4.

556. Dickie, *supra* n. 5, at 14, 26.

557. *Id.* at p. 212.

558. Blok, *supra* n. 23, at 202–203 n. 9.

559. Dickie, *supra* n. 5, at 212.

560. "*Senti le rane che cantano…*, (*You Can Hear Frogs Singing…*)", Portella della Ginestra—*L'Infanzia della trame* (*The Childhood of Plots*) (quoting "Report of Police Commissioner Cosenza of Palermo, Subject: Serious Crimes Committed in Piana degli Albanesi on the Occasion of the Labour Day on 1 May 1947" [May 8, 1947]), "Frogs Singing") https://sites.google.com/site/sentileranechetano.sched/gli-anni/portella-della-ginestra-l-infam.

561. *Id.* (quoting Sandro Provvisionato, "*Misteri d'Italia*," Laterza [1993]).

562. *Id.*

563. *Id.* (quoting Police Commissioner Cosenza's report). The Federterra was the National Federation of Agricultural Workers, a Socialist/Communist-linked union for sharecroppers and other landless peasant farm workers that had been banned by the Fascists in 1926 and revived after World War II by land reformers and property redistributionists. *Wikipedia*, "Federterra," (May 31, 2021, National_Federation_of_Agricultural_Workers_Italy.

564. Dickie, *supra* n. 5, at 212.

565. *Id.* at 212–13.

566. *Id.* at 212.

567. *Id.* at 213.

568. *Id.* at 212–213.

569. *Id.* at 213–14.

570. *Wikipedia*, September 10, 2009, at 2 of 3http://www.en.wikipedia.org/wiki/Salvatore-Giuliano; *see also* Frogs Singing, *supra* n. 560 (quoting Sandro Provvisionato) (identifying Ettore Messana, "a senior official of the Italian State, the head of the Inspectorate of Public Security in Sicily," as having known in advance that the attack would occur).

571. *Id.*

572. Dickie, *supra* n. 5, at 216.

573. *Id.*

574. The Nia Tapes, *supra* n. 13, vol. 1 at 18.

575. *Id.*

576. *Id.*

577. *Id.*

578. Dickie, *supra* n. 5, at 133; Blok, *supra* n. 23, at 121.

579. The Nia Tapes, *supra* n. 13, vol. 1 at 18.

580. *Wikipedia*, "Clare Booth Luce," August 28, 2015 (hereinafter CBL-Wiki https://en.wikipedia.org/wiki/Clare_Boothe_Luce#Ambassador_to_Italy.

581. Evans, *supra* n. 365, at 398.

582. CBL-Wiki, *supra* n. 580, at 6.

583. *Id.* (quoting Joseph Lyons, *CBL, Author and Diplomat* (Chelsea House, 1988) 91.

584. Papers of Clare Booth Luce, United States Library of Congress, Lot 11236-1, Nos. 15(g)–17(G), Photographs of Official Trip to Sicily, December 1953 (Library of Congress Prints & Photographs Division, Washington, DC, 2002).

585. Photograph in Quaglino Macbook, *supra* n. 324, at 22.

586. The Nia Tapes, *supra* n. 13, vol. 1 at 18.

587. *Id.* at 19

588. Davis, *supra* n. 94, at 45–46, 77.

589. Hunt, *supra* n. 106, at 1; "La Cosa Nostra: Sam Carolla," May 19, 2009,.

590. The Nia Tapes, *supra* n. 13, vol. 1. at 12.

591. *Id.* at 19.

592. *Id.* at 18.

593. Dickie, *supra* n. 5, at 16 (quoting Alfredo Niceforo, *Contemporary Barbarian Sicily* [1897]).

594. Sicilian dialect translation by Paolo DiGiovanni, Metairie, Louisiana.

595. *The Catholic Bible: New American Bible, Personal Study Edition* (Oxford University Press, 1995), 745.

596. Obituary of Robert Vincent Ciuffi Sr., May 4, 2020, Obits.nola.com.

597. Obituary of Angelina Bucaro DiGiovanni, *The Times Picayune*, February 10, 1965, at § 1, 2.

[598.] *Succession of Natale Guinta*, Case No. 82-19783, "Sworn Descriptive List of Succession Assets" at 2 (Civil District Court, Parish of Orleans, State of Louisiana) (December 21, 1982) (copy on file with author as "Succession of Guinta").

[599.] "Faubourg" is a French term commonly used in New Orleans to define any old and longstanding neighborhood of the city that historically was one of the suburbs of the city's founding French Quarter core. *See The American College Dictionary* (Random House, 1970), 440. The Faubourg Bouligny is named for Louis Bouligny, who acquired the plantation land where the neighborhood is now located in 1829 from its previous owner, General Wade Hampton of South Carolina. Edward Branley, "NOLA History: The Neighborhoods of Uptown New Orleans," October 12, 2011, https://gonola.com/nola history-the_neighborhoods_of_uptown_new_orleans.

[600.] From 1968 to 2001, Fred McFeely Rogers was the gentle and kindly host of the children's television show *Mr. Rogers' Neighborhood*. The lyrics of the program's theme song bespoke the character and outlook of Mr. Rogers, so starkly different from the worldview of late-nineteenth- and early-twentieth-century Sicilian peasants. *Compare* the Mr. Rogers theme song ("It's a beautiful day in the neighborhood, a beautiful day for a neighbor, could you be mine? Would you be mine?... Let's make the most of this beautiful day. Since we're together, might as well say, would you be my, could you be my, won't you be my neighbor?") https://www.misterrogers.org (1990), *with* Anton Blok's observations of late-nineteenth- and early-twentieth-century Sicilian peasants ("[P]easants appear morose and sullen, and are suspicious towards outsiders... [T]heir folksongs are melancholic and express resignation:... One standard answer to 'How do you do?' is *Cuntrastamu*," which means 'We are resisting' or 'We are struggling.'"). Blok, *supra* n. 23, at 47–48.

[601.] The Nia Tapes, *supra* n. 13, Vol. I at 10.

[602.] *Procura Speciale*, Executed Before Peter Gentile, Notaro Publico (April 15, 1954) (copy on file with author).

[603.] *Id.* at 2.

[604.] The Nia Tapes, *supra* n. 13, vol. 2 at 19–20.

[605.] *Id.* at 20.

[606.] Blok, *supra* n. 23, subtitle; *see* at 93 ("peasants generated new niches for violent entrepreneurs").

[607.] 18 USC § 1001 "[W]hoever, in any matter within the jurisdiction of the executive, legislative, or judicial branch of the Government of the United States, knowingly and willfully—makes any materially false, fictitious, or fraudulent statement or representation;...shall be fined..., imprisoned not more than 5 years or,...both.").

[608.] The Nia Tapes, *supra* n. 13, vol. 1 at 20.

[609.] *Id.*

[610.] *Id.*

611. *Id.*, vol. 2 at 30.

612. Natale's Death Certificate, *supra* n. 288.

613. *Id.* at Lines 10a and 10b.

614. Natale's Obituary, *supra* n. 287.

615. Critchley, *supra* n. 67, at 60.

616. Joan Kent, "Way of Life in New Orleans Dies with Miss Lucy," *The Times-Picayune*, Feb. 7, 1982, at § 1, 5.

617. *Id.*

618. *Id.*

619. Death Certificate of Antonia Guinta, State of Louisiana Office of Public Health—Vital Records Registry No. 640337) (1998) (copy on file with author).

620. The Nia Tapes, *supra* n. 13, vol. 1 at 4.

621. *Id.*, vol. 2 at 31.

622. Barzini, *supra* n. 3, at 263.

623. Davis, *supra* n. 94, at 319.

624. *Wikipedia*, "Paolo Gambino," March 22, 2016,.

625. The Nia Tapes, *supra* n. 13, vol. 2 at 25.

626. Giacomo Puccini, *La Boheme*, Act IV (1896).

627. Richard Collin, "The Little Italians: Some of the Best Pasta This Side of Roma," *The Times-Picayune*, May 19–25, 1979, Lagniappe magazine, at 26.

628. "Metairie Driver Killed in Crash," *The Times-Picayune*, May 6, 1968, at § 1, 1.

629. Barbara Grizzuti Harrison, *Italian Days* (Atlantic Monthly Press, 1989), 461.

630. Eddy Arnold, "My Little Buckaroo," https://www.azlyrics.com/lyrics/eddyarnold/mulittlebuckaroo.html.

631. The Nia Tapes, *supra* n. 13, vol. 1 at 10.

632. Obituary of Ann Guinta Wilkinson, New Orleans Advocate, March 31, 2017, at § B, 4.

633. Jay Wilkinson, *My Dad's Eulogy* (14 copies self-published for family and friends only on file with author) (Walter W. Eckert Binder & Specialty Co, Inc. New Orleans, Louisiana, 2009), 9–10.

634. *About Palermo* 86 (e` un produtto realizzato da: 99idee s.r.l., Via Ausonia, 76, 90100 Palermo (giugno 2001).

635. Edmond Rostand, *Cyrano De Bergerac* (trans. *Gertrude Hall*) (Doubleday & McClure Co., 1808).

636. Natale's Obituary, *supra* n. 287.

637. Natale's Death Certificate, *supra* n. 288, Lines 12c and 16a.

638. Barzini, *supra* n. 3, at 328, 254.

639. Dickie, *supra* n. 5, at 24–25.

640. Barzini, *supra* n. 3, at 164 (quoting Francesco Guicciardini).

641. Federico and Stephen Moramarco, *Italian Pride: 101 Reasons to Be Proud You're Italian* (Citadel Press, 2000), ix–x.

642. The Nia Tapes, *supra* n. 13, vol. 1 at 8.